The Biblical Cosmos

"In this masterful exposition of the sacramental worldview of the Old Testament, Robin Parry explains why the 'flat earth' of ancient Israel continues to be of significance for Christians today. If you're wondering how, with a modern cosmology, we can still believe that Jesus ascended into heaven, this book is a must-read. And if you figure the Old Testament is simply incompatible with the Christian Platonism of the Christian tradition, you just may be startled by the insights of this book."

—Hans Boersma, J. I. Packer Professor of Theology, Regent College, Vancouver

"Delightful. Robin Parry takes the reader on a fascinating tour of biblical cosmology and theology. If you want to enter the minds of the biblical writers, this book will guide you with wit and sound learning."

—Gordon Wenham, Professor Emeritus of Old Testament, University of Gloucestershire, and Tutor in Old Testament, Trinity College Bristol, UK

"Parry expertly guides us through the strange biblical world of a flat earth at center of the cosmos, dragon-infested cosmic waters, a dome overhead, and abode of the dead below. But more than that, Parry invites us to accept this strange biblical world as is and to inhabit it, rather than conforming it to ours. In doing so, Parry opens up fresh ways of envisioning not only the biblical world, but Jesus and our own Christian faith."

—Peter Enns, Professor of Biblical Studies, Eastern University, Pennsylvania

"One of the great challenges for reading the Bible today is how to make sense of a biblical view of the world in our modern scientific era. In this book Robin Parry deftly and thoughtfully lays out the key issues as well as suggesting various ways in which we might begin to respond to them. This book is a must read for anyone serious about reading and making sense of the Bible today."

—Paula Gooder, Theologian in Residence, Bible Society, UK

"Robin Parry gives us what is both a fascinating survey of the cosmos as seen in Holy Scripture and a helpful guide to how Christians can best understand that biblical cosmology today. Thorough, lively, and thought-provoking, I warmly recommend it."

—Michael Ward, author of *Planet Narnia: The Seven Heavens in the Imagination of C. S. Lewis*

"This book is simply stellar! What a fabulously helpful way to introduce the significance of the OT cosmology for today!"

—PLEIADES, open star cluster in the constellation of Taurus

"Roaaaaarrrr!!!!"

—LEVIATHAN, mythical chaos monster

"This book is smokin' hot! I wish I'd read this it when I was alive!"

—SAINT AUGUSTINE, important bishop and theologian bloke[1]

"I feel so honored to have been asked to paint a picture for the cover of this great little travel guide. And to have Leviathan himself agree to pose for it was literally awesome!"

—VINCENT VAN GOCH, artist[2]

---

1. Disclaimer: St. Augustine did not really say this—obviously!

2. Van Goch *really did* paint the cover image . . . kind of. It is a section of *Starry Night over the Rhone* (Sept 1888)—plus a chaos monster that swam over from an old nautical map.

The Biblical Cosmos

A Pilgrim's Guide to the
Weird and Wonderful World of the Bible

Robin A. Parry

with illustrations by
Hannah Parry

CASCADE *Books* • Eugene, Oregon

THE BIBLICAL COSMOS
A Pilgrim's Guide to the Weird and Wonderful World of the Bible

Copyright © 2014 Robin A. Parry. All rights reserved. Except for brief quotations in critical publications or reviews, no part of this book may be reproduced in any manner without prior written permission from the publisher. Write: Permissions, Wipf and Stock Publishers, 199 W. 8th Ave., Suite 3, Eugene, OR 97401.

Cascade Books
A Division of Wipf and Stock Publishers
199 W. 8th Ave., Suite 3
Eugene, OR 97401

www.wipfandstock.com

Scripture quotations are from The Holy Bible, English Standard Version® (ESV®), copyright © 2001 by Crossway, a publishing ministry of Good News Publishers. Used by permission. All rights reserved.

ISBN 13: 978-1-62564-810-5

Cataloging-in-Publication data:

Parry, Robin A.

The biblical cosmos : a pilgrim's guide to the weird and wonderful world of the Bible / Robin A. Parry ; illustrations by Hannah Parry.

xiv + 228 p. ; 23 cm. Includes bibliographical references and index.

ISBN 13: 978-1-62564-810-5

1. Biblical cosmology. 2. Creation—Biblical teaching. I. Parry, Hannah J. II. Title.

BS651 P31 2014

Manufactured in the U.S.A.

We dedicate this book to

Ann Coyle (1958–2014)
—an inspirational woman who modeled love for God,
love for God's people,
love for her family,
and love for God's wee beasties (even insects and reptiles)

Jessica Parry
—daughter, sister, jester, equestrian

Contents

Preface ix
Acknowledgments xiii

Introduction: Welcome to the Biblical Cosmos 1

PART I: A Tour of the Biblical Earth 15

1. Joining the Flat Earth Society: The Big Picture 17
2. Here Be Dragons! The Sea 26
3. Between the Devil and the Deep Blue Sea: Land 48
4. A Land Down Under: Sheol/Hades 71

PART II: A Tour of the Biblical Heavens 89

5. Eyes in Their Stars: The Sky 91
6. Brighter than a Thousand Suns: God's Heaven 120

PART III: The House of God: Temple and Cosmos 137

7. God's in the House: The Temple and the Biblical Cosmos 139
8. Christ's in the House: Jesus and the Biblical Cosmos 151

PART IV: Can *We* Inhabit the Biblical Cosmos? 163

9. *How* Can We Inhabit the Biblical Cosmos Today? 165
10. The Cosmic Temple Today 168
11. The Biblical Heavens Today 180
12. The Biblical Earth Today 197

Bibliography 211
Scripture Index 217

Preface

THIS BOOK WILL BE worrying to many ordinary Christians. Part of what I am saying is that the Bible's understandings of the universe are based on ancient "science" and are no longer the way that we think about the world. This will *sound* to many people like I am saying that the Bible is simply wrong. I am not. Let me assure readers right at the start that I am a Bible-believing Christian. My view is that the books of the Bible are divinely inspired and together are authoritative as Holy Scripture. As such I am committed to the belief that they remain relevant in the modern age and that Jehovah[1] continues to address his people through them. However, I am also committed to the view that we ought to try to understand the biblical texts, as far as we are able, in their ancient contexts. There is a lot more to interpreting the Bible well than reading in this manner; but it

---

1. I should perhaps offer an explanation for my use of the somewhat old-fashioned name Jehovah. This may seem odd because, contrary to what Jehovah's Witnesses say, Jehovah is *not God's name*. Let me explain. God revealed himself to Israel by means of his holy name. This name is reflected in the Hebrew text by four consonants YHWH (or JHVH in older writings). By the time of Jesus, the name was considered so holy that pious Jews would never utter it but would use a range of devices to allude to it without speaking it. Jesus himself and the authors of the New Testament followed this practice and I now do so too. Now one such device was to substitute the word "Lord," *Adonai*, in place of the name. Thus, when JHVH was *read* in the text the word Adonai was *spoken* in its place. When vowels were later added to the Hebrew text the vowels of Adonai were written by the consonants of JHVH as JeHoVaH (trust me on the first a changing to e) to remind readers to say Adonai. So "Jehovah" was not a word that was ever used by Jews and it is not God's name. However, I think that it is actually a very helpful pseudo-name to use. The problem is that substitutes such as "Lord" are titles and not names at all. An audience listening would not know whether someone saying Adonai was reading the name JHVH or the title Adonai. Jehovah, however, contains the consonants of the name itself. As such it clearly gestures towards the name; but it is *not* the name. And for that very reason is helpful, for it allows us to clearly reference the name without saying it. So in this book I will often use the word Jehovah, and when Bible verses use YHWH I have changed the LORD of the translations used to Jehovah.

remains the case that biblical books were written by ancient people in ancient contexts, and we need to give space to hearing them as such. Doing this may well be disorientating for believers; indeed, it can often have the effect of distancing the Bible from us and making it seem very strange and alien. This can be scary—we may fear that the Bible could be lost to us, stranded in the past. And if we left matters there we will not have read the Bible *as Scripture* but simply as an ancient text and we will indeed have lost it in the process. This is not, however, a reason to abandon the attempt to better understanding biblical books in historical context. One ever-present danger for the church is that we can domesticate Scripture; we can mold it into our own image and tame it so that it only reflects back to us what we're expecting it to say. The act of distancing Scripture from ourselves, as one movement within the drama of interpretation, can have the useful function of allowing it to confront us again in its very strangeness; giving it breathing space to say something different and surprising to us. This opens up the possibility that in a second movement within the interpretative act—that of bring our own world into dialogue with that of the Bible—Scripture can speak a fresh word to us. So the first few chapters may well be disorientating but I can only ask the reader to bear with me. My prayer is that by the end of the book you will not be thinking that the Bible is old and out of date but that it is excitingly relevant to our modern understandings of the world in which we live.

Acknowledgments

THE IDEA FOR THIS book has been rumbling away in the back of my mind for some years and I am pleased to finally be able to get it out of my system. I would like to thank those people who helped in one way or another. In particular, those who kindly read and commented on various parts of the book—Tarah Van De Wiele, Michael Ward, Peter Enns, and especially Hans Boersma, who went the extra mile and provided detailed corrections for the entire manuscript. Thanks also to Paula Gooder and Gordon J. Wenham, along with some of those mentioned above, for kindly reading and endorsing the book. I am grateful for the editorial eye of K. C. Hanson, a bloke who knows a lot more about ancient biblical cultures than I ever will. My thanks to Heather Carraher—typesetting guru—for all her great work (and patience). The cover is appropriately weird and wonderful, and for that I offer heartfelt thanks to Christian Amondson, who went above and beyond the call of duty. Respect, dude! Special gratitude is due to my eldest daughter Hannah, who set aside a lot of time to paint pictures for me. I was after a very stark and simple black and white cartoon kind of image and she came up with a style that was just what I wanted. Her other pictures are all straight copies of ancient Near Eastern images so that readers can see some of the things that I speak about in the text.

Introduction

Welcome to the Biblical Cosmos

WE THINK THAT WE have a pretty good grasp of what the cosmos is like. There's us living on the skin of a giant globe, circling a star we call the sun. That star is just one of many millions in the Milky Way galaxy, and the Milky Way, in turn, is just one among many millions of galaxies. So when *we* read the creation story in Genesis 1, in our mind's eye we imagine the world that God created looking something like this picture:

However, as we'll discover, neither the author of Genesis 1 nor his original audience would have thought of the world in this way. Indeed, in many ways the world of the Bible, the cosmos as pictured by the writers and original audiences of biblical texts, was a *very* different cosmos to our own.

Before we get into the "crazy" stuff, however, let's ease into things with some plain and simple "slightly odd" stuff.

The Living Cosmos

The biblical cosmos is a very *vital* place, a place bursting with life. Modern Westerners draw rigid distinctions between animate objects (like animals and plants) and inanimate objects (like the sea and mountains). The former are alive and, in varying degrees, can be conscious. The latter are not alive and have no consciousness. We climb mountains, we look at mountains, we dig in mountains, we paint mountains, but we do not talk to mountains and we certainly do not expect them to talk back. Now ancient Israelites didn't talk to mountains either, but they seem surprisingly willing to talk about the whole of the created order as if it were *in some sense* alive and conscious and able to respond to God in a manner appropriate to it. This phenomena is so common in the Bible we often become oblivious to it, so it worth highlighting some instances.

First, notice that God is regularly said to speak not only to humans and heavenly beings (no surprise there) but also to animals and plants and even to stars, to clouds, to mountains, to the sea, and to sheol (world of the dead). They can be called to obey, to perform certain acts, and to serve as witnesses in a cosmic law court.

Second, notice that these "inanimate" aspects of creation are also spoken of as addressing God or as speaking about God. Stars, waters, trees, and even the mountains and stones cry out *to* and *about* Jehovah.

Stars:

The heavens declare the glory of God;
  the skies proclaim the work of his hands.
Day after day they pour forth speech;
  night after night they reveal knowledge.
They have no speech, they use no words;
  no sound is heard from them.
Yet their voice goes out into all the earth,
  their words to the ends of the world. (Ps 19:1–4, NIV)

Waters above the sky:

Praise him, you highest heavens,
  and you waters above the heavens! (Ps 148:4)

INTRODUCTION

Waters in the sea:

Let heaven and earth praise him,
> the seas and everything that moves in them. (Ps 69:34)

Trees:

let the field exult, and everything in it!
> Then shall all the trees of the forest sing for joy. (Ps 96:12)

Mountains:

[Mount] Tabor and [Mount] Herman joyously praise your name. (Ps 89:12)

And they not only praise but also protest. The Promised Land is polluted by Israel's idolatry and vomits sinful Israel out of it like a body expelling poison.

> But you shall keep my statutes and my rules and do none of these abominations, either the native or the stranger who sojourns among you (for the people of the land, who were before you, did all of these abominations, so that the land became unclean), lest the land vomit you out when you make it unclean, as it vomited out the nation that was before you. (Lev 18:26–28; cf. 20:22)

Third, in some contexts the whole of the heavens or the earth or the seas are spoken of as though they, and not simply individual creatures within them, were conscious. Paul even speaks of creation as a whole as if it were an agent with desires and pains.

> For the creation waits with eager longing for the revealing of the sons of God. For the creation was subjected to futility, not willingly, but because of him who subjected it, in hope that the creation itself will be set free from its bondage to corruption and obtain the freedom of the glory of the children of God. For we know that the whole creation has been groaning together in the pains of childbirth until now. (Rom 8:19–22)

Fourth, notice that humans too will address "inanimate" aspects of creation in certain ritual contexts. In *worship* humans call on creation—on the sun, the moon, the stars, the seas, the mountains, the flora, and fauna—to praise God. For instance,

> Praise him, all his angels;
> > praise him, all his hosts!

3

> Praise him, sun and moon,
>> praise him, all you shining stars!
> Praise him, you highest heavens,
>> and you waters above the heavens!
>
> Let them praise the name of Jehovah!
>> For he commanded and they were created. . . .
> Praise Jehovah from the earth,
>> you great sea creatures and all deeps,
> fire and hail, snow and mist,
>> stormy wind fulfilling his word!
> Mountains and all hills,
>> fruit trees and all cedars!
> Beasts and all livestock,
>> creeping things and flying birds! (Ps 148:2–5, 7–10)

Our natural reaction to this is to say, "Well, sure, but that's only metaphor. That is simply speaking about inanimate things *as if* they were animate." Yes and no. It *is* metaphor; ancient Israelites were well aware that the "speech" of the stars or mountains, say, was not audible or in human languages (see Ps 19:1–4, quoted above). It was not *literally* speech as such. We should not be so quick, however, to suppose that they did not think that there was not something *analogous to* life, to consciousness, to intention, to speech, and to praise in the "inanimate" aspects of creation. To us moderns the universe is mostly like a lifeless machine, but we need to be open to the possibility that the biblical authors saw the world as much more alive than we tend to.

So we can already see that the Bible's universe is somewhat stranger than we may at first think. Prepare for a few surprises in the pages to come.

To really open up the whole issue of the gap between ancient and modern worlds it would be helpful to get a bird's eye view of the biblical cosmos, understood in the light of some of the other cosmologies that were in the air back then. While it may seem a bit of a distraction to try to get your head around ancient Egyptian or Babylonian worldviews, I hope that you'll think it to be worth all the effort in the end. So—here we go . . .

INTRODUCTION

A Bird's Eye View of the Cosmos: Some Ancient Near Eastern Perspectives

In this tour we shall be taking sideways glances at some of the ancient cultures that Israel interacted with, because an appreciation of the wider world inhabited by authors of the Bible can help us to better understand the Bible in its original context. In particular, we will pay attention to ancient Egyptian, Mesopotamian (by which we mean Sumerian, Assyrian, and Babylonian), and Canaanite material. The map below shows where these different cultures were based in relation to each other.

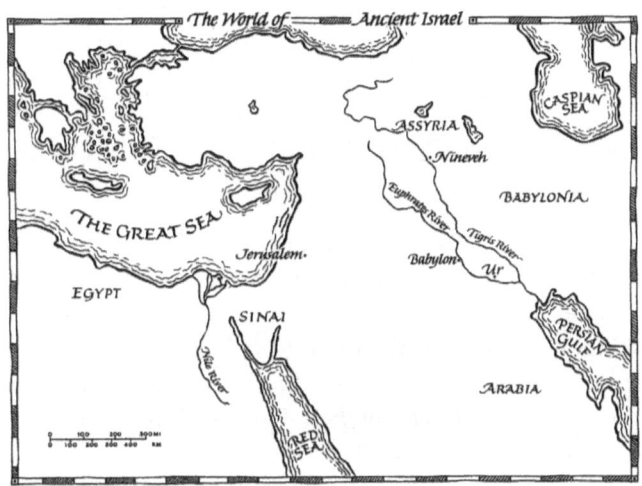

Ancient Egyptian Cosmography

There is no single Egyptian account of creation. However, across all the varied accounts we find some common motifs that seem to capture enduring and central elements in ancient Egyptian views of creation.

The Egyptian cosmos was one in which the earth was a flat expanse, beneath which lay the underworld, and above which soared the sky—a watery place crossed each day by the sun god on a boat. In the image below—a common Egyptian image—the two parts of the Egyptian cosmos can be seen: Nut, the sky goddess arches over Geb, the earth, lying beneath. Heaven and earth are separated by the air god Shu, who holds up the sky. The air god is assisted in holding up the sky goddess by other gods. Above Nut is the infinite expanse of pre-creation chaos, Nu(n). Clearly the very structures of the world are closely associated with gods.

Central to the conception of the universe was Ma'at, the eternal order of the universe, an order associated with justice and truth. Ma'at ordered both the natural world and the human world and was essential for any kind of flourishing. Without Ma'at the world would descend back into disorder. However, Ma'at was under constant threat from the forces of chaos, so both humans and gods needed to fulfill their designated roles in the structure of the world in order to resist this pull towards disorder.

Egyptian cosmology takes great care to balance order and chaos, light and dark, life and death in cyclical patterns. Indeed, every day the battle between life and death takes place as the sun sets, descends to the underworld, and then rises again. And every year it takes place as the Nile floods and then recedes, allowing the land to appear again from the chaotic water, as it had in creation itself, and to burst forth with fresh fertility. This ever waxing and waning conflict between order and chaos is what sustains the cosmos.

Ancient Mesopotamian Cosmography

In ancient Sumer (located in what is now Iraq) the cosmos was divided into two main zones: the heavenly and the earthly. Each of these zones could be subdivided into three heaven zones and three earth zones:

Main divisions	Subdivisions	Belongs to …	Stone Floor
Heavenly realms	*Upper heavens*	Anu, king of the gods	Red stone
	Middle heavens	The Igigi	Blue stone
	Lower heavens	The stars (= gods)	Translucent or blue/grey Jasper
Earthly realms	*Upper earth*	Humanity	
	Middle earth (underground water)	Ea	
	Lower earth (the underworld)	600 imprisoned Anunnaki	

In terms of the cosmos that humans can see, only the upper earth, where we live, and the lower heavens, inhabited by the divine stars, are visible.

Each of the three heavens was associated with a different level of deity and with a different stone. It seems that each heaven had its own solid stone floor, rather like a three story house; the floor of the upper heavens forming the ceiling of the middle heavens, and so on. The stone floor of Anu's heaven—the highest realm of the cosmos—was composed of a red stone, that of the middle heavens of blue stone, and that of the lower heavens was jasper.

Jasper comes in all sorts of colors, but it is likely that the floor of the lower heavens was composed of sky-blue jasper or grey jasper—the sky visible from earth. The constellations were etched onto the stone undersurface of the lower heavens, which, it is reasonable to suppose, were thought to rotate.

We ought to note in passing that the area between the earth's surface and the stars (what we call "the atmosphere") may be considered as the lower part of the lower heaven.

The upper earth is simply what we think of as the earth's surface. That's simple enough to understand. When we come to the middle earth we need to forget Hobbits; this is the realm of Ea, the freshwater god. So the middle earth is an underground watery realm known as the Apsu, the source of springs and rivers. The lower earth is the underworld in which 600 gods known as Anunnaki were imprisoned by the god Bel. Some texts refer to it as "vast earth," "lower land," "the earth of no return," or "earth of the dead."

The universe was pictured as a sphere, divided into two hemispheres. The earth, inhabited by the living, was the flat plane dividing the two hemispheres. The dome above was the sky inhabited by the gods of the living. The hemisphere below was the Apsu (underground water) and below the Apsu was the netherworld inhabited by deities and the ghosts of the dead. These two hemispheres were linked by gates. As in Egypt the sun and moon would pass through both spheres each day.

In Mesopotamian sources the dry land inhabited by humans is always presented as flat and circular, like a round tabletop, surrounded by ocean. The single continent of dry land was described by phrases such as "circle of the lands," "circle of the earth," and the like.

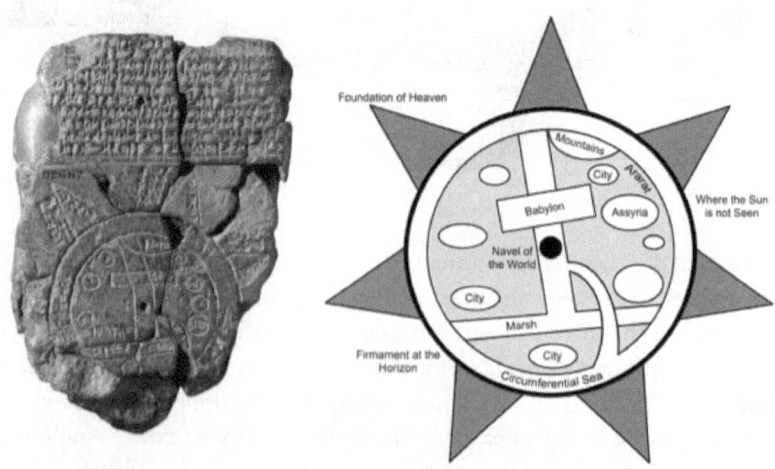

INTRODUCTION

We can see this visually presented in the famous Babylonian map of the world (probably dating back to some time between the eighth and sixth centuries BCE). This map depicts the earth's surface as a central circular landmass on which one can locate key cities of the time, with Babylon itself placed as most prominent. One can also see some prominent geographical features, such as the mountains in southern Turkey to the north, the Euphrates river, the swamps along the lower Euphrates, and (possibly) a shipping channel. Surrounding this continent is a cosmic ocean. Beyond that ocean are triangles of distant uncharted territories (*nagû*), probably thought of as populated political territories and most likely as islands. However, the descriptions of them are vague and indicate that the map's designer knew little about these distant places.

The map is interesting for many reasons but we simply need to note that it intends to chart the scope of the whole earth and that this earth is a circular land mass surrounded by ocean. It is interesting to note that the world of these cartographers was a lot smaller than the world that we now know. For instance, they thought that beyond the mountains of Anatolia (modern Turkey) in the north lay this surrounding ocean. The "totality of the land under heaven," in the minds of the author of a text known as *The Sargon Geography*, extended from the Persian Gulf/Indian Ocean (known as the Lower Sea) to the Mediterranean (known as the Upper Sea), and from Anatolia to Iran. This is just the same as in the world map. There was no Russia, no China, no Scandinavia, no Africa (beyond Egypt), and certainly no Americas.[1] While there was no consensus, and most ancient Mesopotamians likely had no clear opinion on the matter, it is incontestable that their world was a lot smaller than our own.

Mesopotamian sources do not agree about the very ends of the earth. Some texts imagine the surrounding ocean being the uttermost limits of the earth; other texts imagine a mountain range beyond the surrounding ocean acting as a kind of dam (and perhaps also holding up the sky). These mountains contain gates through which the sun could rise and set. It is very clear that there was considerable and understandable fuzziness about exactly what lay at the boundaries of the world.

---

1. It has been estimated that *The Sargon Geography* conceives of the earth's land surface as having an approximate diameter of 4,500 km, although we should not assume that this was a universally shared view.

Ancient Israelite Cosmography: A Quick Overview

The biblical cosmos, like that of other ancient Near Eastern cultures, was essentially a cosmos with a fundamental twofold division between heavenly and earthly realms. Indeed, Scripture often refers to the whole cosmos simply as "heaven and earth." That covers *everything*—there are no other parts of the cosmos beyond heaven and earth. But, as in Mesopotamia, this two-part cosmos can be further subdivided. The divisions are very similar to, though not identical with, those we saw above in ancient Sumer, Assyria, and Babylonia.

Main divisions	Subdivisions		Inhabited by …	
Heavenly realms	*The highest heaven*		God, the divine council, the angels	
	Waters above the skies			
	The firmament (sky dome)		sun, moon, and stars	
	The "atmosphere"		Weather and birds	
Earthly realms	*Land*	*sea*	Humans and animals (wild and domestic)	Fish & sea monsters
	Waters under the earth		Water (and water creatures?)	
	Sheol, the underworld		The dead	

The Old Testament has a differentiated notion of the "heavens" (*shāmayim*). It included the firmament, or sky dome (*raqîaʿ*),[2] but also the space *below* the dome[3] and the space *above* it.[4] Thus, below the dome, in what we call "the atmosphere," is the zone in which weather "happens"—rain, dew, frost, snow, hail, thunder and lightning, wind, and clouds.[5] Here

---

2. Gen 1:8; Pss 19:6; 148:4.

3. Pss 8:8; 79:2.

4. Pss 2:4; 11:4; 139:8.

5. Gen 8:2; Isa 55:10–11; Job 38:29; Deut 33:13; Josh 10:11; 1 Sam 2:10; Zech 6:5; Ps 147:8.

the Bible will often speak of the "birds of the heavens,"[6] because the atmosphere was part of "the heavens." Note, however, that birds fly "in front of"[7] the sky dome (*raqîa'*) and *not* "in" it.[8] The sun, moon, and stars, on the other hand, are set "in" the sky dome.[9]

For ancient Israelites, if one ascended past the birds and past the clouds and past the stars one would need to go through a door in the solid vault of the sky to enter the highest heaven, the dwelling place of God beyond the stars.[10] This dwelling was also spoken of as "in the heavens."[11] Occasionally the Bible will nuance the language of "heaven" to distinguish the different heavens. Thus, for instance, we hear of "*God's* heaven"[12] and the "*highest* heaven,"[13] and Matthew's Gospel distinguishes between the plural "heavens" (where God dwells) and singular "heaven" (where birds and stars can be found).

6. Gen 1:26, 28; 2:20; 6:7; 7:3, 23, etc.

7. Or, "on the surface of..."

8. Gen 1:20.

9. Gen 1:17.

10. 2 *En.* 3:3ff. The Bible only appears to refer to one level of heaven above the stars (as opposed to the two levels in Mesopotamia), although by the time of Jesus some non-biblical Jewish texts refer to as many as seven heavens and it is possible that some New Testament authors were aware of these ideas.

11. Deut 26:15; 2 Chr 30:27; 1 Kgs 8:30, 39.

12. Ps 115:16; Lam 3:66.

13. 1 Kgs 8:27.

We can think of this like different floors in a house. To those living on the ground floor (and remember that this was a pre-flight world in which, without divine assistance, humans could *only* inhabit the ground floor) "upstairs" is the appropriate language to refer to the first and the second floors. The sky dome was the ceiling separating the first and second floors—the stars were the lights in that ceiling. Birds, clouds, stars, and God all lived "upstairs." But, of course, God inhabited the penthouse on the top floor and not the suite on the first floor. And while the first floor in this house is visible from the ground floor, the top floor is not. Non-divine beings cannot see it or enter it (with very rare exceptions).

Beneath the ground was a subterranean freshwater ocean that was the source of springs and rivers, we might think of this as the plumbing for the house, and beneath that was sheol, the world of the dead. Sheol was akin the basement of the house, although it was a basement to which the living had no access and from which the dead had no escape.

Now there was a graded scale of holiness in this cosmos that worked along a vertical axis. Heaven, God's dwelling, was supremely holy, while sheol, the dead zone, was the part of the cosmos furthest away on the holiness spectrum. We could represent that diagrammatically as a cylinder of holiness in which the "further away" one is from God the less holiness there is:

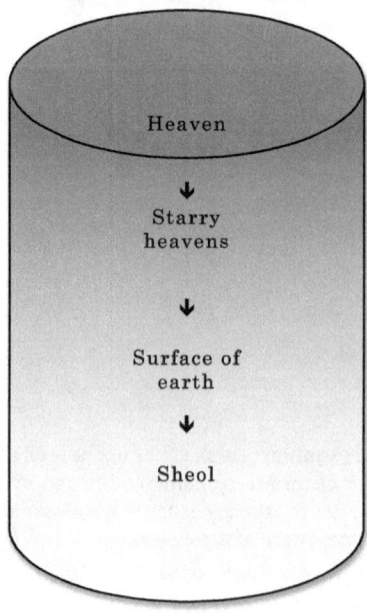

INTRODUCTION

We should not think of the biblical cosmos as composed of completely sealed off units. It is true that the zones are distinct and it is also true that movement between them is restricted. However, there is fluidity. Humans descend to sheol (the underworld) when they die, and, on very rare occasions, can ascend from sheol to the land of the living again (as with the prophet Samuel). On exceptional occasions a human can even ascend to heaven (as in the cases of Enoch and Elijah). Some heavenly beings too can sometimes come down from heaven to earth and then re-ascend to heaven (and some fallen angels are cast into a subterranean prison). But most obviously God is associated with *all* the spheres of creation. Heaven—the highest heaven—is, of course, his throne room, but he also works through the stars, the weather, through historical events on the earth, and even sheol is open before him. In the New Testament, as we will see later in this tour guide, Jesus—God made flesh—moves from heaven to earth to the underworld, then back to earth and finally returns to the right hand of God in heaven. He is thus Lord of *every* sphere of creation.

The Shape of Things to Come

The guide that follows is divided into two main tours, one into each of the two parts of the cosmos—heaven and earth. These tours have various stops along the way that take us into the different zones within the heavenly and earthly realms. Having travelled around the cosmos we will go to Jerusalem and take a third tour around the temple. The reason for that tour and its relevance for understanding biblical cosmology will become clear at the time. Then, before returning to our own cosmos, we will consider the one human being who has actually dwelt in all the zones of the biblical universe—Jesus the Messiah. We shall see that it is Jesus who acts as the ultimate key to understand the cosmos of the Bible. After that it is time to come home, but hopefully by the time we get back to our universe we will better understand the Bible in its own world. However, we cannot leave the tour there. The Bible is not simply an old book locked away in the past; it is divinely inspired Scripture and God continues to speak into our world through it. So the final question we must address is this—what might God be saying to *us* through these ancient biblical cosmologies about the way that *we* should think about the cosmos? The post-tour debrief considers that question in ways that I hope are helpful and show just how relevant the Bible is to the modern world.

PART I
A Tour of the Biblical Earth

I

Joining the Flat Earth Society

The Big Picture

"Behold, he is coming with the clouds, and every eye will see him, even those who pierced him, and all tribes of the earth will wail on account of him" (Rev 1:7). I vividly recall puzzling over this passage when I was at school. I imagined Jesus appearing in the sky over my town in Wales—because it is obvious that Jesus would return to Wales (with Welsh being the language of the angels, and all that)—but the burning question was how the people in Australia could see him too. It was suggested to me that the solution was television, which allowed the biblical prophecy finally to be fulfilled. Call me a cynic, but the idea that Jesus had delayed his parousia simply to give us time to invent TV so that Australians could watch him return seemed a little far fetched! So what is going on? That question is one of those that we hope to get some answer to in this opening tour of the biblical earth.

The earth's surface is the most familiar part of the biblical cosmos, so it seems like a sensible place to begin the tour. You will easily recognize a lot of the same features from your own home: sea, land, mountains, rivers, lakes, trees, deserts, and animals. But before we start to feel too at home we need to look closer. Things that at first sight seem to be ordinary turn out upon second look to be very strange.

PART I—A TOUR OF THE BIBLICAL EARTH

A Flat Earth

The biblical earth, like that of the other cultures in the ancient world, was not a globe but was flat. We see hints of this in all sorts of ways. Biblical language often speaks of:

- "the four corners of the earth."[1]
- "the ends of the earth."[2] This phrase appears over fifty times in the Bible.
- the "pillars" of the earth[3] and its "foundation,"[4] which hold it still and ensure its stability. The biblical earth is thus fixed down and utterly immovable.[5]

A moment's reflection will show that all such language works on a flat-earth model, an earth fixed firmly on pillars and a foundation. One might, of course, take it metaphorically—and indeed we still use much of this language today in precisely such a non-literal sense. That is certainly possible. However, various other biblical texts suggest that it was more-than-metaphor to the original authors and audiences of Scripture. Consider Nebuchadnezzar's dream: "The visions of my head as I lay in bed were these: I saw, and behold, a tree in the midst of the earth, and its height was great. The tree grew and became strong, and its top reached to heaven, and *it was visible to the end of the whole earth*" (Dan 4:10–11). This would obviously only make sense as an image if the earth was flat.

We might also think of Job 37:3, which implies that the lightning God hurls to earth can be seen to the corners of the earth. That too suggests a flat earth. Consider also the devil's

---

1. Isa 11:12; Ezek 7:2; Rev 7:1. It is not clear whether this image simply indicates the four directions of the compass or imagines the earth as a quadrilateral shape.

2. E.g., Isa 41:9; Jer 16:19; Ps 65:5; Job 28:24; 37:3; 38:13; Dan 4:11; Acts 13:47. In the ancient thinking of Israel, the Queen of Sheba, from the southwest corner of the Arabian peninsula, was from the "ends of the earth" (1 Kgs 10:1–13; Matt 12:42). Note too that rulers of ancient Near Eastern empires described themselves as kings of "the whole earth."

3. Pss 75:3; 104:5; Job 9:6; 1 Sam 2:8.

4. 1 Sam 2:8; 2 Sam 22:16; Pss 75:3; 104:5; Job 38:4; Zech 12:1.

5. Pss 93:1; 96:10; 104:5; Isa 45:18; 1 Chr 16:30.

temptation of Jesus in the wilderness: "Again, the devil took him to a very high mountain and showed him all the kingdoms of the world and their glory" (Matt 4:8). On a globe you could not see all the kingdoms of the earth, even from the highest mountain imaginable. Now recall those words concerning Jesus' return with which this chapter opened: "Behold, he is coming with the clouds, and every eye will see him, even those who pierced him, and all tribes of the earth will wail on account of him" (Rev 1:7). It's the same issue. All these images make sense if the world was envisaged as flat.

Interestingly, even when the Bible does use clear metaphors for the earth they are metaphors that assume its flatness. Thus Job 38:13 says that the dawn will "take hold of the skirts of the earth, and the wicked will be shaken out of it." The earth is here like a sheet that is shaken out to flick off the dirt.

But some claim otherwise. I vividly recall being told how the Bible amazingly taught that the earth was spherical:

> When he established the heavens I [Wisdom] was there;
> > when he drew *a circle* on the face of the deep,
> when he made firm the skies above,
> > when he established the fountains of the deep . . . (Prov 8:27–28)

> He has inscribed *a circle* on the face of the waters
> > at the boundary between light and darkness. (Job 26:10)

> Do you not know?
> > Have you not heard?
> Has it not been told you from the beginning?
> > Have you not understood since the earth was founded?
> He sits enthroned above *the circle of the earth*,
> > and its people are like grasshoppers.
> He stretches out the heavens like a canopy,
> > and spreads them out like a tent to live in. (Isa 40:21–22)

It would be really groovy if the Bible's earth were a globe. That would make biblical authors the first people ever to have proposed the idea. Alas, one cannot simply read off a globe from these texts. The Hebrew *ḥûg* can mean curve, circle, or dome. The Proverbs text is ambiguous—"a circle/curve/dome on the face of the deep" could pick up on the common ancient Near Eastern notion of the land as a flat disc in the midst of a sea. However, the Job text seems to play with the same notion as Proverbs and it clarifies the meaning somewhat. The circle on the waters is located at the boundary between light and darkness and is thus not to be identified with the edge of a disc-shaped land but with the furthest horizon. This lay upon the oceans at the point where the sky connected with the earth. Why a curve/circle? Perhaps it referred to the belief, common in the ancient world, of a vast circular sea that surrounded the dry land. Some Egyptian and Babylonian texts associate the edge of this circular sea with the place that the sun rises and sets. This seems to fit Job. Presumably the slight curve of the horizon was thought of as a glimpse of the complete circle inscribed by the sky-dome at its intersection with the sea (imagine an inverted glass bowl lowered until its rim touches a body of water).[6]

Isaiah's "circle of the earth" may also allude to the idea of a roughly circular land mass in the midst of an ocean, though it could possibly refer to the *dome* of the earth (i.e., the solid sky dome of Genesis 1, referred to in Job 22:14 as the dome/vault [*ḥûg*] of heaven) above which God is enthroned in the highest heaven. More likely, "earth" is being used to refer not merely to the dry ground ("earth" as opposed to "sea") but to the whole ground floor of the cosmos, composed of land *and sea* ("earth" as opposed to "heaven").[7] In this case the "circle of the earth" is an image of a flat, circular sea surrounding the land. Above this circular tabletop of an earth sits God who looks down from the great height of heaven.[8]

Some have also suggested that Job 26:7 pictures the earth as a globe located in space, something the author could not have known apart from divine revelation. Here is the verse in context:

> The dead tremble
>   under the waters and their inhabitants.
> Sheol is naked before God,
>   and Abaddon has no covering.
> He [God] stretches out the north over the void
>   and *hangs the earth on nothing.* (Job 26:5–7)

It is the context that points us towards the meaning of this somewhat ambiguous verse. The text here is clearly working with a three-decker universe

---

6. We have *no* evidence to indicate that ancient Israelites extrapolated from the obvious fact that the horizon has a slight curve to the conclusion that the earth was a globe. The curved horizon was clear to all ancient peoples and it clearly did not lead them to believe in a ball-shaped earth. The biblical evidence suggests that the same was so with Israel.

7. E.g., Gen 1:1–2.

8. As an aside, the prophet of Isaiah 40–55 could have spoken of the earth as a sphere had he wanted to. The word *kadûr*, meaning "ball," was available for use. Cf. Isa 22:18.

model. Below is sheol, world of the dead (vv. 5–6); above is heaven (vv. 9, 11). In verse 7 the north, most likely referring to the northern part of the sky, is pictured as a tent stretched out. A tent is a common biblical image for the sky.[9] The point is that while the tent of the sky is supported by pillars at the four corners of the earth (v. 11) there is nothing holding it up in the middle, no central pole. It is *God* who stretches the sky across and holds it up. The earth itself, while it too has a foundation of pillars (see Job 38:4–6), is also suspended over nothing. The pillars stabilize the earth but they do not rest on the back of anything else. *God* is the one who suspends it there. Job 26:7 is not an ancient vision of the earth as a globe in space.

So, when all is said and done, the case for a spherical earth in Scripture falls flat, if you excuse the pun.[10]

An Earth-centric Cosmos

In our cosmology the sun lies at the center of a solar system and the earth orbits it. But, of course, such an idea was undreamt of before the work of Nicolaus Copernicus (1473–1543). The biblical cosmos was *geo*centric—the sun, moon, and stars went around a fixed earth.

First, consider the biblical texts that refer to the immobility of the earth. For instance,

> Worship Jehovah in the splendor of holiness;
> tremble before him all the earth (*'ereṣ*);
> yes, the world (*tēbēl*) is established;
> it shall never be moved. (1 Chr 16:29–30, cf. Pss 93:1; 96:10)

---

9. Job 9:8; Isa 40:22; 44:24; 45:12; 51:13; Jer 10:12; 51:15; Zech 12:1; Ps 104:2.

10. We find a move away from a flat earth to a spherical earth model in ancient Greece. Perhaps as early as the sixth century BC some philosophers speculated that the earth is a globe (Pythagoras was said to be among the originators of the idea, and we can find it in the work of Parmenides, Empedocles, Plato, and Aristotle, among others), but it was not until the third century BC that astronomy established the idea. By the first century AD the notion was widely spread and was probably known to some of the New Testament authors.

The name most closely associated with the fully developed spherical-earth-cosmology model is that of Claudius Ptolemy (90–168 AD). His cosmological system became that of the civilized world—including that of the church—until the time of Copernicus. Of course, while the ancient Greeks grasped that the earth was a globe they still thought, as did the biblical writers, that earth was static and that the sun orbited it.

PART I—A TOUR OF THE BIBLICAL EARTH

Presumably this cosmic stability is aided by the firm pillars upon which God founded the earth.[11]

> For the pillars of the earth (*'ereṣ*) are Jehovah's,
>> and on them he has set the world (*tēbēl*). (1 Sam 2:8)
>
> When the earth (*'ereṣ*) totters, and all its inhabitants,
>> it is I [Jehovah] who keep steady its pillars. (Ps 75:3)
>
> He [God] set the earth on its foundations,
>> so that it should never be moved. (Ps 104:5)

Second, look at the following texts that describe the astral bodies circuiting the earth.

> The sun rises, and the sun goes down,
>> and hastens to the place where it rises. (Eccl 1:5)
>
> The Mighty One, God Jehovah,
>> speaks and summons the earth
>> from the rising of the sun to its setting. (Ps 50:1)

Now, of course, we still retain this language of the sun rising and setting and have no trouble using it in everyday conversation. We are simply speaking about *how things look from where we are standing*. We are well aware that such language should not be taken as a denial that we live in a solar system. Biblical authors too were simply talking about how the world appeared to them from observation: it *looks like* the sun rises and moves across the sky; it *feels like* the earth is static. However, the big difference is that we now posses a lot of data that was simply not available to ancient people; data that shows us that in fact things are *not* exactly how they appear to be. Ancient Israelites did not possess this information and had absolutely no reason to suppose that the universe was any different from how it seemed to be. To them, to talk of a static earth and circling stars, sun, and moon was simply to talk of how the cosmos *was*. Thus, even when metaphors or similes are employed by biblical authors to describe the sun they still operate on the same geocentric model. For instance:

---

11. In addition to the texts cited see, 2 Sam 22:16; Job 38:4; Zech 12:1.

> In them [the heavens] he has set a tent for the sun,
>> which comes out like a bridegroom leaving his chamber,
>> and, like a strong man, runs its course with joy.
> Its rising is from the end of the heavens,
>> and its circuit to the end of them,
>> and there is nothing hidden from its heat. (Ps 19:4c–6)

Here the sun is like a bridegroom leaving his chamber at sunrise and like a strong man running across the sky joyfully.

Biblical authors would also not infrequently speak of catastrophic events in terms of the sun and moon being darkened and *the stars falling from the sky*.[12] Even if such language was understood metaphorically—as a way of highlighting the cosmic significance of certain historical events—the metaphor works on an understanding of the stars being considerably smaller and closer to earth than we take them to be; to be objects that circle the earth and which can at least be *imagined* as falling to earth. The image makes no sense on a modern understanding of planet earth and the stars.

This pre-Copernican cosmology helps us to understand a couple of biblical stories in which the sun did not follow its usual route.

Hezekiah and the Reversing Shadow

Hezekiah, king of Judah, was dying. The prophet Isaiah had said as much. But Hezekiah pleaded with God and God told the prophet to convey the assurance that his prayer had been heard and that he would be healed. The story continues:

> And Hezekiah said to Isaiah, "What shall be the sign that Jehovah will heal me, and that I shall go up to the house of Jehovah on the third day?"
>
> And Isaiah said, "This shall be the sign to you from Jehovah, that Jehovah will do the thing that he has promised: shall the shadow go forward ten steps, or go back ten steps?"
>
> And Hezekiah answered, "It is an easy thing for the shadow to lengthen ten steps. Rather let the shadow go back ten steps."
>
> And Isaiah the prophet called to Jehovah, and he brought the shadow back ten steps, by which it had gone down on the steps of Ahaz. (2 Kgs 20:8–11)

---

12. Matt 24:29.

Hezekiah was looking for an impressive sign and that is a pretty impressive sign! Making the shadow go back ten steps required moving the sun backwards in the sky, making it reverse its route somewhat before moving forward again.

Joshua and the Static Sun

Joshua and the Israelites went to the defense of their allies Gibeon when the Gibeonites were attacked by a coalition of five Canaanite kings.[13] God assisted Joshua's forces by throwing the Canaanites into a panic, making them vulnerable, by "throwing large stones from heaven on them. . . . There were more who died because of the hail stones than the sons of Israel killed with the sword" (Josh 10:11). Then we read:

> At that time Joshua spoke to Jehovah in the day when Jehovah gave the Amorites over to the sons of Israel, and he said in the sight of Israel,
> "Sun, stand still at Gibeon,
> and moon, in the Valley of Aijalon."
> And the sun stood still, and the moon stopped, until the nation took vengeance on their enemies.
> Is this not written in the Book of Jashar? The sun stopped in the midst of heaven and did not hurry to set for about a whole day. There has been no day like it before or since, when Jehovah heeded the voice of a man, for Jehovah fought for Israel. (Josh 10:12–14)

So God enabled Israel to finish the task by *making the sun stand still in the sky* for a day![14] Make no mistake; the author was *not* suggesting that this was a common occurrence. Quite the contrary—it was unique! Nevertheless, the sun stopped moving.

Now as astonishing as this event was to the author of Joshua it is even more so for us. This is because in a solar-centric model like our own for the sun to stand still in the sky for a day requires the earth to stop spinning for

---

13. Joshua 10.

14. We should note that one scholar, John Walton, has proposed a plausible alternative interpretation of this story. He suggests the story does *not* picture the sun as stopping. Rather, it relates to omens. Having the sun in the east (over Gibeon) and the moon in the west (over Aijalon) standing in opposition on the 14th of the month was a very good omen but on other days was a bad omen. Walton argues that "stop," "stand," and "wait" is technical terminology used in omen literature. Joshua prayed for God to send a celestial omen that would freak the Amorites out—and God did.

a day, and that has all sorts of repercussions! But these were not problems for people in Bible times. For them the earth stood still and the sun moved. Thus, while it was awesome that the sun should stand still (because it was unique) it was not particularly problematic.

Now that we have caught a glimpse of the whole earth with the sun moon and stars orbiting it we are ready to begin the tour itself.

2

Here Be Dragons!

The Sea

> In the beginning, God created the heavens and the earth. The earth was without form and void, and darkness was over the face of the deep. And the Spirit of God was hovering over the face of the waters. (Gen 1:1–2)

We shall begin our tour of the biblical universe by travelling out to sea because, as we will discover, ancient Israelites thought that the world began in a state of watery chaos. It was from this dark, primeval waterworld that the ordered cosmos emerged. So if we are to start at the very beginning we need to get out into a boat and push off from the shore.

The sea is an awesome place bursting with life, but also a vast, wide, deep, dark, and dangerous place for human beings. It is overwhelmingly powerful and uncontrollable. Ancient people had never explored the bottom of the seas so their depths were largely unknown. As God asks Job, "Have you entered into the springs of the sea, or walked in the recesses of the deep?" (Job 38:16). Absolutely not! In the same way, their expanse was also unexplored. All that was known was that the sea went further than any people had ever sailed. And it was an inhospitable place for humans that could be braved by seafarers, but only at risk of their lives. Even seasoned sailors lost out to the power of the sea in the midst of violent and unpredictable storms. It was a restless, ever-moving, undifferentiated mass that spoke to the ancients of great wonder and life but also deep mystery, mortal danger, raw power, and utter chaos. And it was inhabited by fearsome beasts:

> Those who sail the sea tell of its dangers,
> and we marvel at what we hear.
> For in it are strange and marvelous works,
> all kinds of living things,
> and huge creatures of the sea. (Sir 43:24–25)

Biblical authors were familiar with several "seas." The big sea was the Mediterranean, and was understandably referred to as "the Great Sea" and "the Western Sea." Inland and to the south was the Dead Sea, known as the "Salt Sea," "the Eastern Sea," or "the Sea of Arabah." In the north was the little inland Sea of Galilee, known as "the Sea of Chinnereth." Finally, because of its importance in the exodus story, there was "the Red Sea" (*Yam Suph*) by Egypt.[1]

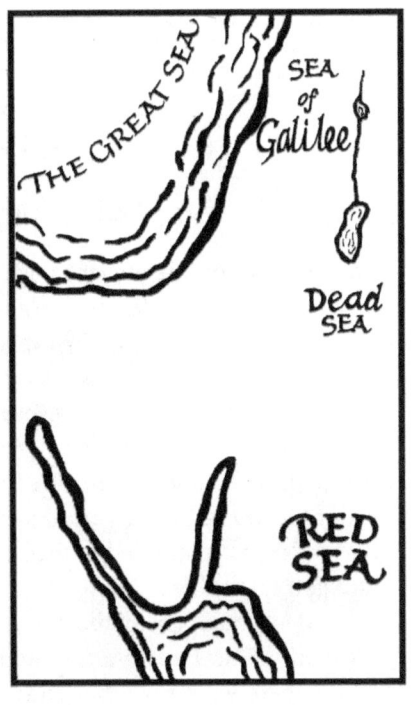

The Mediterranean Sea, running along Israel's west coast, was hugely significant to the civilizations around it. It had long been an important source of food and became increasingly important for trade, cultural exchange, and migration. Certain cities became very wealthy on the riches brought by sea trade. And the water's edge was the location of important sea-related trades such as the extraction of salt (used as a preservative), sourcing building materials (sand and quarried stone) with easy access to sea transport, and the production of purple dye for the über-rich. (Natural purple dye comes from the secretions of certain sea snails. It took the secretions of 240,000 snails to dye one kilogram of wool or silk! Hence its association with the very wealthy.)

Familiar though it was with various seas, ancient Israel was not a seafaring nation. The Bible does speak of the occasional Israelite sea traveler, like the prophet Jonah or the apostle Paul (both of whom had life-threatening

---

1. Although the *Yam Suph* was often associated with the Red Sea, we are not sure precisely which body of water this name refers to.

trouble at sea),[2] and the Gospels testify to a small-scale fishing industry on Lake Galilee, but for the most part Israel left the sea to others.

While not a seafaring people, Israel was familiar with those who were. Their neighbors, the Philistines, had migrated across the sea from the Aegean region in the 1200s BC and settled along the coast, becoming a thorn in the side of Israel. Further north along the coast was the ancient, wealthy, and well-fortified harbor city of Tyre. This city's financial success was based on its maritime trade. Kings David and Solomon had good trading relations with Tyre.[3] Israel's southwestern neighbor Egypt had also long benefitted from the riches of the Mediterranean, and later powers known to Bible writers, such as Greece and Rome, went to great lengths to flex their muscles at sea. So it is no surprise to discover that the sea washes up on the pages of Scripture.

The Primal Sea

Water, Water, Everywhere...

To better appreciate ancient understandings of the sea we need to try to grasp their mythological beliefs about of its place in creation.

In Egyptian mythology everything begins in a vast sea (a god called Nun) and in darkness. This is the ancient Egyptian equivalent of "nothing" or "void." That image makes sense because sea appears to be an unlimited and unpredictable mass. Nun is not the creator god, but in this watery chaos Atum, the creator god, generates himself (!) and then creates the other gods. From the sea rises a large primordial mound of land. The waters and the darkness are constrained in their allocated places and on this land the creator god causes life to burst forth.

Mesopotamian mythology too sees creation beginning from a pre-creation ocean. *Enuma Elish*, the Babylonian creation myth, explains that before there were any other gods and before heaven and earth were set in place, there were only Apsu (the freshwater ocean) and Tiamat (the saltwater ocean). The sky and the earth and everything else were born from this primeval father (Apsu) and mother (Tiamat), whose waters mingled. Several other gods were created from these waters, but they were noisy

---

2. Acts 27; 2 Cor 11:25–26 says that Paul was shipwrecked and adrift at sea three times.

3. 1 Chr 14:1; 2 Chr 2:3–4 (and parallel texts in 1 Kings). Though in later periods various biblical prophets spoke oracles of doom against it (Amos 1:9–10; Isaiah 23; Jer 27:3; 47:4; Ezekiel 26; 29).

and annoying, and freshwater Apsu planned to kill them. Saltwater Tiamat warned the most powerful of these gods, Ea, of Apsu's plan. Ea then killed Apsu and established himself as chief god. Tiamat decided to take vengeance for the death of her husband so Ea's powerful son Marduk engaged her in battle. He slew her and from her divided watery corpse created the heavens and the earth. Here is an Assyrian depiction of a chaos dragon like Tiamat.

In this cultural environment it is perhaps no surprise that Genesis 1 also sees a cosmic sea prior to God's creative activity. "The earth was without form and void, and darkness was over the face of the deep (*tĕhôm*). And the Spirit of God was hovering over the face of the waters" (1:2). This primeval state was pure darkness and ocean, chaotic disorder unable to support life, without form and void.

It was from this dark, watery chaos that God created cosmos. The first three days are all about putting the primeval darkness and water into ordered zones to create environments in which life can thrive. First, he pushes back the darkness with light, keeping it within the bounds of nighttime (1:3–5). (What God actually creates on Day One is not simply light, i.e., bright stuff, but *time*. He creates ordered *temporal* spaces, day and night, into which he will later place bright objects, the sun, moon, and stars.) Next he divides the waters vertically, pushing some of the water up, behind a protective barrier—the firmament or sky-dome. This created a space between the waters above the waters below (1:6–8). Then he pulled the waters back on the horizontal plain, separating the land from the sea (1:9–13). The primeval condition was one "without form" so the first three days concern God's activity of in-forming a world.

This primeval watery chaos has not gone; it is still there, but is held back within certain boundaries by God. In fact, the world of biblical writers is *surrounded* by this dangerous water. The primeval waters remain above the sky-dome,[4] as can be seen from texts such as the following:

> Praise him, you highest heavens,
> > and *you waters above the heavens!* (Ps 148:4)

> It is he who made the earth by his power,
> > who established the world by his wisdom,
> and by his understanding stretched out the heavens.
> > When he utters his voice, there is a tumult of *waters in the heavens* ... (Jer 10:12–13)

God's throne room in heaven is above the heavenly waters and he rules over them.

> The voice of Jehovah is over the waters;
> > the God of glory thunders,
> > Jehovah, over many waters ...
> Jehovah sits enthroned over the flood;
> > Jehovah sits enthroned as king forever. (Ps 29:3, 10; cf. 104:1–3)

The terrestrial ocean itself, with which humans were familiar and upon which they sailed, was also a remnant of these very same primeval waters.[5]

Not only was water above and around, but the land itself was founded *upon* waters (held fast by its pillars). Thus there was yet more primeval water *beneath the earth*, sometimes referred to as "the abyss" or "the deep." This belief in an earth that "floats" upon an ocean also mirrors a view common across the ancient Near East, from Egypt in the west to Sumeria and Babylon in the east. Several biblical passages speak of water below the earth:

> The earth is Jehovah's and the fullness thereof,
> > the world and those who dwell therein,
> for *he has founded it upon the seas*
> > and *established it upon the rivers*. (Ps 24:1–2)

---

4. Which, as an aside, means that recent creationist theories of a water canopy around the earth that collapsed in the Flood are not only unprecedented in the history of the church but also unbiblical. The water canopy *remains in place*.

5. Gen 1:7.

> Give thanks to the Lord of lords,
>> for his steadfast love endures forever . . .
> to him *who spread out the earth above/on* (Heb. *'al*) *the waters*,
>> for his steadfast love endures forever. (Ps 136:3, 6)

> You shall not make for yourself a carved image, or any likeness of anything that is in heaven above, or that is in the earth beneath, or that is in *the water under* (*taḥat*) *the earth*. (Exod 20:4)

As we will see in the next chapter, this primeval ocean that the earth "floated" upon was considered to be the source of the water in springs and rivers.

In the context of a world surrounded by water those Bible passages celebrating God's setting of boundaries for the sea make sense. The sea was dangerous and should God ever stop holding these chaotic waters at bay the world would collapse.

> When he [God] established the heavens, I [Wisdom] was there;
>> when he drew a circle on the face of the deep,
> when he made firm the skies above,
>> when he established the fountains of the deep,
> *when he assigned to the sea its limit,*
>> so that the waters might not transgress his command . . .
> (Prov 8:27–29)

> Do you not fear me? declares Jehovah.
>> Do you not tremble before me?
> *I placed the sand as the boundary for the sea,*
>> *a perpetual barrier that it cannot pass;*
> *though the waves toss, they cannot prevail;*
>> *though they roar, they cannot pass over it.* (Jer 5:22)

> He [God] gathers the waters of the sea as a heap;
>> he puts the deeps in storehouses. (Ps 33:7)

Here Be Dragons!

Israel was not alone in the ancient world in associating the sea with chaos and the danger of descending back into chaos. Indeed, it was a common association. Ancient Near Eastern mythologies told of a cosmic battle between a sky god and a sea monster in which the sea monster is vanquished. In the Ugaritic version, Baal, the storm god, battles and beats Yam, the sea god.⁶ In the Babylonian myth already mentioned, *Enuma Elish*, the fight is between Marduk (the sky god) and Tiamat (a sea dragon goddess). Marduk slays Tiamat and splits her body in half. From one half he makes the sky and

from the other half he made the earth. The well-known creation story in Genesis 1 in which God separates the waters above from the waters below is a non-violent, monster-less version of this same idea.

Nevertheless, we do find the sea monster myth elsewhere in the Hebrew Bible. There are echoes of it in biblical language about God rebuking the sea,⁷ guarding the sea,⁸ and controlling the sea.⁹ But sometimes the chaos monsters slither into full view:

> The pillars of heaven tremble
> > and are astounded at his [God's] rebuke.
> By his power he stilled the sea;
> > by his understanding he shattered Rahab. (Job 26:11–12)

> You rule the raging of the sea;
> > when its waves rise, you still them.
> You crushed Rahab like a carcass;
> > you scattered your enemies with your mighty arm. (Ps 89:9–10)

The first text above is a reflection on the wonders of creation. Rahab¹⁰ is a chaos sea beast shattered by Jehovah. So dramatic is this event that the

---

6. As an aside, the Hebrew word for "sea" is also *yam*.
7. Ps 106:6–9; Isa 50:2; Nah 1:4.
8. Job 7:12.
9. Job 38:8–11; Pss 89:9; 107:29; Prov 8:29.
10. The name Rahab is possibly connected to a root meaning "be boisterous, agitated," like the sea.

HERE BE DRAGONS!

pillars of heaven themselves, observing the fight, tremble in awe at God's angry rebuke.[11] This "rebuke" (*gĕʿarâ*) is more of an explosive blast of breath than a verbal rebuke; the kind of blast that can dry up the sea.[12] But it is not simply force that God uses to defeat Rahab—he uses his divine wisdom and understanding. Understanding is something that chaos does not have.

Psalm 18 pictures Jehovah as a lightning-hurling storm deity battling the sea as he comes to the rescue of the psalmist. So awesome is the Lord that the sea runs off in fear, laying the sea floor exposed, before he even arrives.

> He [God] rode on a cherub and flew;
>> he came swiftly upon the wings of the wind.
> He made darkness his covering, his canopy around him,
>> thick clouds dark with water.
> Out of the brightness before him
>> hailstones and coals of fire broke through his clouds.
> Jehovah also thundered in the heavens,
>> and the Most High uttered his voice,
>> hailstones and coals of fire.
> And he sent out his arrows and scattered them;
>> he flashed forth lightnings and routed them.
> *Then the channels of the sea were seen,*
>> *and the foundations of the world were laid bare*
> *at your rebuke, O Jehovah,*
>> *at the blast of the breath of your nostrils.*
> He sent from on high, he took me;
>> he drew me out of many waters. (Ps 18:10–16)

---

11. Cf. Job 9:13.
12. Isa 50:2; Nah 1:4.

And then there is Leviathan:[13]

> Yet God my King is from of old,
> > working salvation in the midst of the earth.
> You divided the sea by your might;
> > you broke the heads of the sea monsters on the waters.
> You crushed the heads of Leviathan;
> > you gave him as food for the creatures of the wilderness.
> You split open springs and brooks;
> > you dried up ever-flowing streams. (Ps 74:12–15)

The Leviathan of this psalm is the Israelite version of the monster Litanu, a seven-headed chaos beast linked with the sea. Here is a part of an Ugaritic poem in which Mot (god of death) is angry with Ba'al (the storm god) for defeating Litanu:

> Because you [Ba'al] smote Litanu the slippery serpent
> [and] made an end of the wriggling serpent
> the tyrant with seven heads . . .

---

13. The name Leviathan probably means "coiled one."

What is particularly interesting is the similarity of this Ugaritic poem and the following text from the Bible: "In that day Jehovah with his hard and great and strong sword will punish Leviathan the slippery serpent, Leviathan the twisting serpent, and he will slay the dragon that is in the sea" (Isa 27:1). The language is strikingly similar

Ugaritic	Hebrew
Ltn (Litanu)	*Lvytn* (Leviathan)
btn brḥ (slippery serpent)	*nḥsh brḥ* (slippery serpent)
btn ʿqltn (wriggling serpent)	*nḥsh ʿqltn* (twisting serpent)

There can be little doubt that Isaiah is drawing on Canaanite mythology and adapting it for Israelite religion. These sea dragons personify the chaos that must be defeated and put in its place so that order and life can flourish. For the authors of the Bible it is *Jehovah*, the God of Israel, who takes on the role of dragon slayer.

However, this is not the only thread in the Bible describing God's relationship with the sea monsters. There is a second strand in which the dragons are God's fierce pets, creatures that *only God* can command. Job 41 is a classic instance of this second strand. Leviathan, as a sea monster, is presented churning up the waters into a white foam:

> He makes the deep boil like a pot;
>> he makes the sea like a pot of ointment.
> Behind him he leaves a shining wake;
>> one would think the deep to be white-haired. (Job 41:31–32)

And this fearsome beast is completely untamable. God uses his relationship with Leviathan as a means of contrasting himself with Job. Could Job hunt and capture Leviathan? Hardly!

> Can you draw out Leviathan with a fishhook
>> or press down his tongue with a cord?
> Can you put a rope in his nose
>> or pierce his jaw with a hook? (Job 41:1–2)

Job, unlike God, cannot tame such a beast to make it a pet. The very thought is laughable.

> Will he make many pleas to you?
>> Will he speak to you soft words?
> Will he make a covenant with you
>> to take him for your servant forever?
> Will you play with him as with a bird,
>> or will you put him on a leash for your girls? (Job 41:3–5)

"Lay your hands on him/ remember the battle—you will not do it again!" (Job 41:8). This beast is large and strong with armor plated scales that neither swords nor spears nor arrows can pierce, and terrifying teeth. Worse still, he breathes fire!

> His sneezings flash forth light,
>> and his eyes are like the eyelids of the dawn.
> Out of his mouth go flaming torches;
>> sparks of fire leap forth.
> Out of his nostrils comes forth smoke,
>> as from a boiling pot and burning rushes.
> His breath kindles coals,
>> and a flame comes forth from his mouth. (Job 41:18–21)

But much as this dragon is a threat to humans, he is not God's enemy. He is one that God can hunt and capture and tame; one that makes a covenant with God to serve him; that God can play with as with a bird.

Chaos monsters pose no problem for Jehovah. Indeed, they are his servants. The famous Genesis 1 creation story tells the tale of creation without seeing God engaging in any combat with monsters. Now there may well be echoes of the monsters in Genesis 1. We do begin with dark watery chaos, and note that the Hebrew word for "the deep" (*tĕhôm*) in verse 2 may echo the name Tiamat, the sea dragon goddess of *Enuma Elish*. But if there is an echo here it is only very faint. There is no battle; God creates by issuing effortless commands. And the water and darkness are not removed from creation but incorporated into it. Indeed, they are described as *good* when, on Days One to Three, they are put in their right place and kept within bounds. There are great sea dragons (*tannîn*, the same word used to describe Leviathan in Psalm 74 and Isaiah 27) in Gen 1:21, but they are simply creatures that God created and their creation "was good." A similar take on Leviathan is found in Psalm 104.

> Here is the sea, great and wide,
> > which teems with creatures innumerable,
> > living things both small and great.
> There go the ships,
> > *and Leviathan, which you formed to play in it.*
> These all look to you,
> > to give them their food in due season. (Ps 104:25–27)

This is no evil enemy, it is a creature looked after by God and created to "play" in the ocean.

This balance between the conflict and the no-conflict motifs is important. In terms of the way that the biblical material was compiled and organized into a canonical whole, the no-conflict Genesis 1 story is placed first and becomes the lens through which the other passages are to be understood. In other words, the primeval waters are a powerful and chaotic force in God's creation but are only a bad thing when not constrained, when out of control. But God can command them and compel them to serve good purposes. Indeed, they praise God in their submission to his will. Leviathan, God's ferocious pet, represents the forces of chaos woven into the very fabric of God's good creation. These forces are dangerous to humans and beyond human control, but they are not beyond divine control. In certain contexts

God's command of the dragons is pictured in terms of a ferocious battle, but even then there is never any question of the outcome. The dragons cannot possibly win.

Read in the light of Genesis 1 the conflict passages become very vivid ways of describing the power of chaos and of God's surpassing power in taming it. It is also worth noting that the conflict-with-dragons motif is rare in creation contexts in the Bible. It usually crops up when God is resisting political powers, portrayed as monsters, in the midst of history and fighting to rescue his people. God is the divine warrior who comes to deliver his chosen ones. Even in such contexts there are echoes of creation through conflict—such echoes come along with the ancient Near Eastern motif that has been borrowed—but in the Bible they usually become images of *new creation through salvation*.

Tales of the Sea

Understanding this perspective on the sea also opens up our understanding of some other well-known biblical stories. Here are a few to ponder.

Noah's Flood: Uncreating the World

The story of Noah's flood is a story in which the waters of chaos were no longer held at bay and the world ended! Modern people struggle making sense of the story because we cannot understand how there could be a global flood in which the tops of the highest mountains were submerged.[14] Where on earth could so much water come from, and what happened to it afterwards? But we are trying to understand the story from the wrong cosmology. In our understanding of the earth there isn't enough water for the job, but in a biblical cosmology there most certainly is, for the world is surrounded by water. The book of Genesis tell its audience exactly where the water came from: "In the six hundredth year of Noah's life, in the second month, on the seventeenth day of the month, on that day all *the fountains of the great deep burst forth*, and *the windows of the heavens were opened*" (Gen 7:11).

Contrary to common claims, even by scholars, biblical authors did *not* think that the rain came from holes in the sky. They were well aware that rain came from clouds.[15] However, this was no ordinary rain. On this

---

14. Gen 7:19–20.

15. 1 Kgs 18:45; Pss 135:7; 147:8; Prov 16:15; 25:14; Ecc 11:3; Isa 5:6; 45:8; Zech 10:1.

occasion—and *only* on this occasion—the rain *did* come through holes in the sky-dome. Water also burst forth from the subterranean ocean beneath the earth. *That* is how there was enough water to flood the earth.

The significance of the flood story is that it is told as a story of the undoing of Genesis 1, as a move towards *de*-creation. God is unraveling the separations he had put in place between the waters above and the waters below, and between the land and the sea. The terrifying story of Noah's flood—and to the ancient mind it really was terrifying—is almost a return to the primeval chaos of Gen 1:2.

And it would have been the end of the world had God not "remembered Noah" and shut up the fountains of the deep and closed the windows of the heavens,[16] promising never to flood the earth again.[17] As a sign of this end to hostility God reversed his archer's bow and extended it away from himself towards the earth as a sign of peace. Genesis speaks merely of a "bow" in the sky, but we call this divine archer's bow a rainbow.[18]

The Israelites Crossing Sea: Defeating the Dragon

Everyone knows the story of the Israelites, led by Moses, crossing through the "Red Sea." To our minds it is an amazing miracle showing God's great power. But for biblical authors it was more than that.

A strong battle motif can be seen in Exodus 14 in the story of the crossing of the sea itself. As the Egyptians approach the trapped Israelites Moses assured the people that "Jehovah will fight for you." God then tells Moses to stretch out his staff and divide the sea. This Moses did, and a strong wind from Jehovah blew all night, dividing the waters, allowing the Israelites to pass through the sea without getting wet. God, in other words, commanded the waters to step aside, allowing Israel to pass through, but then to collapse back in again as the Egyptians attempt the passage. The song in Exodus 15

---

16. Gen 8:1–2.

17. Gen 9:11–12. As an aside, God does sometimes use local floods as a means of judging a city. For instance, God says he will cause the deep to cover Babylon (Jer 51:42) and the seaport of Tyre (Ezek 26:19).

18. I owe this rainbow insight to Dr. Eric Smith, who kindly showed me an Assyrian image of a ruler extending a bow in just this way.

goes overboard in its use of the language of battle and triumph to describe the crossing. Jehovah used the sea as a weapon to defeat Egypt. The sea—a dangerous primal power—is under God's complete control.

However, the conflict motif in other biblical texts relating to the crossing sometimes turns in more monstrous directions. Several texts speak of the divine warrior Jehovah's awesome presence terrifying the sea into submission in the exodus,[19] while in other passages the divine warrior slays the sea monsters. In Isaiah, Jehovah's victory over Pharaoh is portrayed as a victory over Rahab, the sea dragon:[20]

> Awake, awake, put on strength,
>> O arm of Jehovah;
> awake, as in days of old,
>> the generations of long ago.
> *Was it not you who cut Rahab in pieces,*
>> *who pierced the dragon?*
> *Was it not you who dried up the sea,*
>> *the waters of the great deep,*
> *who made the depths of the sea a way*
>> *for the redeemed to pass over?* (Isa 51:9–10)

The sea was Pharaoh's weapon against Israel, blocking their escape. But Jehovah turned that weapon back against Egypt. God defeated the sea by controlling it, and in so doing defeated Egypt. The exodus is spoken of here in terms of an act of creation. This may seem weird to us. We can appreciate that it is an act of salvation, but how can it be an act of creation? Well, the reason is that salvation is being understood as an act of *new creation* in the midst of the old creation. It is an act of holding back chaos so that life and order can flourish.

Psalm 74:12–15 (quoted earlier) may also allude to the crossing of the sea in the exodus as a battle between God and Leviathan. Notice the language it uses: "God . . . working *salvation*. . . . You

---

19. Pss 77:16; 106:9; 114:3, 5.
20. Egypt is also referred to as Rahab in Isa 30:7 and Ezek 29:3–5 speaks as Pharaoh as a dragon living in the rivers of Egypt.

divided the sea by your might; you broke the heads of the sea monsters on the waters. You crushed the heads of Leviathan; . . . You *split open springs and brooks*; you *dried up ever-flowing streams*." What is interesting is that both Isa 51:9ff. and Psalm 74 are addressed to God to ask him to deliver the people as he did in the days of the exodus. The chaos monster that they faced in Egypt is in need of repelling again so that there can be salvation, which means new creation.

It is worth pointing out that the dragon motif was used in these passages of political-historical events. This should alert us that in such contexts Israelites did not imagine a *literal* scaly beast that could be seen with the eyes.[21] We need to allow for more sophistication in their use of mythological motifs than that. The powers that threaten to unravel the meaningfulness of history are portrayed as chaos monsters that need killing for stability and meaning to return.

The final "end" of Egypt's story, in some texts, is more positive.[22] There is salvation in the end for *even Rahab and Babylon*, God's archenemies: "Among those who know me [Jehovah], I mention Rahab [Egypt] and Babylon" (Ps 87:4).

Jonah and the Gargantuan Fish: God's Dangerous Pets

God told Jonah to go east to Nineveh in Assyria, so Jonah got into a boat and went . . . west, across what we call the Mediterranean Sea. Running off to sea to escape God is a pretty daft idea because the sea itself is under God's control, as are its wee beasties (and the not so wee ones).

First God sends a terrific sea storm that threatens to destroy the boat. The sailors are powerless and terrified. Eventually, Jonah asks the sailors to throw him overboard in order to save the ship. God then sends a "gigantic fish" (*dāg gādôl*) to swallow Jonah and, in effect, rescue him. We typically think of this "fish" as a whale, but the book of Jonah does not say this. The word used, *dāg*, is simply the generic word for fish. However, this is no ordinary fish! It is *huge* and swallows Jonah down in a single gulp. (Tales of giant fish have been around as

---

21. Though *some* passages do appear to envisage an actual Leviathan swimming in the sea (Ps 104:25–26; Job 41).

22. Isa 19, etc.

long as people have sailed the seas—Lucian, in his second-century parody of such tales, *True History*, claims to have seen fish in the Atlantic Ocean that were over 150 miles long!!! One such monster swallowed down his whole ship without even having to chew it.)

It is quite possible that the fish was a cosmic sea monster of the kind we have considered above. It is interesting to note that when the Hebrew text was translated into Greek the word chosen to translate *dāg* was not *ichthus* (fish), nor *enalion* (sea creature), but *kētos*, meaning gargantuan fish or sea monster. This was a word with dark and scary connotations. When Jesus in Matthew's Gospel speaks of the beast that swallowed Jonah it is, of course, a *kētos* (Matt 12:39–40), a vast and lethal sea monster. This is not the friendly whale of modern children's Bibles, smiling sweetly as it rescues Jonah.

Another thing worth noting in this story is the prayer that Jonah prays from the belly of the fish. He prays,

> For you cast me into the deep (*tĕhôm*),
>   into the heart of the seas
>   and the flood surrounded me;
> all your waves and your billows
>   passed over me. (Jonah 2:3)

Jonah has been thrown into the chaotic and dangerous depths of the sea. He speaks of sinking, being surrounded by "the deep," of being tangled in seaweed, and then of going down *further still*—of descending to the roots of the mountains into "the land whose bars closed upon me forever," "the pit" (2:6), "the belly of sheol." Jonah speaks as if he were *dead*—in sheol, the realm of the dead. Christian readers through history have, following Jesus' lead (Matt 12:39–40), noted this link between being in the belly of the fish and being in the realm of death and have seen Jonah's tale as paralleling Jesus' own story of descending into death for a period and then returning back to life. But the association of the giant fish with the realm of the dead further enhanced its monstrous image. This fish, certainly for early Christian readers, *was death*.

Yet, monster though it may be, this is one of God's lethal pets, serving God's purposes. The fish is the means not of Jonah's terrible end but, unexpectedly, of his salvation from the sea. Even the dragons serve God.

Jesus Calms the Waves: Putting the Sea in Its Place

Here is Mark's version of the well-known story:

> And leaving the crowd, they took him with them in the boat, just as he was. And other boats were with him. And a great windstorm arose, and the waves were breaking into the boat, so that the boat was already filling. But he was in the stern, asleep on the cushion. And they woke him and said to him, "Teacher, do you not care that we are perishing?" And he awoke and rebuked the wind and said to the sea, "Quiet! Be silent!" And the wind ceased, and there was a great calm.
>
> He said to them, "Why are you so afraid? Have you still no faith?" And they were filled with great fear and said to one another, "Who then is this, that even the wind and the sea obey him?" (Mark 4:36–41)

Notice first that Jesus spoke to the wind and to the sea as if they were personal agents. Notice too *how* he spoke. He "rebuked" the wind and he commanded the sea to "be silent" and cease its thrashing. The language of "rebuke" and the command to "be silent!" are both found in Jesus' words to the evil spirit in Mark 1:25: "Jesus *rebuked* [the spirit], saying, '*Be silent,* and come out of him!'" So the language of the story suggests a sense of conflict and calls to mind the Old Testament motif of God's battle with the sea. There too God *rebukes* and *stills* the sea.[23] The wind and the sea are no match for Jesus either; to the amazement of the disciples, they obeyed him, just as they obey Jehovah. Indeed, when Jesus commands the sea he is acting *as Jehovah*, the divine warrior defeating the chaotic waters.

Jesus Walking on Galilee: Divine Sovereignty over the Sea

We all know the story of Jesus walking on water.[24] And for most of us it is simply a great show of his power and authority but, truth be told, we don't really see the point of it. However, Jesus did not actually walk on water. You *did* read that correctly. Jesus did not walk on the water . . . he walked on the *sea*. There's a difference and it is important. Here is Mark's version:

> And when evening came, the boat was out on the sea, and he was alone on the land. And he saw that they were making

---

23. Job 26:11–12; Pss 18:15; 104:7; 106:6–9; 107:29–30; Isa 50:2; Nah 1:4.
24. Mark 6:47–53; Matt 14:23–34; John 6:16–21.

headway painfully, for the wind was against them. And about the fourth watch of the night he came to them, *walking on the sea*. He meant to pass by them, but when they saw him *walking on the sea* they thought it was a ghost, and cried out, for they all saw him and were terrified. But immediately he spoke to them and said, "Take heart; it is I. Do not be afraid." And he got into the boat with them, and the wind ceased. And they were utterly astounded, for they did not understand about the loaves, but their hearts were hardened. When they had crossed over, they came to land at Gennesaret and moored to the shore. (Mark 6:47–53)

This is not simply a great party trick to show off his power. This is, in the words of John's Gospel, a *sign*—a powerful deed with a meaning. And that meaning was very much tied up with the meaning of the sea. The Jewish Scriptures had spoken of God, the powerful creator, as the one who walks on the sea, exercising his great power over it: "[God] who alone stretched out the heavens/ and *trampled the waves of the sea*" (Job 9:8). The Greek translation of Job 9:8 says that God "walks about on the sea as on the ground." Mark uses this same word for Jesus walking about (*peripateō*) on the sea. Jesus is acting out the role of God in Job 9!

Jesus, like Jehovah, exercises complete control over the chaotic sea and walks upon its waves as on the dry ground. And in case ancient readers were dumb enough to miss the point, Jesus' words of comfort to his disciples in verse 50 should clarify things. Jesus says, literally, "Be confident, *I am*." This is deliberately ambiguous. On the one hand, it simply means "Take heart, it is me, Jesus." On the other, it is an allusion to God's self-designation, "I am."[25] In other words, in this story Jesus is acting *as Jehovah himself*, Lord of the Sea.[26]

The Sea in Daniel and Revelation: Beastly Powers!

The mythic association of the sea with dangerous monsters crops up in the apocalyptic books of Daniel and Revelation.

---

25. Isa 43:10–11; see also 41:4.

26. Matthew expands the story with an account of Peter attempting to join Jesus. Interestingly, when he speaks about Peter he switches his vocabulary. Matthew tells his readers that Jesus was "walking on the *sea*" (14:25–26; cf. John 6:19). Peter, however, was walking "on the *water*" (14:28–29). This was presumably because Peter was not the divine warrior defeating chaos monsters.

The prophet Daniel had a disturbing vision in which he saw four great beasts come up out of the sea.[27] Each was composed of the parts of various animals blended in unnatural combinations, and each represented a human political kingdom that was more animalistic than human. The beastly kingdoms stand in contrast to "one like a son of man" (Dan 7:13), a human figure who represents "the saints of the Most High" (Dan 7:18, i.e., Israel). His rule was truly human. We do not need to understand the details of the vision. We simply need to observe the understandable symbolic origin of the beasts—the sea. As such, they are forces of chaos and opponents for the divine warrior.

In Revelation this image of Daniel's is picked up and reapplied to a new situation. In chapter 13 John has a vision of a blasphemous beast with seven horns and ten heads that rises out of the sea. As with Daniel's beasts, this ugly brute was composite, like a leopard with bear's feet and a lion's mouth. This sea monster was a symbol for Rome and its emperor, a great political power, granted temporary authority by the dragon (Satan), and in opposition to the church and God. As in Daniel's vision, this was not a literal monster, but the imagery used by both Daniel and Revelation draws on the longstanding tradition of God's battle with chaos monsters from the sea.

Perhaps now we can understand a peculiar comment near the end of the book of Revelation to the effect that in the new creation there will be *no more sea*.[28] We might think of that as a disappointing idea—no more beach holidays, scuba diving, or wind surfing. That is not the point. This is not about water as such. This is about the ever-present danger of chaos and its eventual permanent removal.

"Living" Water?

The Bible shows a lack of interest in classifying marine biology, but biblical authors do celebrate the lush abundance and variety of marine life. In Genesis 1 God dealt with the problem of the formless primeval chaos by forming it—separating the waters—and once the seas were in their place God saw that it was *good*. God then dealt with the problem of the lifelessness of the primeval state by filling it with life. Here is the account of the Wednesday of creation week:

> And God said, "Let the waters swarm with swarms of living creatures . . ." So God created the great sea monsters and every

27. Dan 7:1–8.
28. Rev 21:1.

> living creature that moves, with which the waters swarm, according to their kinds ... And God saw that it was good. And God blessed them, saying, "Be fruitful and multiply and fill the waters in the seas ..." And there was evening and there was morning, the fifth day. (Gen 1:20–23)

We see God's great delight in having the seas swarming with life of all kinds. This the psalmists also celebrate:

> Here is the sea, great and wide,
>> which teems with creatures innumerable,
>> living things both small and great. (Ps 104:25)

Fish, among other creatures (including bushes!), can be thought of as discerning the hand of God in events:

> But ask the beasts, and they will teach you;
>> the birds of the heavens, and they will tell you;
> or the bushes of the earth, and they will teach you;
>> *and the fish of the sea will declare to you.*
> Who among all these does not know
>> that the hand of Jehovah has done this? (Job 12:7–9)

The fish and sea creatures are also obedient to God. The sea creatures obey the Lord, who addressed them directly:

> And Jehovah *appointed a great fish to swallow* up Jonah. And Jonah was in the belly of the fish three days and three nights. ... And Jehovah *spoke to the fish*, and it vomited Jonah out upon the dry land. (Jon 1:17; 2:10)

We see this in the Gospels also, where Jesus arranges for amazing catches of fish for his disciples.

Sea beasts can also be called to worship God: "Praise Jehovah from the earth / you great sea monsters (*tannîm*) and all deeps ..." (Ps 148:7).

Not only the inhabitants of the sea, but *the sea itself* is addressed by God—and, in ritual contexts, by humans—as if it were conscious. Jesus, as we have seen, spoke directly to the sea. The sea also acts and speaks in response to God. Thus God "calls" for the waters and they respond.[29] During the exodus, he "rebuked the Red Sea";[30] both it and the Jordan river "looked

---

29. Amos 5:8; 9:6.
30. Ps 106:9—or whatever body of water *yam supf* refers to.

and fled" when Jehovah led Israel out of Egypt;[31] "they were afraid; indeed the deep trembled" (Ps 77:16). In the awesome presence of God, nature—the sea included—quakes:

> Was your wrath against the rivers, O Jehovah?
> Was your anger against the rivers,
>   or your indignation against the sea,
> when you rode on your horses,
>   on your chariot of salvation?
> You stripped the sheath from your bow,
>   calling for many arrows. *Selah*
> You split the earth with rivers.
> The mountains saw you and writhed;
>   the raging waters swept on;
> the deep gave forth its voice;
>   it lifted its hands on high. (Hab 3:8–10)

In non-ritual normal-life contexts humans do not speak to the sea but *in worship* humans can call on the terrestrial seas[32] and the heavenly seas[33] to praise Jehovah. The waters, in turn, were expected to offer up joyful praise to God; a praise not in words so much as in crashing and roaring obedience.

Interestingly the dominion that God gave humanity in Genesis 1 extends to "the fish of the sea," but no mention is made of the sea itself. That remains beyond human rule. This may explain why the sea never responds to humans in the Bible—it does not obey human orders[34] and it never addresses humans—nor do humans ever call it to. God is the creator of the sea[35] and thus its line-manager, so it is to *God alone* that it responds.

By now you may be feeling a little sea sick. It is time to make our way back to the safety of dry land and to begin the next phase of the pilgrimage.

---

31. Ps 114:3, 5.
32. Pss 96:11; 98:7; 148:7; 1 Chr 16:32.
33. Ps 148:4.
34. Moses' activity with the staff at the "Red Sea" might suggest otherwise. However, note that Moses simply "stretched out his hand over the sea [follow a direct divine command to do so], and *Jehovah drove the sea back* . . ." (Exod 14:21).
35. Exod 20:11; Pss 95:5; 146:6; Jonah 1:9; Neh 9:6; Prov 8:24–28.

3

Between the Devil and the Deep Blue Sea

Land

It's time to step ashore onto the dry land. As a race of landlubbers we probably feel more at home here. Let's begin by taking a look at some of the features of the earth—mountains, deserts, rivers, and springs. At least we know what they are all about, right? But even here things are not as we expect. Consider the words of this psalm:

> Great is Jehovah and greatly to be praised
> > in the city of our God!
> His holy mountain,
> > beautiful in elevation,
> > is the joy of all the earth,
> Mount Zion, in the far north,
> > the city of the great King.
> Within her citadels God
> > has made himself known as a fortress. (Ps 48:1–3)

Notice that Mount Zion is said to be "in the *far north*." The thing is, Zion is actually in the *south* of the Israel. What on earth is going on? Was their sense of direction really *that* poor? This is just one of several peculiar issues we hope to consider in this part of the tour. To unravel the mystery of Zion's migration up north we need to take a walk up into the hills.

Mountains

In certain ancient Near East cultures some mountains were more than simply... well... mountains. They were seen as having a cosmic significance—of being places that linked heaven, earth, and the netherworld; locations where the earth could reach up and touch the heavens and whose roots descend into the underworld. Mountains were places where the gods met, ruled, dispensed their decrees, and sent forth the water of life, and even locations where cosmic battles might take place. Cosmic rule and stability issued from these holy hills.

Even ancient cultures in locations that were exceptionally flat—like Egypt or Mesopotamia, for which mountains only existed on the horizon—gave *some* significance to hills. Thus, the famous temple towers of Mesopotamia—the ziggurats (see picture)—likely represent temple-mountains, stairways to heaven. (The biblical tower of Babel was probably thought of as one such temple-mountain.) And, as previously mentioned, some ancient Egyptian creation myths spoke of a primeval hillock on which creation took place.

However, to really appreciate the role of mountains in some parts of the ancient world we need to look to the peoples who lived in mountainous areas: Hurrians, Hittities, and Canaanites. We shall take a quick peek at Canaanite holy mountains.

In Canaanite mythology the chief god, El, lived atop "the Mount of El" in a tent. There, in some myths, the divine council of gods met to eat and drink and then, under the leadership of El, to make decisions about the running of the cosmos. It is from this mountain that the powerful divine decrees issue forth. El's mountain was also seen as a paradisical source of water that gave fertility to the earth.

The god Ba'al's royal throne was on Mount Zaphon, far north of Palestine. It was the location of much banqueting but also of Ba'al's battle with his enemies. After his victory he urged his ally Anat to put on the face of the goddess of fertility and to come to him. He built a temple that celebrated and brought about cosmic fertility and harmony. So on this mountain matters of life and death were decided by mortal combat.

The land of Canaan was a land with a lot of hills and Israel inhabited the hill country to the west of the Jordan. So it is no surprise to find that mountains also play an important role in Israelite understandings of the cosmos. Biblical authors often complain against idolatry among the chosen people, and the location of much of this idolatry is shrines to pagan gods located in "the high places," on the tops of hills and mountains.¹ This was a natural place for gods to be worshipped. Indeed, some passages indicate that *Jehovah himself* was also worshipped in high places.

Consider the story of Solomon sacrificing to God at Gibeon, a "great high place." Jehovah appeared to him in a dream and offered to grant whatever he requested. The king pleased the Lord by asking for wisdom.² The story is interesting because God at least tolerates Solomon's worship of him at a high place, even though the biblical narrator is uneasy about it.³ However, for the most part the Bible is very negative about worship at high places, because of their association with gods other than Jehovah, and it seeks to focus worship on one location, chosen by the Lord⁴—a location that was mobile for a while but which eventually settled down in Jerusalem.

Yet it was not only pagan gods who had a fondness for heights; Jehovah, the God of Israel, was also linked to mountains. Here are a few worthy of note:

- *Mount Moriah* on which Abraham was to sacrifice his son Isaac and where he had such a game-changing encounter with God.⁵ As such it was described as "the mountain of Jehovah."

- *Jacob's ladder.* The sacred mountain tradition may also be seen in Jacob's dream—during his overnight stay in Bethel—of a stairway set up on the earth with its top reaching the heavens. Upon this "ladder" God's angels ascend and descend.⁶ That place, realized Jacob, was "the house of God" (*Beyt-El*), "the Gate of Heaven." Many scholars think that Jacob's dream was of something like a Mesopotamian *ziggurat*, a symbolic mountain temple that serves as a stairway between heaven and earth.

1. 1 Kgs 13:32–33; 14:23; 2 Kgs 14:4; 16:4; 17:9; 21:3; Jer 7:31, etc.
2. 1 Kgs 3:4–15.
3. 1 Kgs 3:2–3.
4. Deut 12; 16:6, 15, etc.
5. Genesis 22.
6. Gen 28:10–22.

- *Mounts Gerizim and Ebal.* Moses commanded that after the Israelites entered the Promised Land they should build an altar on Mount Ebal, offer sacrifices to the Lord, and inscribe the words of his covenant law on memorial stones. Then some of the Levites stood on Mount Gerizim to declare the blessings that would come on the people if the obeyed the covenant and some of them stood on Mount Ebal to declare the curses that would follow disobedience.[7]
- *Mount Carmel,* the scene of Elijah's epic battle with the prophets of Ba'al—or, more precisely, of Jehovah's battle with Ba'al.[8] In the Canaanite myth mentioned above Ba'al fights and wins victory on his mountain, but in this story Jehovah is "the God who answers by fire" and he whips Ba'al's ass!
- *Eden.* Yes, you heard me right. The prophet Ezekiel says that Eden, the primeval paradise in which God and humanity dwelled together, was located on God's "holy mountain."[9] And when you think about it, a mountain seems like a sensible place for deity.
- *Jesus and mountains.* There is a bumper sticker that reads "Climb mountains—Jesus did!" He most certainly did. Let's focus on Matthew's Gospel. *The mountain of temptation:* Jesus was taken by the devil to a high mountain and shown all the kingdoms of the world in order to test him. *The mountain of teaching:* Just like Moses, Jesus delivered his most famous sermon on a mountain.[10] *The mountain of prayer:* Jesus went up a mountain alone to pray.[11] *The mountain of healing:* Jesus healed crowds of sick people atop a mountain.[12] *The mountain of glory:* Jesus was transfigured at the top of a mountain. This was a visionary revelation for a select group of disciples of his heavenly identity. There with him were Moses and Elijah (both men who had met God atop Mount Sinai). So important was this event that 2 Peter

---

7. Deut 27:4–13.
8. 1 Kgs 18:20–40.
9. Ezek 28:13–16.
10. Matthew 5–7.
11. Matt 14:23.
12. Matt 15:29–31.

refers to the mountain as "the holy mountain."[13] *The mountain of commissioning:* After the resurrection Jesus met his disciples on top of a mountain in Galilee and sent them out into all the world.[14]

So mountains, real and visionary, pepper Israel's experience of God. But two mountains dominate all the others associated by biblical authors with Jehovah—Mount Sinai and Mount Zion.

Mount Sinai

We no longer know the location of Mount Sinai (or Horeb, as it is called in Deuteronomy). But in the book of Exodus it was the holy ground where Jehovah revealed himself to Moses in the burning bush, commissioning him to bring his enslaved people out of Egypt,[15] and where Moses later led the children of Israel after the exodus from Egypt in order to make a covenant with Jehovah and to receive the Law. Indeed, Sinai is preeminently associated with the giving of the Law to Israel via Moses. A vast chunk of the Pentateuch, during which God's commands are given, is set at Mount Sinai.[16] (The link of the divine mountain and the issuing of divine decrees is reminiscent of the Canaanite god El.)

It was not simply the Law but also the instructions for the making of the tabernacle, the mobile tent in which God would dwell with his people and which became the pattern for the later temple in Jerusalem. The pattern for this tabernacle was shown to Moses on the mountain.[17] (Might one think of the tent in which the Canaanite god El dwelt on his mountain?)

The holy presence of God on Sinai is associated with dramatic thunder and lightning and a dark cloud.[18] (This too reminds us of the Canaanite tradition in which a god could reveal himself in thunder and lightning and cloud.)

Another interesting passage in the divine encounter at Horeb was when Moses and the elders went up the mountain and worshipped. God appeared walking on blue (*sappîr*) paving, probably representing the dome of the sky over which he rules from heaven above the sky. (The god Ba'al's palace in Zaphon also had blue paving, and remember too the solid stone blue floor of the first two layers of heaven in Mesopotamian cosmology.)

13. 2 Pet 1:18.
14. Matt 28:16.
15. Exodus 3–4.
16. Exod 19:1—Num 10:13.
17. Exod 26:30; cf. 25:9, 40; 27:8; Num 8:4.
18. Exod 10:14–20; 20:18.

Moses and the elders then feast before Jehovah (just as the gods El and Ba'al also host banquets on their mountains).[19]

Sinai was also the sacred mountain to which the prophet Elijah much later fled from the wrath of Queen Jezebel.[20] There he encountered God, not in the thunder and lightning, as Moses did, but in the silence and in the "still small voice." Sinai is thus not just any old mountain, but is *"the mountain"*[21] or "the mountain of God."[22] Indeed, not only is the mountain named after its association with God, but God too is named after his association with the mountain. He is "Jehovah, the One of Sinai."[23] Certain biblical texts look to God coming in awesome power from Sinai with his angelic armies:

> Jehovah came from Sinai
> > and dawned from Seir upon us;
> > he shone forth from Mount Paran;
> he came from the ten thousands of holy ones,
> > with flaming fire at his right hand. (Deut 33:2)

> The chariots of Jehovah were two myriad,
> > thousands the archers of my Lord.
> > They came from Sinai with the Holy Ones. (Ps 68:18)

One difference between Sinai and the mountain of El is that Sinai, despite its importance, was not God's *permanent* abode. It was a location that God chose to associate with and appeared on but not a location one had to visit to meet with God. God's tabernacle, unlike El's, was *mobile* and the cloud of God's presence could travel from Sinai with Israel. Once in the Promised Land God's tabernacle was located at various sites that God "chose to place his name" (Gilgal, Shiloh, Nob, and Gibeon) and as long as those locations had God dwelling there they were sacred. It was not, in other words, the sacred place that made it a fitting abode for Jehovah but

---

19. Exod 24:9–11.
20. 1 Kings 19.
21. Exod 19:2; Deut 4:11; 5:4–5, etc.
22. Exod 3:1; 4:27; 18:5; 24:13
23. Judg 5:5; Ps 68:8.

rather the other way around—the presence of Jehovah made the place holy. Eventually the presence of God with his people found a permanent location in the solid structure of Solomon's temple in Jerusalem on the second key mountain in Scripture, Mount Zion.

Mount Zion

Mount Zion is the mountain, more of a hill really, on which the Jerusalem temple was located. (According to the book of Chronicles it was the same hill on which Abraham had almost sacrificed Isaac.)[24] But because of its association with the presence of Jehovah it assumed a status far out of proportion to its unimpressive stature. It attracted to itself, like a magnet, a range of motifs associated with sacred mountains.

Let us return to Ps 48:1–3 with which we began this chapter. Recall that Zion, located in the south, is said to be "in the *far north*." What is that all about? The Hebrew word for "north" is *ṣāpôn*, the same word as the name of Baʻal's mountain, Zaphon, located in the far north. The psalm is implicitly claiming that Zion usurps Mount Zaphon as the divine dwelling place. Note that in the psalm God is Zion's fortress and protector. God as military protector of Zion is a common theme in parts of the Bible and reflects the motif of Baʻal military victory when he protects Mount Zaphon from its enemies. Like Zaphon, Zion is attacked by enemies,[25] an event that can cause nature itself to shake and shudder. Jehovah steps in and smashes the enemy, but unlike Baʻal in the Canaanite myth, who as a seasonal god suffers periodic defeat by Mot, Jehovah is never defeated—Zion is impregnable[26] (unless, as in some prophets and historical books, Jehovah abandons it because of the sin of the people). So what appears to be bad geography actually turns out to be a shrewd adaptation of Canaanite mythology.

Zion, as Jehovah's dwelling place, is described as glorious and the perfection of beauty, and the place where Israel can meet her God. And the prophets saw its future as even more glorious. In the famous vision of Isa 2:2–4 (= Mic 4:1–4):

> It shall come to pass in the latter days
>   that the mountain of the house of Jehovah
>   shall be established as the highest of the mountains,
>   and shall be lifted up above the hills;

24. 2 Chr 3:1.
25. Psalms 2; 46; 48; 76.
26. E.g., Isa 29:1–8; 31:1–6.

and all the nations shall flow to it,
> and many peoples shall come, and say:

"Come, let us go up to the mountain of Jehovah,
> to the house of the God of Jacob,

that he may teach us his ways
> and that we may walk in his paths."

For out of Zion shall go the law,
> and the word of Jehovah from Jerusalem.

He shall judge between the nations,
> and shall decide disputes for many peoples;

and they shall beat their swords into plowshares,
> and their spears into pruning hooks;

nation shall not lift up sword against nation,
> neither shall they learn war anymore.

The *highest* of the mountains? Really? It's tiny! But in the vision all the nations shall come to receive God's divine decrees from the *preeminent* holy mountain in the world! Other mountains will be dwarfed!

In the prophet Ezekiel's vision of the future restored temple in Jerusalem, life-giving water flows from under the throne of God out into the holy land bringing fertility even to the Dead Sea.[27] No actual spring ever existed on Zion but as a sacred hill, as *the* sacred hill, it has to have one.[28] So the vision of the glorious future-Zion shows it bursting with water.

Biblical mountains then are not simply great hunks of rock—they are locations associated with divine encounters. More than that, the hills are occasionally spoken of as being in *some* sense alive, and sometimes with the sound of music. "Let the hills sing for joy together" (Ps 98:8) urges the psalmist. And why not? A worshipping hill is a happy hill, so they say: "The hills gird themselves with joy" (Ps 65:12), "the mountains skipped like rams, the hills

---

27. Ezek 47:1–12; Cf. Zech 14:8; Joel 4:18; Isa 33:20–22.

28. Echoing the Canaanite idea of life-giving waters flowing from the mountain of El.

like lambs" (Ps 114:4). Mountains and hills, being at least metaphorically alive, can be directly addressed by God[29] and by human beings.[30]

So much for mountains. What of other land locations?

Wilderness and Deserts: Where the Wild Things Are

Wilderness was not a comfortable place for many ancient Near Easterners. It was, for the most part, hot and dry desert with few water and food sources and, consequently, sparse plant life and animal life. The wilderness was thus an inhospitable and precarious place to be. Indeed, it was not simply the lack of water but the devastating desert storms that made the wilderness such a "terrible land."[31] As God says to Job, it is "an uninhabited land, a desert in which there is no man" (Job 38:26). Added to that, the animals that did inhabit deserts were, from an Israelite perspective, wild and unclean beasts.

In the geography of the ancient Near East, deserts were seen as liminal in-between places representing the zone between civilization and order, on the one hand, and chaos and disorder, on the other; between life, on the one hand, and death, on the other. To be cast out of a community into the desert was to be sent away from the ordered human world and thereby to lose one's social status. In the symbolic thinking of ancient Israel the barren desert, associated with death, was further away on the holiness spectrum from the temple, associated with the living God. It is not that going into the wilderness made one unclean, but simply that the wilderness was symbolically further from the life end of the spectrum and as such represented uncleanness.

This transitional space between order and chaos had a fuzzy boundary. Sometimes the Bible will picture divine judgment in terms of a city being decimated and abandoned to the desert. No longer inhabited by humans it is now the domain of the wild desert creatures. The city has, in effect, ceased to be a beacon of order and civilization and has descended towards chaos, becoming a part of the desert. Here's an oracle about the coming destruction of Edom:

> And the streams of Edom shall be turned into pitch,
>   and her soil into sulfur;
>   her land shall become burning pitch.

---

29. Ezek 6:3–4; Mic 6:2.
30. Hos 10:8 (cf. Luke 23:30); Mic 6:1; Ps 148:9; Matt 17:20.
31. Isa 21:1.

> Night and day it shall not be quenched;
>   its smoke shall go up forever.
> From generation to generation it shall lie waste;
>   none shall pass through it forever and ever.
> But the hawk and the porcupine shall possess it,
>   the owl and the raven shall dwell in it.
> He shall stretch the line of confusion over it,
>   and the plumb line of emptiness.
> Its nobles—there is no one there to call it a kingdom,
>   and all its princes shall be nothing.
> Thorns shall grow over its strongholds,
>   nettles and thistles in its fortresses.
> It shall be the haunt of jackals,
>   an abode for ostriches.
> And wild animals shall meet with hyenas;
>   the wild goat shall cry to his fellow;
> indeed, there the night bird settles
>   and finds for herself a resting place.
> There the owl nests and lays
>   and hatches and gathers her young in her shadow;
> indeed, there the hawks are gathered,
>   each one with her mate. (Isa 34:9–15)

The land will be desolate, swallowed up by the desert, and the wild creatures will make their homes there.

In the symbolic geography of the ancient Near East the desert was often seen as a place of death, closely associated with the netherworld, and the natural habitat for evil spirits. There are some hints in the Bible of the association between demons and deserts. The book of Leviticus contains one such possible wilderness demon in its prescriptions for Yom Kippur, the Day of Atonement. This was the day in which all the sin of the community that had built up over the year and had not been dealt with was sorted in one swift blow, lest the ongoing dwelling of God with his people be threatened. As part of the rite two goats are selected:

> Then he [Aaron, the high priest] shall take the two goats and set them before Jehovah at the entrance of the tent of meeting. And Aaron shall cast lots over the two goats, one lot for Jehovah and *the other lot for Azazel*. And Aaron shall present the goat

on which the lot fell for Jehovah and use it as a sin offering, but the goat on which the lot fell for Azazel shall be presented alive before Jehovah to make atonement over it, that it may be sent away *into the wilderness to Azazel*. (Lev 16:7–10)

So one goat is sacrificed to God while, uniquely in Israelite rituals, the other is not killed but sent into the desert "to Azazel." Symbolically, it carried the sins of the people away into the wilderness. It is not entirely clear what Azazel means. Perhaps the most common opinion is that Azazel was a desert-dwelling demon. There is something to be said for this (and by the time of Jesus some Jews certainly understood Azazel to be a demon, one of the fallen "sons of God" of Gen 6:1–4).[32] The goat is not sacrificed to the demon—that would have been forbidden in Israelite law—but sin is sent to the demon on the goat. Return to sender. The goat is sent as far away from the holy presence of God as possible, into the wilderness unto a demon.

The desert-demon association is possibly found elsewhere too:

- It is worth noting that after his baptism Jesus "was led by the Spirit into the wilderness to be tempted by the devil" (Matt 4:1). "And he was in the wilderness forty days, being tempted by Satan. And he was with the wild animals, and the angels were ministering to him" (Mark 1:13). Forty days in the desert being tested, just as Israel was tested in the desert for forty years. They failed; he passed. While Satan in the Gospels is most certainly not restricted to the desert, it is, symbolically speaking, a fitting place for him.

- The Gadarene demoniac lived away from human communities, alone on the mountains and among the tombs. Luke adds, as an aside, "For many a time it had seized him. He was kept under guard and bound with chains and shackles, but he would break the bonds and be *driven by the demon into the desert*" (Luke 8:29). Again the demons are linked with deserts and death.

- In the book of Revelation, the seer John writes: "And he carried me away in the Spirit into a wilderness, and I saw a woman sitting on a scarlet beast that was full of blasphemous names, and it had seven heads and ten horns" (Rev 17:3) A wilderness is an appropriate place for such an unholy sight.

Yet there is also a sense that demons are not happy in deserts. They too find deserts less than ideal living conditions—they aspire instead to inhabit people. Jesus said, "When the unclean spirit has gone out of a person, *it*

---

32. *1 En.* 8:1–3; 10:4–8; *Apoc. Ab.* 13:4–9; DSS 4Q203.

passes through waterless places seeking rest, and finding none it says, 'I will return to my house from which I came.' And when it comes, it finds the house swept and put in order. Then it goes and brings seven other spirits more evil than itself, and they enter and dwell there. And the last state of that person is worse than the first."[33]

However, precisely because they were "off the grid," deserts could serve as places of shelter from danger for both brigands[34] and Bible heroes like David, fleeing from Saul.[35] That said, they were precarious places to exist and often God had to step in to ensure the survival of the hero. Here is one such story:

> So Abraham rose early in the morning and took bread and a skin of water and gave it to Hagar, putting it on her shoulder, along with the child [Ishmael], and sent her away. And she departed and wandered in the wilderness of Beersheba.
>
> When the water in the skin was gone, she put the child under one of the bushes. Then she went and sat down opposite him a good way off, about the distance of a bowshot, for she said, "Let me not look on the death of the child." And as she sat opposite him, she lifted up her voice and wept.
>
> And God heard the voice of the boy, and the angel of God called to Hagar from heaven and said to her, "What troubles you, Hagar? Fear not, for God has heard the voice of the boy where he is. Up! Lift up the boy, and hold him fast with your hand, for I will make him into a great nation."
>
> Then God opened her eyes, and she saw a well of water. And she went and filled the skin with water and gave the boy a drink. And God was with the boy, and he grew up. He lived in the wilderness and became an expert with the bow. (Gen 21:14–20)

One thinks also of the manna from heaven and the water from the rock the Lord provided for Israel in the desert[36] or the ravens who supplied Elijah with food[37] or the woman in the vision of Revelation 12 who was hidden from the serpent in the wilderness in a place prepared by God where provisions were available.[38]

---

33 Luke 11:24–26.

34. Job 30:3, 8.

35. 1 Sam 23:14.

36. Exodus 16; 17:1–7.

37. 1 Kgs 17:1–6.

38. It is a sign of God's power that he can hide the woman in the wilderness, the serpent's own back yard, and still keep her hidden.

In some ways Israel's time wandering forty years in the wilderness was even sometimes considered a *good* time. However, this was nothing to do with romantic notions of the desert. The desert was still seen as a dangerous and hostile place. What was good was that Jehovah was with his people and that he protected them and provided for them, *even in such a hostile place.*

In the end it lies in God's power to turn fertile land into wilderness or to turn wilderness into fertile land.

> He turns rivers into a desert,
> > springs of water into thirsty ground,
>
> a fruitful land into a salty waste,
> > because of the evil of its inhabitants.
>
> He turns a desert into pools of water,
> > a parched land into springs of water.
>
> And there he lets the hungry dwell,
> > and they establish a city to live in;
>
> they sow fields and plant vineyards
> > and get a fruitful yield. (Ps 107:33–37)

As such, God promised to lead the Jews who were captives in Babylon in the sixth century BC back to the Promised Land through the desert—a second exodus, as it were. But as they go he will transform the wilderness into a rich and fertile place. He will even modify the topography to make the journey easier.

> A voice cries:
> "In the wilderness prepare the way of Jehovah;
> > make straight in the desert a highway for our God.
>
> Every valley shall be lifted up,
> > and every mountain and hill be made low;
>
> the uneven ground shall become level,
> > and the rough places a plain. (Isa 40:3–4)
>
> When the poor and needy seek water,
> > and there is none,
> > and their tongue is parched with thirst,
>
> I Jehovah will answer them;
> > I the God of Israel will not forsake them.
>
> I will open rivers on the bare heights,
> > and fountains in the midst of the valleys.

> I will make the wilderness a pool of water,
>   and the dry land springs of water.
> I will put in the wilderness the cedar,
>   the acacia, the myrtle, and the olive.
> I will set in the desert the cypress,
>   the plane and the pine together,
> that they may see and know,
>   may consider and understand together,
> that the hand of Jehovah has done this,
>   the Holy One of Israel has created it. (Isa 41:17–20)

This fabulous vision is one of several biblical texts that imagines a transformation of wilderness into a water-fed and fruitful space. Which naturally leads us to take a look at rivers and springs.

Rivers and Springs

Where does the water in rivers and natural springs come from? It just seems to seep out of the earth itself. The peoples that ancient Israel had contacts with—Egyptians, Mesopotamians, Canaanites, and Greeks—thought that the water that came out of the earth was fed from a vast underground ocean upon which the earth rested like a lily pad on a pond. Bible writers also appear to share this ancient belief that rivers and springs originate in a vast subterranean ocean and break forth through gaps in the earth.

One common pairing in the ancient Near East was of fertilizing waters from above (rain) with those from below (the springs fed by the underground ocean). For instance, from Ugarit:

> No dew. No rain
> No welling up of the Deep.

We find the same parallel in Scripture. Thus, Jacob prays blessing on Joseph as follows:

> ... the Almighty who will bless you
> with blessings of heaven above,
> blessings of the deep sea (*tĕhôm*) that lies beneath ... (Gen 49:25)

This is most likely a reference to agricultural fruitfulness, a fruitfulness that depends on fresh water from the rains above and from springs and rivers. The latter are described as "blessings of the deep sea that lies beneath."

The blessing of Moses upon the tribes mirrors Jacob's blessing:

And of Joseph he said,
"Blessed by Jehovah be his land,
 with the choicest gifts of heaven above,
 and of the deep sea that lies beneath." (Deut 33:13)

Here any doubts about the reference to rain and springs/rivers in Genesis are dispelled. It is very clear that verses 13–16 are concerned with abundant agricultural blessings. As such the "gifts of heaven above" must refer to rain, and the "gifts . . . of the deep sea that lies beneath" must refer to rivers and springs that emerge from the deep ocean beneath the earth.[39]

We might finally note that one of the sources of the water during Noah's flood was "all the springs of the great deep (*tĕhôm*)" (Gen 7:11; 8:2). These springs were most likely *land-based* springs (cf. the use of *tĕhôm* in Gen 49:25 and Deut 33:13 above) rather than underwater springs. They were springs through which the underground sea would normally seep but which on this fateful occasion gushed forth with catastrophic consequences.

There is more to say about rivers and springs in the symbolic world of the Bible than simply noting their origin in the ocean beneath the earth. Rivers and springs were sources of life-giving water. As such they normally have positive associations, although the destructive experience of rivers in flood did lend them a different set of meanings in some contexts.[40] The life-giving aspect of rivers and springs made them a natural image to use in picturing the renewal of the Promised Land,[41] the eternal life that God gives to his people,[42] or the agent of this gift of life—the Holy Spirit of God.[43]

More than giving life, rivers and springs are themselves seen as "alive" in some way. Thus, rivers can be rebuked by God when acting in a chaos

---

39. See the same parallel in Prov 3:19–20. We also find underground water back in the Genesis 2 creation story. "When no bush of the field was yet in the land and no small plant of the field had yet sprung up—for the Jehovah God had not caused it to rain on the land, and there was no man to work the ground, and a 'mist' (*'ēd*) was going up from the land and was watering the whole face of the ground" (Gen 2:5–6). The word translated "mist" only occurs here in the Bible so its exact meaning is not clear. What is clear is that this (*'ēd*-water was "going up" from the land to water it and is contrasted with rainwater from above. In an ancient Near Eastern context it was most likely thought of as originating in the subterranean ocean.

40. 2 Sam 5:20; Job 22:11; Ps 88:17; Luke 6:48.

41. Ezekiel 47.

42. John 7:38.

43. John 4:10, 13–14; 7:37–39.

monster role[44] and can worship God when in a more submissive role ("Let the rivers clap their hands"[45]).

Rivers also served as important symbolic boundary markers. As we have already seen, in an ancient Near Eastern worldview the main landmass was surrounded by a cosmic ocean or river (both terms were used to describe this expanse of water). This river serves as the boundary of the land. Other important boundary rivers for Israelites were the "Red Sea" and the river Jordan. The former marked the break with Egypt, leaving the sphere of the Pharaoh's control; the latter marked entry into the Promised Land. Both crossings were attended by a miraculous act of God temporarily removing the water out of the way so that his people could cross out of Egypt and then into Canaan, the land of promise.[46]

We shall end the first part of the earth tour by considering this idea of promised land.

The Promised Land

Ancient Israelites saw the land in which they lived as a land that God had given to them by divine promise to their ancestor Abraham.[47] The theme of the promise of the land looms *very* large in the Old Testament. Indeed, we could say that the whole plot is the story of the relationship of God, his people, and the land of promise. God promises the patriarchs that their descendants will inherit the land, Moses leads the people from slavery in Egypt to the land, and Joshua leads them into it; the period of the judges is one of seeking to get a secure foothold in the land, a story that reaches its peak in the kingdoms of David and Solomon. After that it is downhill, reaching a low point in the exiles of the northern and southern kingdoms from the land by Assyria and Babylon respectively. Then the story turns again in a more positive direction as the exiles return to the land and start to rebuild Jerusalem and its temple. So any understanding of the Bible's perspectives on land requires an understanding of its perspectives on *this particular* land.

---

44. Nah 1:4; Hab 3:8.
45. Ps 98:8.
46. Exodus 14; Joshua 3.
47. Gen 12:7; 13:14–17; 15:7, 18–21; 17:8; 24:7. The promise is repeated to Jacob (Gen 28:4, 13; 35:12; 48:4) and inherited by the descendants of his twelve sons.

The Promised Land Like Eden

The land of Canaan is presented in the Bible in ways that are intended to echo the Garden of Eden, God's dwelling place. The land is presented as flowing with milk and honey,[48] an amazingly lush garden paradise.

> For Jehovah your God is bringing you into a good land, a land of brooks of water, of fountains and springs, flowing out in the valleys and hills, a land of wheat and barley, of vines and fig trees and pomegranates, a land of olive trees and honey, a land in which you will eat bread without scarcity, in which you will lack nothing, a land whose stones are iron, and out of whose hills you can dig copper. (Deut 8:7–9)

> But the land that you are going over to possess is a land of hills and valleys, which drinks water by the rain from heaven, a land that Jehovah your God cares for. The eyes of Jehovah your God are always upon it, from the beginning of the year to the end of the year. And if you will indeed obey my commandments that I command you today, to love Jehovah your God, and to serve him with all your heart and with all your soul, he will give the rain for your land in its season, the early rain and the later rain, that you may gather in your grain and your wine and your oil. And he will give grass in your fields for your livestock, and you shall eat and be full. (Deut 11:11–15)

The fruit of the land is so astonishing that the Israelite spies Joshua sent in to reconnaissance the land cut a single bunch of grapes that was so big it took two of them to carry it on a pole between them.[49] These are all idealized visions of the land that echo the paradise of Eden. When the prophet Joel describes the desolation of the Promised Land by an army (of locusts?) he pictures it like the destruction of Eden:

---

48. Deut 11:9; 26:15.
49. Num 13:23.

> The land is like the garden of Eden before them [the locusts],
>> but behind them a desolate wilderness,
>> and nothing escapes them. (Joel 2:3)

Some of Israel's prophets during the time of the exile from the land promised a return to the land akin to a return to Eden.

> For Jehovah comforts Zion;
>> he comforts all her waste places
>
> and makes her wilderness like Eden,
>> her desert like the garden of Jehovah;
>
> joy and gladness will be found in her,
>> thanksgiving and the voice of song. (Isa 51:3)

> And they will say, "This land that was desolate has become like the garden of Eden, and the waste and desolate and ruined cities are now fortified and inhabited." (Ezek 36:35)

The restored land will be a lush garden,[50] a new creation.[51] Like Eden the Promised Land is the place that God has chosen to dwell with his people, a sanctuary location where blessing flows from heaven to earth. As such we may even think of the Promised Land as intended to be a scaled down version of the whole creation, and Israel is like Adam, created outside the garden and placed into the garden by God.[52] This land is more than just land. It represents creation as a paradise, a temple garden for God to live with his people.

Two Angles of the Promised Land's Borders

The borders of the Promised Land are mapped out in two quite distinct ways in the Bible. The first mapping pattern—found in Numbers, Deuteronomy, Joshua, and Ezekiel—considers Israel's western boundary to be marked by the Mediterranean Sea and the eastern boundary to be marked by the *Jordan river* (although the north-eastern boundary goes far into Syria and Lebanon).[53]

---

50. Isa 58:11; Jer 31:12.
51. Jer 3:16; 23:3; Ezek 36:11; Zech 10:8.
52. Gen 2:8.
53. Num 34:1–12.

PART I—A TOUR OF THE BIBLICAL EARTH

The second mapping pattern—found in Genesis, Exodus, and 1–2 Samuel and 1–2 Kings—sets the western boundary at *the Nile* and the eastern boundary at the *Euphrates river*. Thus in Genesis God promises Abram to "give this land, from the river of Egypt [the Nile] to the great river, the river Euphrates" (Gen 15:18). In Exodus God says, "I will set your border from the Red Sea to the Sea of the Philistines [the Mediterranean], and from the Wilderness to the Euphrates" (Exod 23:31; cf. 1 Kgs 5:1; Deut 1:7; 11:24).

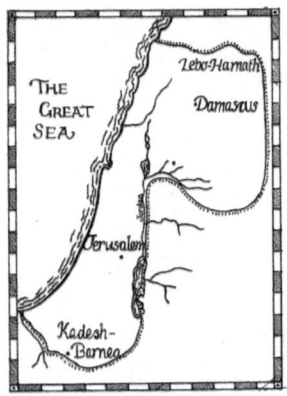

The First Border Pattern

What is interesting is that both these maps were held together in a certain tension in the Bible. We even find both together in the same chapter. Thus on one occasion God promises the land from the Mediterranean to the Euphrates and yet in the same episode says that the land is entered by crossing the river Jordan from the west.[54]

Historically Israel at its height ruled over much of the land in the first mapping (though the northeastern area was never under its control) but didn't even came close to ruling all the land in the second mapping, nor is there any evidence that it sought to do so. So what is going on here?

Several features of these maps deserve comment. First, notice the importance of water as a boundary marker. This may call to mind the Babylonian world map we looked at in the introduction. There too a river/ocean marks the boundaries of the earth. Evidence from Egypt, Phoenicia, and Greece suggests that the same idea was found there as well. So both boundary maps of Israel may allude to this mythic idea of the world framed by water. The meeting place of expanses of water and land serves as a symbolic boundary between order and the threat of chaos. The link that we have already noticed between the Promised Land and creation suggests that the Land was conceived of by some as a microcosm of creation. As such water boundaries make a lot of sense and serve to reinforce that association. In such symbolic geography it makes some sense that if one was to push the western boundary beyond the Jordan one would have to keep pushing it until stopped by the next major river, the Euphrates, even if the land in between was of little or no interest.

---

54. Deut 11:24, 31; Josh 1:2, 4. The land between the Jordan and the Euphrates has an ambiguous status—both inside and outside the Promised Land. Some biblical traditions see the borders of the Promised Land extended to include the Transjordan tribes while others see the border remaining at the Jordan.

The Second Border Pattern

Second, unlike many territorial maps, the boundaries are not descriptions of what is the case *now*. They are offered, rather, as promises of what will be the case at some point in the future.

Third, it has been suggested that the two maps reflect Israel as conceived in relation to two of the great empires that it was engaged by—Egypt and Babylonia. The first mapping pattern (the Jordan map) encompasses the boundaries of the province of Canaan under Egyptian rule. In the symbolism of the exodus story, God liberated Israel from slavery in Egypt and then gave them the land of Canaan, liberated from Egyptian dominance. So the borders of map 1 are simply the Egyptian-defined borders of Canaan rather than a description of Israel's exact borders at any specific moment in its history. The map forms part of Israel's resistance to Egyptian rule.

The second mapping pattern (the Euphrates map) reflects the politics of the Neo-Babylonian period. The map presents Israel as a power almost all the way up to Babylon itself. Babylonian imperial geography considered all the land and peoples west of the Euphrates as conquered people. The biblical map turns this around. The land west of the Euphrates is *not* the land of the conquered but the land of promise. Thus both maps represent one way in which Israel resisted major imperial powers. The maps symbolically push these imperial enemies back behind river boundaries.

Fourth, the second map is not actually intended as a boundary map in any formal or technical sense—a comparison with ancient Near Eastern boundary documents shows that it is *far* too vague for that. It is rather a symbolic map picturing a future world rule for the little nation of Israel akin to the empires of Assyria and Babylon.[55] The world is represented in its wholeness by elements that reflect it and its boundaries—sea, rivers, wilderness, and mountains.

The Centrality of the Promised Land

Many Jews by the time of Jesus and later saw the Promised Land as being located at the center of the world. Jerusalem was located at the center of Judah,[56] as its navel,[57] but more than that, at the center of the whole earth,[58] "the center of the navel of the world."[59]

It is possible that this belief can be found further back, in the Old Testament itself. In particular, two texts in Ezekiel are often thought to contain the idea. First, "Thus says the Lord Jehovah: 'This is Jerusalem. I have set her *in the center of the nations*, with countries all around her'" (Ezek 5:5). Second, concerning Gog, an end-time enemy of Israel who will attack the promised land, God says: "On that day, thoughts will come into your [Gog's] mind, and you will devise an evil scheme and say, 'I will go up against the land of unwalled villages. I will fall upon the quiet people . . . who were gathered from the nations, . . . *who dwell at the center of the earth*'" (Ezek 38:10–12). The Hebrew word for "center" here, *tabbûr*, certainly has the meaning of navel in post-biblical Hebrew, and it is indeed possible that in Ezekiel's Hebrew the idea is also that Israel (or perhaps Jerusalem itself) is located at the navel of the earth.

Some later Christian writers saw Golgotha, where Jesus was crucified just outside the city walls of Jerusalem, as the center of the earth. For instance, Cyril of Jerusalem, in the fourth century, spoke of Jesus extending his arms on Calvary to embrace the ends of the earth, "for this Golgotha is the mid-point of the earth" (*Catechesis* 13.28). After all, had not God been spoken of by the psalmist as "working salvation in the midst of the earth" (Ps 74:12)? The beautiful Hereford Mappa Mundi offers a thirteenth-century

---

55. Cf. Psalm 2, etc.
56. *Letter of Aristeas* 83.
57. Josephus, *War* 3:51–52.
58. 1 *En.* 26:1–2.
59. *Jub.* 8:19; cf. *b. San.* 37a.

visual presentation of this same idea. On the map we see the whole earth as pictured by these medievals, and there, right at the centre, is Calvary, just outside Jerusalem.

Alongside the vertical model of holy space, represented by the cylinder of holiness on page 12, the Bible also contains a *horizontal* model of holy space.

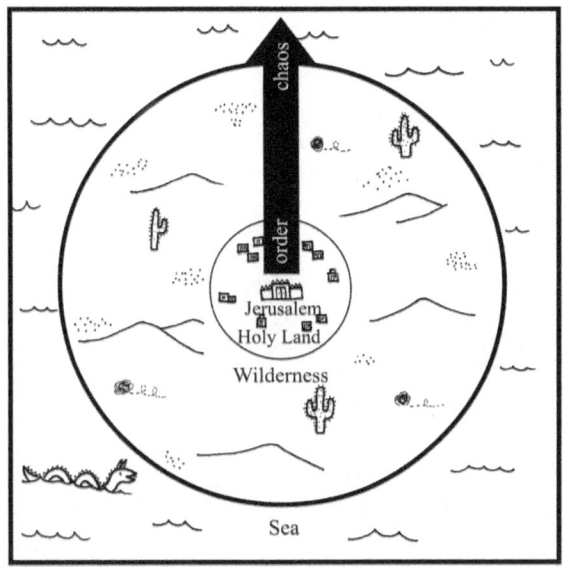

This model moves from a center of total holiness outwards towards a periphery, with decreasing holiness and order the further from the center one moves. At the periphery lies chaos. For Israel the center was Jerusalem's temple surrounded by the holy land, promised by God to the patriarchs. Beyond that was wilderness and beyond the wilderness lay the sea.

The story of the exodus from Egypt can be read as a story of the God-guided journey of Israel from the periphery to the center. Israel was in Egypt, the land of slavery and chaos and death. God delivered them by leading them through the boundary-marking sea (*yam suph*, literally, "sea of the edge"). There God defeated the chaos dragon and led Israel into an in-between place, the wilderness. Here was great danger—hunger, thirst, and hostile peoples—but God provided and protected. He led the people to the land where they would dwell with him and find rest. This is not simply mundane geography or history as we know it—this is *meaning-full* geography and history, rich in sacred symbolism.

There is plenty more that we could say about the land and especially its inhabitants, both human and animal. But we have seen enough for the time being. Now it is time to head underground into the deep and dark chambers of sheol.

4

A Land Down Under

Sheol/Hades

Here is a story from a Christian evangelistic newspaper a few years ago. It was not printed as a joke.

Geologists Drilling 9 Mile Hole Hear the Screams of Lost Souls in Hell

The shrieks of condemned souls have been heard coming from the world's deepest hole, where terrified researchers fear they've unleashed the evil forces of hell upon the earth. "The information we're collecting is so astounding that quite frankly, we're afraid of what we might find down there," declares Dr. Viktor Azzakov, director of the project to drill a nine-mile-deep hole in remote Siberia. Geologists were dumbfounded when, after drilling several miles into the bedrock, the drill bit began to spin wildly. "The only explanation is that the very centre of the earth is hollow," states amazed Dr. Azzakov. Another surprise was the extreme heat detected in the depths of the earth. "Our calculations indicate temperatures of 2,000 degrees Fahrenheit," notes Dr. Azzakov. "This is ten times higher than we expected. It almost seems as if a fiery inferno is raging within the earth's core."

The latest discovery, however, is so earth-shattering that scientists are afraid to continue with the project. In an attempt to listen to the shifting of the earth's different levels, a high-sensitivity microphone was extended into the shaft. What they heard turned the logical-minded Russian scientists into trembling wrecks! "There was a faint high-pitched noise, which we thought was our equipment," explains Dr. Azzakov. "But after we made some adjustments, we realised it was indeed coming from the earth's centre. We could hardly believe our ears. What we were listening to was the unmistakable sound of a human voice, screaming in pain." "Although one voice was prominent, we could also make out, as if in the background, the screams of thousands, perhaps millions of tormented souls." Since the ghastly discovery, half the scientists have resigned in fear. "Hopefully, whatever's down there will stay down there," adds Dr. Azzakov.

I confess that when I read this my jaw dropped open in amazement ... that anyone would be so naïve as to take such a story seriously. We all know what you'd find in our cosmos if you drilled down into the ground—lots of hard and hot stuff: rocks, metals, magma, and the like. You would certainly *not* find chambers full of dead people being tormented!

But I was perhaps a little too hasty. Like us, biblical authors were well aware that if you dug down into the ground you'd find rocks and metals but they also appear to have believed that further down—at basement level, if you will—was the realm of the dead, sheol. This final stop on the earth tour takes us into the dark and dismal depths of the pit. But before that, on our way down, we can take a look out of the window and see some miners.

Mines

There is plenty of evidence of mining in the ancient world, with rocks, gems, and metals put to diverse uses, from building materials to pottery to weaponry to jewelry. Job 28 contains a wonderful poem about the dark hidden places beneath the earth that are inaccessible to beast and bird but which intrepid humans can penetrate in order to extract their wealth:

> Surely there is a mine for silver,
>> and a place for gold that they refine.
> Iron is taken out of the earth,
>> and copper is smelted from the ore.
> Man puts an end to darkness
>> and searches out to the farthest limit
>> the ore in gloom and deep darkness.
> He opens shafts in a valley away from where anyone lives;
>> they are forgotten by travelers;
>> they hang in the air, far away from mankind; they swing to and fro.

> As for the earth, out of it comes bread,
>> but underneath it is turned up as by fire.
> Its stones are the place of sapphires,
>> and it has dust of gold.
> That path no bird of prey knows,
>> and the falcon's eye has not seen it.
> The proud beasts have not trodden it;
>> the lion has not passed over it.
> Man puts his hand to the flinty rock
>> and overturns mountains by the roots.
> He cuts out channels in the rocks,
>> and his eye sees every precious thing.
> He dams up the streams so that they do not trickle,
>> and the thing that is hidden he brings out to light. (Job 28:1–11)

Yet, the poet continues, wisdom and insight are even more precious and even more elusive than these treasures.[1]

Ancient Near Easterners employed the rich resources of the earth in a variety of ways and so they were willing to face the dark and danger of the world under the ground . . . to a point. But they also believed that deep in the belly of the earth was the realm of the deceased, the pit, which was inaccessible to the living. *That* is where we are heading now.

The Realm of the Dead in the Ancient Near East

The peoples around Israel entertained all sorts of intricate beliefs about the underworld.

Egypt

Ancient Egyptians had gradually developed a range of very elaborate views on the post-mortem existence of the soul[2] in the underworld (*Duat*), not all of them entirely consistent.

---

1. Job 28:12–19.
2. I am using "soul" as a blunt word to cover a range of Egyptian words for the afterlife self. The *ka* was like a spiritual body within the physical body that could survive apart from that physical body. Life is impossible without a *ka*. The *ba*, often pictured as a bird with the human head of the deceased, seems to emphasize the disembodied self as mobile. When the deceased reached its blessed goal it is described as an *Akh*.

To understand Egyptian views of the afterlife we need to appreciate Egyptian views of the sun. The sun, symbol of life and divinity, was a god named Re. The sky was a cosmic ocean above the air that he would row across on a boat during the day. At night Re would sail through the netherworld, the *Duat*. Sunset was thus his death but each sunrise he was reborn.

Re's journey through the underworld was fraught with danger, not least from the Apophis monster, representing chaos and often pictured as an endless serpent. Re's rebirth was possible because when he was in the *Duat* he merged with Osiris, god of the underworld. We could perhaps think of Re as the soul and Osiris as the corpse of a single deity. During the day the body and its corpse are separated while Re sails the sky and Osiris is in his tomb, but during the night body and soul gradually reunite until at midnight, when Re is at his weakest, they merge thereby reinvigorating Re, who gradually then rises again into a new day.

Now a Pharaoh who died sought to join with Re and Osiris, indeed to *merge* with Re and Osiris, so that he too could successfully navigate the underworld and then emerge to sail the cosmic ocean as a god. If all went well, and that was not at all guaranteed, Osiris and Re's story would be the Pharaoh's story. The Pharaoh's body—identified with the god Osiris—would never leave its crypt but the Pharaoh's soul—identified with the sun god Re—would descend into the underworld at night, merge with its body/Osiris, then rise *with* and indeed in some sense *as* the sun god himself into the celestial sphere.

In later Egyptian texts, as witnessed in the *Book of the Dead*, the hope of such an afterlife was "democratized" and extended beyond Pharaohs to private individuals, at least those with enough wealth to pay for the necessary requirements relating to proper burial.

At death a human being—composed of a body and a soul—was disintegrated. The goal was to achieve a new re-integration of these parts in the afterlife when the soul had journeyed through the underworld to *Duat*.

The underworld is a huge area beneath the earth connected with, among others, the gods Osiris, Anubis, and Horus; it contains islands, rivers, lakes, fields, caverns, lakes of fire, and the like. Burial chambers could serve as entry points into (and out of) *Duat* for spirits. The dead soul must embark on a dangerous journey through the underworld in order to reach the afterlife—first, the Marshland of Rushes (a kind of reed marsh paradise) and then beyond the underworld to the celestial ocean.

On this perilous voyage the soul would have to contend with gatekeeping gods and monsters and face a final judgment on their life—the weighing of the heart. Here their heart, the seat of the emotions and intellect, is placed on an unbiased scale and weighed against the feather of Maat, the goddess who personifies truth, order, and justice.

If one's sins weighed more than the feather then one's soul was devoured by Ammit, "she who swallows the dead."

There was a range of gruesome afterlife punishments including torture, decapitation, being burned in fire pits, being sacrificed, being dismembered, being cooked and eaten, and being consigned to a watery limbo to float forever like one drowned. The chances of messing up big time were large and so the dead person needed all the help that they could get. To this end they were equipped with esoteric knowledge to help them pass various tests and an armory of magical spells, words, and items of power that could control the irrational forces of the underworld, coercing gods to do the will of the deceased.

Mesopotamia

In ancient Mesopotamia it was believed that when a person died a ghost (Sumerian, *gidim*; Akkadian, *eṭemmu*) was formed, distinct from the body, which then leaves the body behind. The personality of the dead person continued as the ghost going down all the way past the Apsu (the underground freshwater ocean) to the netherworld. Only one text indicates the depth of the underworld and that places it at 100 leagues below sea-level.

The underworld was often called "Great City" and seems to have been thought of as a massive underground metropolis, with palaces, a giant temple complex, a courtyard, and dwellings for the dead. It was a dark place and had a (dry) river, (infertile) fields, and even (wool-less) sheep! It was ruled by the goddess Ereshkigal (as seen in the picture here) and her consort Nergal (or Ninazu), and, in later stories, a range of other fearsome gods with power over death.

When a person died and their ghost was formed it went on a journey to the underworld, although not a great deal is made of this journey. Some texts speak of a road—"the road of no return"—to the underworld, others of a stairway, and others of a river, the Hubur, that flows past the entrance and must be crossed to enter the city via the seven great gates with their fourteen gatekeepers.[3] On their arrival in the city the dead offer gifts to the gods. Then the fate of the ghost is decided. This fate was not based upon any moral evaluation of the life of the deceased person; it was simply the decree of the gods.

Within the underworld the ghosts take their place in the society of the dead. They live in houses, eat meals, fulfill their new social roles, and can be reunited with deceased loved ones.

The living would regularly offer food and drink to the dead (because the food and drink in the netherworld was crap, sometimes *literally*). If one looked after the ghosts well then things should go well. Pity the ghost that had no one living to care for it. Some of them got really hacked off and came to the living world to hunt for food or to punish those who should have cared for them but failed to. Such punishment could be in the form of bad luck and illness. If the living had any hassle with ghosts they would appeal to the sun god, Utu, for help in his role as the one who mediated between the two hemispheres of existence.

---

3. Traditions on the river differ. In one tradition it is a dry riverbed, in the other it is a great river with a boatman.

The afterlife was by no means a sure ticket to paradise. In *The Epic of Gilgamesh* the dying Enkidu tells his companion Gilgamesh of a vision he had of being confronted by a man with frightening features "like a Thuderbird," hands like lion's paws, and claws like an eagle's talons. The man grabbed Enkidu by the hair, struck him, bound him like a dove, and led him captive "to the house of darkness, seat of Irkella":

> to the house which no one who enters leaves,
> > on the path that allows no journey back,
> to the house whose residents are deprived of light,
> > where soil is their sustenance and clay their food,
> where they are clad like birds in coats of feathers,
> > and see no light but dwell in darkness. (VII 185–90)

Enkidu entered the House of Dust and discovered the dead, past rulers and priests, and underworld gods ruled over by their queen, Ereshkigal. This vision of the afterlife, with its dark perpetual imprisonment and poor diet, holds out little hope for those facing death. Unlike in Egypt, there is no hope for any ascent to the celestial realm.

There are other important ancient afterlife beliefs, such as those found at Ugarit and those from ancient Greece, but we have said enough to provide a feel for the kind of ideas in circulation among the peoples ancient Israelites had some contacts with.

The Realm of the Dead in Ancient Israel

What is perhaps most surprising about the religion of the Old Testament is how *little* interest it shows in the afterlife and the domain of the dead. Israel had no epics about guided tours of the underworld nor any elaborate tales of the journey of a dead person through judgment to sheol. The religious literature of Israel was very much focused on life with Jehovah *this side* of the grave.

Nevertheless, we do find references from Old Testament texts written across several centuries (suggesting the stability of the concept over time) that reflect a belief in an underworld realm of the dead, sheol.

PART I—A TOUR OF THE BIBLICAL EARTH

Going Underground

The first thing to say about sheol is that it is located deep within the earth. This is seen in the language used to describe it:

(a) it is "below"[4]

(b) it is called "the pit"[5] and "the depths of the earth"[6]

(c) one goes "down" to sheol and "ascends" from it

(d) one digs towards it[7]

(e) it is associated with dust and worms[8]

(f) in the ancient cosmos it is the opposite of heaven (which is in the sky)[9]

We can also see its subterranean location in a couple of well-known narratives. The book of Numbers tells a story in which Korah & co. cause many among the people to turn against Moses and Aaron, God's appointed leaders. Bad move! We read:

> And Jehovah spoke to Moses, saying, "Say to the congregation, Get away from the dwelling of Korah, Dathan, and Abiram." Then Moses rose and went to Dathan and Abiram, and the elders of Israel followed him. And he spoke to the congregation, saying, "Depart, please, from the tents of these wicked men, and touch nothing of theirs, lest you be swept away with all their sins." So they got away from the dwelling of Korah, Dathan, and Abiram. And Dathan and Abiram came out and stood at the door of their tents, together with their wives, their sons, and their little ones. And Moses said, "Hereby you shall know that Jehovah has sent me to do all these works, and that it has not been of my own accord. If these men die as all men die, or if they are visited by the fate of all mankind, then Jehovah has not sent me. But if Jehovah creates something new, and the ground opens its mouth and swallows them up with all that belongs to them, and they go down alive into sheol, then you shall know that these men have despised Jehovah."

---

4. Deut 32:22; Ps 86:13; Job 11:8; Prov 9:18; Isa 7:11.
5. Jonah 2:6; Ps 40:2; Isa 14:15; Ezek 32:23.
6. Ps 71:20.
7. Amos 9:2.
8. Job 17:16; Isa 14:11.
9. Job 11:8; Ps 139:8; Isa 7:11; Amos 9:2.

And as soon as he had finished speaking all these words, the ground under them split apart. And the earth opened its mouth and swallowed them up, with their households and all the people who belonged to Korah and all their goods. So they and all that belonged to them went down alive into sheol, and the earth closed over them, and they perished from the midst of the assembly. And all Israel who were around them fled at their cry, for they said, "Lest the earth swallow us up!" (Num 16:23–34)

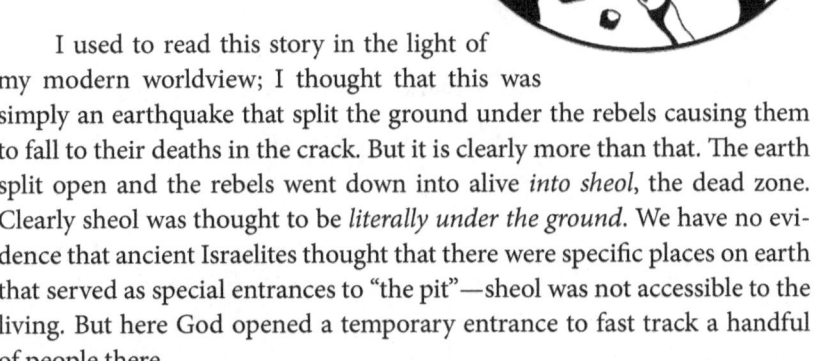

I used to read this story in the light of my modern worldview; I thought that this was simply an earthquake that split the ground under the rebels causing them to fall to their deaths in the crack. But it is clearly more than that. The earth split open and the rebels went down into alive *into sheol*, the dead zone. Clearly sheol was thought to be *literally under the ground*. We have no evidence that ancient Israelites thought that there were specific places on earth that served as special entrances to "the pit"—sheol was not accessible to the living. But here God opened a temporary entrance to fast track a handful of people there.

A second story concerns the "witch" of En-Dor.[10] Contacting the dead was common in the ancient world but *strictly forbidden* in Israel.[11] King Saul, in sheer desperation for some supernatural guidance, secretly consults a medium at En-Dor.

> Then the woman said, "Whom shall I *bring up* for you?" He said, "*Bring up* Samuel for me."
> When the woman saw Samuel, she cried out with a loud voice. And the woman said to Saul, "Why have you deceived me? You are Saul." The king said to her, "Do not be afraid. What do you see?" And the woman said to Saul, "I see a god *coming up out of the earth*." He said to her, "What is his appearance?" And she said, "An old man is *coming up*, and he is wrapped in a robe." And Saul knew that it was Samuel, and he bowed with his face to the ground and paid homage.

10. In Hebrew she is called "the mistress of the pit."
11. Lev 19:31; 20:6; Deut 18:9–14; Isa 8:9.

Then Samuel said to Saul, "Why have you disturbed me by *bringing me up?*" Saul answered, "I am in great distress, for the Philistines are warring against me, and God has turned away from me and answers me no more, either by prophets or by dreams. Therefore I have summoned you to tell me what I shall do." (1 Sam 28:11–15)

The direction from which the spirit comes is repeated five times—he arises *up* from out of the earth. That makes perfect sense because the dead dwell under the earth.

Darkness

So what is sheol like? Israelite authors say very little about it but there are little clues scattered here and there.

First, and most important, the domain of death was the opposite of the living God. The Old Testament often seeks to distance God, who is deeply and essentially *alive*, from death. So in most Old Testament texts those in sheol are further from God than the living. This is why the pious worshippers of Jehovah contemplate it with some dread.[12] Those in the pit cannot remember God or praise him;[13] they are cut off from God.[14]

Yet, even though sheol is, in many ways, the opposite of Jehovah's realm, it was still totally open before him;[15] God has complete access to the realm of the dead.[16] Alas, this did not mean that the inhabitants of sheol had any access to God; they did not.

The language used to describe this quasi-existence in the depths of the earth is vague but depressing.

    a) It is a location of deep and permanent *darkness.*[17]

---

12. Pss 16:10; 30:3; 49:15; 86:13.
13. Pss 6:6; 88:12; Isa 38:18; Jonah 2:5.
14. Ps 88:5.
15. Job 26:5; Prov 15:11.
16. Amos 9:2; Ps 139:8.
17. Job 10:21; Ps 88:6, 12; Lam 3:6; Sir 22:11.

b) It is a place imagined as having bars[18] and gates[19] and from which one cannot escape[20]

c) Nothing much happens—the inhabitants are weak[21] and almost totally inactive; they just lie still and no one speaks much.[22] Indeed some texts envisage the dead as being forgotten by the living[23] and as themselves knowing nothing.[24]

Psalm 88 gives a good feel for this perspective on the netherworld. The psalmist faces a dire situation in which he contemplates with dread the possibility of his own death and what it would mean. He prays to God for deliverance.

> Let my prayer come before you;
> > incline your ear to my cry!
> For my soul is full of troubles,
> > and my life draws near to sheol.
> I am counted among those who go down to the pit;
> > I am a man who has no strength,
> like one set loose among the dead,
> > like the slain that lie in the grave,
> like those whom you remember no more,
> > for they are cut off from your hand.
> You have put me in the depths of the pit,
> > in the regions dark and deep . . .
> Do you work wonders for the dead?
> > Do the departed rise up to praise you?
> Is your steadfast love declared in the grave,
> > or your faithfulness in Abaddon?
> Are your wonders known in the darkness,
> > or your righteousness in the land of forgetfulness?
> > (Ps 88:2–6, 10–12)

---

18. Jonah 2:6.
19. Isa 38:10.
20. Job 16:22.
21. Isa 14:10.
22. Pss 94:17; 115:17; Ezek 32:21.
23. Isa 26:14.
24. Eccl 9:5–6.

The pit puts proud humans in their place. In Isaiah we find a taunt over the king of Babylon who has died and descends to the pit. He is greeted by other rulers who are now mere shades.[25] In life the monarch had suffered from acute delusions of grandeur, imagining that he could even reach higher than God's own throne! That's a giddy height from which to fall! And fall he would, right down to sheol.

> sheol beneath is stirred up
> >   to meet you when you come;
> it rouses the shades to greet you,
> >   all who were leaders of the earth;
> it raises from their thrones
> >   all who were kings of the nations.
> All of them will answer
> >   and say to you:
> "You too have become as weak as we!
> >   You have become like us!"
> Your pomp is brought down to sheol,
> >   the sound of your harps;
> maggots are laid as a bed beneath you,
> >   and worms are your covers.
> How you are fallen from heaven,
> >   O Day Star, son of Dawn!
> How you are cut down to the ground,
> >   you who laid the nations low!
> You said in your heart,
> >   "I will ascend to heaven;
> above the stars of God
> >   I will set my throne on high;
> I will sit on the mount of assembly
> >   in the far reaches of the north;
> I will ascend above the heights of the clouds;
> >   I will make myself like the Most High."
> But you are brought down to sheol,
> >   to the far reaches of the pit. (Isa 14:9–15)

---

25. Isa 14:9–11.

The taunt goes on to describe how all will stare at the king of Babylon and marvel that one who was so powerful in life is so reduced in death.[26] Ezekiel pictures a similar scene in which the Egyptian army is slain by the sword and descends to "the world below," the pit. The mighty rulers already there say, "They have come down, they lie still, the uncircumcised, slain by the sword." Assyria is there; so too is Elam, Meshech-tubal, Edom, the princes of the north, and the Sidonians. They all "bear their shame with those who go down to the pit" (Ezek 32:17–32).

The inhabitants of sheol are rarely named in the Bible, but some texts refer to them as "shades" (*rĕpā'îm*).[27] The same root, *rp'm* ("shades"), occurs in Hebrew, Ugaritic, and Phoenician to refer to the dead, but in Ugarit the *rpum* were divinized ancestors with some positive ongoing role for the living. Not so in the Bible. The biblical dead are weak, subdued, and almost entirely inactive. Contact with them is forbidden.

Sheol is the great leveler: *everyone* goes there in the end[28]—rich and poor,[29] mighty leaders[30] and social outcasts, the godly[31] and the wicked;[32] *all* find themselves in sheol.

Life after Sheol?

There was a discomfort felt by some Old Testament writers about this state of affairs. Sheol was a perfectly fitting fate for the wicked. Indeed, most of the time sheol is used to designate the fate of the wicked[33]—sinners,[34] the foolish rich,[35] scoffers,[36] and the immoral.[37] Death is an appropriate end for those who reject the way of the living God. But the righteous? The fitting thing seems to be for God to rescue the righteous from the grip of sheol, and many a psalm speaks in just this way.[38] Language about deliverance from

---

26. Isa 14:16–20. Cf. Matt 11:20–24; Luke 10:12–15.
27. Job 26:5; Ps 88:10; Isa 14:9; Prov 21:6.
28. Ps 89:48; Eccl 9:10.
29. Job 3:13–19.
30. Isaiah 14; Ezekiel 32.
31. Gen 37:35; 42:38; Ps 88:3; Isa 38:10.
32. 1 Kgs 2:6, 9; Pss 9:17; 31:17; 49:14; Prov 5:5; 7:27; Isa 5:14, etc.
33. Pss 9:17; 31:17; 141:7, etc.
34. Job 24:19.
35. Ps 49:14.
36. Isa 28:15, 18.
37. Prov 5:5; 7:27; 9:18.
38. E.g., Pss 14; 30:3; 40:2; 71:20; 86:13; 88:6.

sheol is hyperbole, referring to rescue from life-threatening situations rather than from *actual* death. However, although such rhetoric does not refer to a literal salvation for the righteous from sheol it does indicate a discomfort with the notion of God's holy people entering this perpetual twilight zone.

There are just a few glimmers in the Old Testament of the possibility of life after sheol. Psalm 16:10–11 seems to suggest that God's faithful one would not be given up to sheol but would have fullness of joy and pleasures in God's presence forevermore. Again, Ps 49:15 seems to envisage a ransom from sheol for the psalmist—something impossible for a human but possible for God:

> Truly no man can ransom another,
>   or give to God the price of his life,
> for the ransom of their life is costly
>   and can never suffice,
> that he should live on forever
>   and never see the pit.
> For he sees that even the wise die;
>   the fool and the stupid alike must perish
>   and leave their wealth to others.
> Their graves are their homes forever,
>   their dwelling places to all generations,
>   though they called lands by their own names.
> Man in his pomp will not remain;
>   he is like the beasts that perish.
> This is the path of those who have foolish confidence;
>   yet after them people approve of their boasts.
> Like sheep they are appointed for sheol;
>   death shall be their shepherd,
> and the upright shall rule over them in the morning.
>   Their form shall be consumed in sheol, with no place to dwell.
> *But God will ransom my soul from the power of sheol,*
>   *for he will receive me.* (Ps 49:7–15)

Towards the very end of the Old Testament period a belief in resurrection from the dead began to arise (another bad pun). We see this only at the very edges of the Old Testament as something *possible* for the life-giving

God,[39] as an image for the restoration of the nation of Israel,[40] and as a future for some of the dead.[41] But by the time of first century AD certain segments of Judaism—including the movement associated with Jesus of Nazareth—had developed a full-blown belief in the coming resurrection of the dead. Sheol would not, after all, have the last word! We'll return to this theme in chapter 8.

Later Developments of Underworld Traditions

Jewish ideas about sheol (translated in the Septuagint by the Greek word *hades*) continued to develop. It became increasingly common to think of the body remaining in the grave and of the spirit descending into subterranean chambers.[42] All the dead descend to these chambers, but some texts started to distinguish the fate of the righteous and the wicked there. *First Enoch* 22, for instance, speaks of three or four compartments, with inhabitants divided according to their goodness when alive. Some texts refer to the righteous dead as those "asleep,"[43] while the wicked dead are "haunted."[44] Sheol/hades thus increasingly came to be seen as a place of suffering for the wicked.[45]

Jesus' parable of the rich man and Lazarus may reflect this idea of different compartments in hades separated by a wide, uncrossable chasm.[46]

> The poor man died and was carried by the angels to Abraham's side. The rich man also died and was buried, and in hades, being in torment, he lifted up his eyes and saw Abraham far off and Lazarus at his side. And he called out, "Father Abraham, have mercy on me, and send Lazarus to dip the end of his finger in water and cool my tongue, for I am in anguish in this flame." But Abraham said, "Child, remember that you in your

39. Deut 32:39; 1 Sam 2:6.
40. Hos 6:1–2; Ezek 37:1–14.
41. Isa 26:19; Dan 12:2.
42. *L.A.B.* 32:13; 15:5; 21:9; *2 Bar.* 30:1; *4 Ezra* 4:35.
43. *4 Ezra* 7:32; *2 Bar.* 11:4.
44. *Pss. Sol.* 17:14.
45. *Jub.* 7:29; *1 En.* 63:10.
46. I say "may" because it is not clear that Jesus is intending to communicate theology about the afterlife here: (a) Jesus' parable is not about the afterlife but about the use of wealth in this life; (b) the parable uses a well-established folk tale that existed in various forms and Jesus may have simply been adopting it to make a point about wealth; (c) the teaching concerning afterlife punishment in this parable is significantly different from that found in the rest of Jesus' teaching. So we need to be very cautious in using the parable to establish doctrine regarding the afterlife.

lifetime received your good things, and Lazarus in like manner bad things; but now he is comforted here, and you are in anguish. And besides all this, between us and you a great chasm has been fixed, in order that those who would pass from here to you may not be able, and none may cross from there to us." (Luke 16:22–26)

Hades by this time was seen to be both more depressing (for the rich man) and less depressing (for the poor man) than in the Old Testament. But it was still seen as located literally under the earth. Thus St. Paul speaks of every creature in the universe using the following categories: those "in heaven," those "on earth," and those *"under the earth"* (Phil 2:10). And the book of Revelation speaks of "every creature in heaven and on earth and *under the earth* and in the sea" (5:13).

In the book of Revelation hades was the abode of the dead *until* the end of the age when the dead are raised from hades and judged. Then death and hades are thrown into the lake of fire and come to an end.[47] So, contrary to popular belief, hades in the New Testament is probably not thought of as the final fate of anyone, but rather as an intermediate state, a holding room until the final judgment day.

Death as a Substantial Reality

One final thought before leaving this depressing place. We tend to think of death as, for want of a better word, an *event*. It is something that happens to us—we die. We also sometimes think of it as a *state* of some kind. Thus, we can speak of *being* dead. Other times we think of death as a void, a nothing (not something one can *be*). Sometimes we even picture death as a "person"—the Grim Reaper. However, all these conceptualizations strain to grasp the mystery that is death.

Ancients also thought of death as an *event* (people die) and as a *state* (people are dead). Only rarely was death thought of as nothingness—some mode of post-mortem existence (or semi-existence) was usually envisaged. But death was more substantial than this. As we have seen in this leg of the tour, death could be considered as a *place*, a spatial location, far removed from the "land of the living," and even further removed from heaven, the abode of the living God. For ancient Israelites, to be dead is to be one of the shades held captive in the deep subterranean pit.

---

47. Rev 20:13–14.

There is, however, even more to say about death. As with the rest of the biblical cosmos, sheol could sometimes be spoken of as if it were *a sentient entity, a being.* Judah, says Isaiah in words laden with sarcasm, made a covenant agreement with it.[48] It has a large and greedy appetite and opens its mouth to swallow people,[49] it entangles them with its cords and drags them down,[50] and it can be stirred up by new arrivals, arousing its shades to meet them.[51] Unlike the rest of creation it does not praise God,[52] yet God can speak directly to it: "O Death, where are your plagues? O sheol, where is your sting?" mocks Jehovah (Hos 13:14).

Some biblical writers, most notably the Apostle Paul, take this personification of death even further. In ancient Near Eastern religions death was closely linked with a deity, a god who was part of the cosmic system. Paul similarly sometimes speaks of both Sin and Death as if they were substantial beings with intentions. Death and Sin are kings, joint regents who have reigned over humanity from the time of Adam,[53] but who have no dominion over the risen Lord.[54] Jesus has defeated the cosmic powers Sin and Death in the most unexpected way—by means of his own innocent death. Thanks to this definitive victory, at the end of the age Sin and Death, the last enemy, will be finally and completely vanquished.[55]

After this grizzly descent to the depths it is time that we take the tour on upwards and ascend to the heavens. The second tour will depart shortly.

---

48. Isa 28:15, 18.
49. Isa 5:14; Hab 2:5; Ps 141:7; Prov 27:20.
50. 2 Sam 22:6; Ps 18:5.
51. Isa 14:9.
52. Isa 38:18.
53. Rom 5:14, 17, 21.
54. Rom 6:9.
55. 1 Cor 15:26, 54–56.

PART II
A Tour of the Biblical Heavens

5

Eyes in Their Stars

The Sky

WHAT DO YOU SEE when you look up into the night sky? Whatever it is, it is almost certainly not what people living in the ancient Near East, including ancient Israel, saw when they looked up. It is hard for us to make the leap of imagination that it takes to see the sky through ancient eyes.

In the Disney movie *The Lion King* (1994) there is a wonderful scene in which Simba the lion, Timon the meerkat, and Pumba the warthog are lying on their backs staring at the night sky.

> *Pumba:* Timon, ever wonder what those sparkly dots are up there?
>
> *Timon:* Pumba, I don't wonder; I *know*.
>
> *Pumba:* Oh, what are they?
>
> *Timon:* They're fireflies . . . fireflies that got, er, stuck up on that . . . big bluish-black thing.
>
> *Pumba:* Oh gee. I always thought they were balls of gas burning billions of miles away.
>
> *Timon:* Pumba, . . . with you everything's gas.
>
> *Pumba:* Simba, whadda you think?
>
> *Simba:* Well, I don't know . . .
>
> *Pumba:* Oh c'mon kid. Give, give, give. We told you ours . . . please . . .
>
> *Simba:* Somebody once told me that the great kings of the past are up there watching over us.
>
> *Pumba:* Really?

> *Timon:* You mean a bunch of royal dead guys are watching us?
> [Timon and Pumba start laughing. Simba, embarrassed, joins in]
> *Timon:* Who told you something like that?
> *Simba:* Yeah, yeah
> *Timon:* what mook?
> *Simba:* Yeah, pretty dumb, huh?

So what are stars? Burning balls of gas? Or the dead kings of the past? Here we have the clash between a scientific and a "primitive" worldview. For the audience, the joke is that we know that in the *real* world it is Pumba, the dumb warthog, who is actually correct about the nature of the stars. But, within the world of the story, it is Simba who turns out to be right. The dead lion kings of the past do indeed inhabit the night sky and watch over those living on earth. This conflict between Simba's "dead kings" and Pumba's "burning balls of gas" neatly highlights the difference between our modern scientific cosmologies and the mythic cosmologies of the ancient world, the Bible included. In this part of the tour I wish to help us to understand biblical views on the sun, moon, and stars. But first, the weather.

Weather

Before we get too high up into the heavens it would be good to take a look out of the window as we ascend and briefly consider the weather. We think of weather in terms of modern meteorology and climatology but biblical weather is not about "natural" phenomena, if by that we mean events that happen independent of divine influence. Biblical weather is always occurring within the sphere of God's sovereignty—the winds, for instance, do his bidding[1] and the storms are unquestionably under divine control.[2] Weather, in fact, is a means by which God is manifest in creation. To take the most obvious biblical example, in the thunderstorms, noted for their destructive power,[3] Jehovah appears riding the storm clouds into battle; he wields their lightnings as weapons, as arrows,[4] manifesting his power and glory;[5] their

---

1. Pss 78:26; 104:4, 30; 107:25; 148:8.
2. Pss 107:25,29; 148:8.
3. Pss 55:8; 58:9; 83:15; 107:25.
4. Pss 18:14; 38:2; 77:17–18; 78:48; 105:32; 144:6.
5. Ps 50:3.

thunders are his voice, his battle cry.[6] (God's other meteorological weaponry included winds[7] and hail.[8])

However, at the same time as revealing God, the weather also conceals him. In particular, the clouds of a divine appearance, a theophany, serve this dual role.[9] The most important biblical example of this revealing/concealing weather is the dark clouds atop Mount Sinai when Moses and the children of Israel were camped at the bottom. The thunder and lightning struck terror into the hearts of the people, manifesting God's power and glory, and yet it simultaneously hid God from view. When God rides the storm all that is ever seen is the storm itself, *never God*.

Before moving up higher, and lest we begin to think that biblical weather is all about the scary side of God, we ought to note that it also manifests God's goodness and blessing. Rain from heaven, in particular, is a divine provision, a means of blessing the land with fertility.[10]

The clouds are disappearing below us now and up ahead we can see the stars coming out.

Ancient Near Eastern vs. Modern Views about Celestial Bodies

Where Are the Sun, Moon, and Stars Located?

Before trying to make sense of biblical views of the sun, moon, and stars it will be helpful to get some feel for how the ancients thought about the *location* or *habitat* of such celestial entities. Here we need to forget our scientific understandings about "space" and look with fresh eyes. Genesis 1 provides a good entry point into that discussion. In Genesis 1, as we have previously seen, God spends Days One to Three shaping and marking off the different zones of the creation, and days four to six filling them.

---

6. Pss 18:13; 77:17–18; 104:7.
7. Pss 1:4; 11:6; 18:42; 35:5; 48:7; 83:13, 15; 103:16.
8. Exod 9:18–34; Ps 18:12–13; 78:47–48; 105:32–33; Hag 2:17.
9. Pss 18:9; 18:11–12; 68:4; 77:17; 89:6, 37; 97:2; and 104:3.
10. Pss 65:9–10; 68:9; 104:13; 147:8.

Create habitable zones	Fill the zones
Day 1: light and dark separated	*Day 4:* sun, moon, stars
Day 2: waters above separated from waters below by a firmament	*Day 5:* sky creatures (birds) and sea creatures
Day 3: water separated from dry land	*Day 6:* land creatures (incl. humans)
Day 7: rest	

Each "zone" is created by means of an act of separation. To understand the zone inhabited by the sun, moon, and stars we need to consider Day Two:

> And God said, "Let there be a firmament (*raqîaʿ*) in the midst of the waters, and let it divide the waters from the waters." And God made the firmament, and divided the waters which were under the firmament from the waters which were above the firmament: and it was so. And God called the firmament heaven. And the evening and the morning were the second day. (Gen 1:6–8)

As we have already seen, this concerns a cosmic mass of primeval water that God "tames" by creating a habitable space between the "waters below" and the "waters above." These "waters above" are not clouds nor "the atmosphere" but rather a vast sea above the sky, beyond the space now inhabited by the sun, moon, and stars. What kept these oceanic waters at bay was the "firmament" (Heb. *raqîaʿ*)—a solid sky dome holding back the life-threatening waters.

To us the idea of a solid sky seems absurd, but all peoples in the ancient world thought of the sky as solid. We find the same view, for instance, in ancient Sumerian, Hittite, Egyptian, Assyrian, and Babylonian texts.[11] The Bible is here simply reflecting the then-universal view of a solid sky.

The celestial lights, according to Gen 1:17, were placed by God "*in* the firmament (*birqîaʾ*) of the heavens." They were fixed, it appears, *in* the solid vault of the sky. Ancient Israelites were very well aware that the stars moved so we must suppose that this vault was imagined to rotate.

In Ps 19:5[6] the rising sun is said to "come forth" from his "chamber" beneath the horizon. How the sun got from where it set back to where it

---

11. There was speculation concerning what the sky was made from—some kind of metal (suggestions included tin, brass, iron, etc.) or clay or some type of crystalline substance. Ezekiel 1:22 suggests the latter.

rises is not explained. In other ancient Near Eastern cultures it was thought to pass through gates in the sky and then on a night voyage through the underworld. The Old Testament does speak of "gates,"[12] "doors,"[13] and "windows"[14] in the sky and it may well be that the sun passed through a portal such as these.[15] The only reference to its journey between sunset and sunrise is found in Ecclesiastes: "The sun rises, and the sun goes down, and hastens to the place where it rises" (Eccl 1:5).

Classifying Celestial Entities

Having clarified the location of celestial bodies, we need to get some sense of how ancient Near Easterners classified such entities.

Type of celestial entity	Ancient typology of astral entities	
Sun		
Moon		
Stars	Falling stars	*Comets, etc.*
	Fixed stars	*Stars (grouped in constellations)*[16]
	Wandering stars	*Mercury*
		Venus
		Mars
		Jupiter
		Saturn

Table 1: Ancient views of astral entities

---

12. Gen 28:17.
13. Ps 78:23.
14. Gen 7:11; 8:2.
15. Certainly later Jewish literature thought in these terms. See the astronomical book of Enoch (*1 Enoch* 72–82).
16. Stars and constellations have been identified in Babylonian astronomical texts. The Bible also appears to mention certain specific stars and constellations, although we cannot be sure which ones are referred to. For instance, *Kîyûn* (Amos 5:26) may be Saturn, viewed as a god; *kîmâ* (Job 9:9; 38:31; Amos 5:8) may be the Pleiades.

Types of celestial entity	Modern typology of astral entities
Stars	*(incl. the sun)*
Planets	*(incl. Mercury, Venus, Mars, Jupiter, Saturn, and the earth itself)*
Moons	*(incl. our moon)*
Comets, asteroids, etc.	

Table 2: Modern views of astral entities

A simple comparison of ancient and modern typologies of astral entities will reveal just how different our classification schemes are. To us, the sun is a star composed, mostly, of hydrogen and helium—a "ball of gas burning billions of miles away," as Pumba put it. It forms the centre of our solar system with all the planets in orbit around it. To the ancients, while the stars and the sun were all heavenly bodies and were associated with the gods, the sun was not thought to be just a star—it was clearly in a league of its own—nor was it conceived of as the center of a solar system. The earth was not a planet in orbit around the sun—the sun was a god that moved across the vault of the heavens.

In the ancient world, including ancient Israel, the moon was not what we think of as a moon. To us a moon is a celestial body in orbit around another celestial body, such as a planet—a natural satellite, as it were—and *the* moon is the natural satellite that orbits our planet, earth. But, of course, the earth was not "a planet" in the ancient Near Eastern conception of the cosmos—there were no planets—and the moon was a *unique* celestial object, not simply one moon amongst many. We also need to remember that the moon was not thought of as a great "lump of rock" glowing only because it *reflects* the light of the sun. The moon was understood to be a *source* of light.[17]

The ancients watched the sky very closely and knew the stars far more intimately than most modern people do. It was clear that the stars fell into three categories: those that were fixed in constellations, those that seemed to shoot across the sky, and those that seemed to wander free. We now know these "wandering stars" to be planets, visible to the naked eye—Mercury, Venus, Mars, Jupiter, and Saturn. But, as we have already said, there were no planets in the ancient understandings of the cosmos. The "wandering stars" appeared to be like all the other stars, save in their behavior. For that reason

---

17. Gen 1:16.

they were singled out as special and were associated with various specific deities (an association still preserved in our names for the planets).

To the modern mind, stars are "balls of gas burning billions of miles away"—some of them being considerably larger and brighter than our own sun. For the ancients the stars were very far away and inaccessible to humans, but they would never have imagined just *how far* away the stars actually are.

Celestial Entities and the Gods in the Ancient Near East

For ancient peoples there were most certainly "eyes in their stars." The stars were very closely associated with gods. It is not always completely clear whether the stars were thought to be literally identical with gods, to be mere symbols of gods, or to be the heavenly bodies of gods that transcended those bodies. The data is complex, but a strong case can be made for the last option. What is indisputable is that the sun, moon, and stars were *very closely* linked with deities. So in ancient Mesopotamia, from as far back as our evidence goes, there were gods associated with the moon (Nana/Sin/Suen), the sun (Šamaš), and various stars (e.g., Inana/Ištar and Ninsianna as Venus, Marduk as Jupiter and sometimes Mercury, Ninurta as Mercury or Sirius or Saturn, and Nergal as Mars).

Given that gods were also regularly pictured in humanlike terms (having giant human-like bodies) and non-humanlike terms (for instance, the moon god as a bull-calf) it seems that while the stars may have been gods, there was more to those gods than the stars. Here, for instance, is an Assyrian depiction of the Pleiades constellation as a warrior deity in human form. In other words, stars and gods were not *simplistically* identified but gods did manifest themselves in stars.

In the mythological texts about the gods some of them are seen as having "astral bodies" and thus as being visually embodied in stars. (Their human-like bodies were not manifest in the visible world except as idols and in art.) In Omen texts and other astronomical texts about the stars they are seen as being images of gods in much the same way that idols in temples were images of gods. A telling passage in this regard is found in *Enuma Elish*: "[Marduk] created the stations for the great gods, setting up the stars, their [i.e., the great gods'] likenesses, as constellations." The meaning of "the stars, their likenesses" seems to be that the stars represent astral counterparts to the gods. Thus the stars were the repositories of the presence of the gods—existing on the boundary of the physical and metaphysical aspects of reality. This, incidentally, is why the behavior of astral bodies was understood to be messages from the gods—their will made manifest for those humans who could interpret the signs through astrology.

These astral deities were the objects of cultic devotion—praise, sacrificial offerings, and intercessions. Here, for instance, is a prayer to the moon god, Sin:

> O Sin, radiant god, luminary of [heaven], firstborn son of Enlil, [foremost one] of Ekur, You reign as king of the uni[verse], you s[et] your throne [in] the [shining] heavens, You set out a superb linen, you [don] the resplendent tiara of lordship whose waxing never fails! . . . O luminary Sin [. . .] . . . At sight of Sin, the stars are jubilant, the night rejoices. Sin takes his place in the centre of the shi[ning] heaven.

This pattern of astral worship was also known in West Semitic cultures such as those of the Canaanites, Israel's neighbors.

Divine Stars in Ancient Israel?

The Worship of Celestial Entities in Ancient Israel

Ancient Israelites were well aware that their neighbors worshipped the sun, moon, and stars, and the evidence suggests that such astral worship was not unknown in Israel. Jehovah, through Amos, complained against the northern kingdom:

> "Did you bring to me sacrifices and offerings during the forty years in the wilderness, O house of Israel? You shall take up *Sikkût* your king, and *Kîyûn*—your images (*ṣalmêkem*) of a star (*kôkab*), your gods (*'ĕlohêkem*) that you made for yourselves, and I will send you into exile beyond Damascus," says Jehovah, whose name is the God of hosts. (Amos 5:25–27)

In the southern kingdom, Josiah "deposed the priests whom the kings of Judah had ordained to make offerings in the high places at the cities of Judah and around Jerusalem; those also who burned incense to Baal [not an astral deity], to *the sun and the moon and the constellations and all the host of the heavens*" (2 Kgs 23:5). Later, the prophet Jeremiah proclaimed a coming desecration of idolaters: "'At that time,' declares Jehovah, 'the bones of the kings of Judah, the bones of its officials, the bones of the priests, the bones of the prophets, and the bones of the inhabitants of Jerusalem shall be brought out of their tombs. And they shall be spread before *the sun and the moon and all the host of heaven, which they have loved and served, which they have gone after, and which they have sought and worshiped*'" (Jer 8:1–2; cf. Zeph 1:5). While we need to bear in mind prophetic rhetoric, this suggests that astral worship was *widespread* in Israel (from the kings to the general populace). Ezekiel, in a vision, sees an "abomination"—twenty-five men in the inner court of the temple in Jerusalem "with their backs to the temple of the Jehovah, and their faces toward the east, worshiping the sun toward the east" (Ezek 8:16).

The very fact that such worship was strictly forbidden—in Deuteronomic law, worship of the sun, moon, and stars by Israelites was punishable by stoning[18]—would indicate that it presented something of a temptation: "beware lest you raise your eyes to heaven, and when you see *the sun and the moon and the stars, all the host of heaven*, you be drawn away and bow down to them and serve them, things that the Jehovah your God has allotted to all the peoples under the whole heaven" (Deut 4:19).

The piety required is well-expressed by Job:

> if I have looked at [i.e., worshipped] the sun when it shone,
>   or the moon moving in splendor,
> and my heart has been secretly enticed,
>   and my mouth has kissed my hand,
> this also would be an iniquity to be punished by the judges,
>   for I would have been false to God above. (Job 31:26–28)

Similarly, astrology, though widely practiced in the ancient world, was frowned upon by the guardians of Israel's faith:

> You are wearied with your many counsels;
>   let them stand forth and save you,
> those who divide the heavens,
>   who gaze at the stars,
> who at the new moons make known
>   what shall come upon you. (Isa 47:13)

---

18. Deut 17:2–6.

PART II—A TOUR OF THE BIBLICAL HEAVENS

Astral Entities and the Divine Council

However, surprising as it may be to many, there are reasons to think that some biblical authors did consider the sun, moon, and stars to be very closely associated with, perhaps even *identified with*, heavenly creatures—the members of the divine council.

First, I need to say a little about the divine council. All the ancient cultures around the Mediterranean had a concept of a divine council. This was a council of the gods that administered the cosmos. In Ugarit—the ancient West Semitic culture closest to ancient Israel—the divine council had four layers in its hierarchical structure.

1. El, the chief god, and his wife, Athirat. (You can see an image of El on p. 101.)
2. The sons of El—the gods. There appear to have been seventy of them. Among them are Anat, Athtart, Athtar, Shapshu, Yarih, Shahar, and Shalim.
3. The craftsmen gods.
4. Minor deities including the messenger gods (*ml'km*)—servants.

So in Ugarit the council of El is called "the assembly of the gods," "the circle of El," "the assembly of the sons of El." The divine council was a large divine family, with servants, who convened on El's sacred mountain. Now it appears that the sons of El were *astral* deities. They are called "star gods" and "the assembly of stars" and individual members have astral associations: Yarih was the moon god, Shapshu was the sun-goddess, Shahar was the dawn and Shalim the dusk, Athtar and Athtart appear to be the morning and evening star (Venus), and Rephesh possibly represents Mars.

Ancient Israel's divine council was not dissimilar, although it only had three layers.

1. El, the *chief* god (i.e., "*the* god" or, what we would call, "God with a capital G") and ruler of the council
2. The "sons of El" or "gods"[19]
3. The messengers (*ml'km*, i.e., angels)

---

19. Incidentally, in Psalm 8, I suggest that when we read that humans were created "a little lower than ʾelōhîm," it is neither "*the* god" (i.e., Jehovah) nor run of the mill "angels" that are in mind, but the members of the divine council—the sons of El.

We need to appreciate that in ancient Israel, the category of ʾelōhîm (gods) was not reserved for Jehovah. ʾElōhîm were beings that inhabited the spirit world. So the category included Jehovah, but also the other members of the divine council.[20] This, however, should not lead us to suppose that biblical faith was polytheistic. In the Bible Jehovah was not just any old ʾelōhîm. He was one of a kind—utterly unique. He alone is called *"the* god" (*ha'elōhîm*).[21] He alone was *before* all things and *created* all things (including all the other ʾelōhîm).[22] He alone rules over all things. There is *no* sense in which he is simply one among equals. Thus, worshippers can proclaim, "Who is like you, O Jehovah, among the gods?" The answer is that *no one* is like Jehovah[23]—he is the "God of gods."[24] The ʾelōhîm are thus rightly called to worship him.[25]

Our interest in this chapter is in the members of the divine council. In the OT they are called, amongst other things, "gods" (ʾelōhîm),[26] "sons

---

20. Psalm 82. Possibly the spirits of dead people also (1 Sam 28:13).
21. Exod 18:16; 1 Kgs 18:39.
22. Isa 45:18; Pss 33:6; 148:1–5.
23. Exod 15:11; Deut 10:17; Pss 86:8; 95:3; 96:4; 135:5.
24. Ps 136:2.
25. Ps 29:1.
26. Ps 82:1.

of God Most High" (*El-elyon*),[27] "princes,"[28] and "holy ones."[29] They are assigned governance by Jehovah over the seventy nations of the world.[30] Their responsibility is to do justice—although they do not always achieve this.[31]

Now, just as Ugaritic literature refers to the divine council as "the assembly of stars," so too parts of the OT seem to associate the members of the divine council with stars. Given that many readers are likely to find this claim rather implausible, I will take a little more care in giving my reasons. There are several lines of evidence that seem to support this claim:

Ezekiel 1:4–28a

While at the Chebar canal in Babylon, Ezekiel experienced a dramatic vision in which he saw a fiery cloud come from the north. He saw "the likeness of four living creatures" that had human and animal features: the form of a man, the feet of a calf, four wings, and heads with four faces—human, lion, ox, and eagle.[32] It is likely that these are the four Babylonian seasonal constellations: Leo (the lion), Scorpio (who had a human face), Taurus (the bull), and Pegasus (the thunderbird/eagle). In Babylonian astrology these four constellations depict the four directions of the sky, being about 90 degrees from each other. Thus they represent the entire sky with God's throne at the centre.

> Ezekiel has made immediate sense of his vision. He is looking into the night sky and interprets the constellations in line with Babylonian understanding. For this reason Ezekiel is called an astral prophet. He learns God's will from the stars in the sky. The fact that the rim of the wheels (v. 18; see vv. 15–21) on which the living creatures moved are "full of eyes" confirms this. The ancients called stars "eyes," and thought them to be living entities. Constellated stars, called "full of eyes," were perceived as animate beings like persons or animals. Since Ezekiel sees all four constellations moving at once, his vantage point was high above the entire cosmos (vv. 4–11).

27. Ps 82:6.
28. Job 37:7–8.
29. Ps 89:6–7; Zech 14:15; Job 5:1.
30. See chapter 6.
31. Psalm 82.
32. Ezek 1:4–14.

> According to ancient star lore, the constellations support the firmament, that solid bowl-like object that covers the earth. That is precisely what Ezekiel saw (vv. 22–23) . . . .[33]

That the creatures are constellations is supported by the observation that above them is the solid crystalline firmament (*raqiaʿ*) and above the firmament is the throne of God. Ezekiel's vision is of stars, the sky dome, and the throne in heaven.

Job 38:4–7

> Where were you [Job] when I [Jehovah] laid the foundation of the earth? . . .
> On what were its bases sunk,
> > or who laid its cornerstone,
> > when the *morning stars* sang together
> > and all the *sons of God* shouted for joy?

The first thing to observe here is that the "sons of God" (i.e., the members of the divine council[34]) seem to be identified with "the morning stars." The two lines in verse 7 are parallel and the subjects of each line would appear to be the same or, at very least, linked. We may also note that the stars/sons of God were not involved in creating—Jehovah did that—but they were around when God made the earth and they responded to God's creative activity with joy.

Job 4:18 and 15:15

Job 4:18 and 15:15 seem to contain the same idea and need to be interpreted in the light of each other:

- "Even in his servants he puts no trust, / and his angels he charges with error." (4:18)
- "Behold, God puts no trust in his holy ones, / and the heavens are not pure in his sight." (15:15)

---

33. Pilch, "The Call of Ezekiel," 37.
34. See the use of the term "sons of God" in Job 1:6; 2:1.

PART II—A TOUR OF THE BIBLICAL HEAVENS

By "heavens" the poet most likely has the heavenly bodies in mind. This would also make the stars as equivalent to "his servants," "his angels," and "his holy ones." The point of 15:14–16 is that God is *so* pure that *even* his heavenly servants seem impure by comparison—if even the stars/heavenly beings cannot be pure in his sight, how much less can human beings?

Isaiah 14:12–15

How you are fallen from heaven,
    O Day Star, son of Dawn!
How you are cut down to the ground,
    you who laid the nations low!
You said in your heart,
    "I will ascend to heaven;
above the stars of God
    I will set my throne on high;
I will sit on the mount of assembly
    in the far reaches of the north;
I will ascend above the heights of the clouds;
    I will make myself like the Most High."
But you are brought down to Sheol,
    to the far reaches of the pit.

This lament is generally thought to employ an old West Semitic myth, perhaps concerning the fall of one of the astral gods. This myth is applied parabolically to the king of Babylon (referred to as a divine figure, "Helal, son of the Dawn," v. 12). In this context "the stars of El" in v. 13 are almost certainly understood as divine beings. That suggestion is reinforced by the mention of "the mount of assembly" in the "far reaches of the north" (i.e., Ba'al's mountain, Mount Ṣaphānu, north of Israel; see chapter 3). It is not an accident that this oracle pictures the divine assembly meeting in ṣāpôn. Here, in this oracle against the king of Babylon, the mountains of El (the Mount of Assembly) and Baal (Mount Ṣaphānu) are merged into a single divine mountain on which the divine assembly meets. The king of Babylon is portrayed as having the hubris of thinking that he could ascend to become like ʿelyôn (the Most High)—and rule the divine assembly itself! This makes it highly likely that the "stars of El" are the divine council members that the king intends to ascend above.

EYES IN THEIR STARS

Psalm 89:5–7

Let the *heavens* praise your wonders, Jehovah,
> your faithfulness in the assembly of the holy ones!
For who in the *skies* can be compared to Jehovah?
> Who among the sons of God is like the Jehovah,
a God greatly to be feared in the council of the holy ones,
> and awesome above all who are around him?

The focus here is clearly on Jehovah and the divine council. Note the phrases "the assembly of the holy ones," "the sons of God," "the council of the holy ones" who are "around" Jehovah. These sons of God are identified with "the heavens" and "the skies." Note too that the skies (*šaḥaq*) (89:6) in which the sons of God dwell are said in the same psalm to be the dwelling place of the moon (89:37), so we are speaking of the astral realm.[35] Thus, here too it is likely, though not certain, that the sons of God are linked to stars.

Isaiah 24:21–23

On that day Jehovah will punish
> *the host of heaven*, in heaven,
> and *the kings of the earth*, on the earth.
They will be gathered together
> as prisoners in a pit;
they will be shut up in a prison,
> and after many days they will be punished.
Then the moon will be confounded
> *and the sun ashamed*,
for Jehovah of hosts reigns
> on Mount Zion and in Jerusalem,
> and his glory will be before his elders.

---

35. We find the same parallel of "sons of God" and "heavens" in Deut 32:43 in LXX and 4QDeut^q (not in MT which was almost certainly changed for theological reasons).

Here "the host of heaven" are the heavenly equivalent of "the kings of the earth" (note the parallel in v. 21). Both will be punished (v. 22). Then "the moon will be confounded, and the sun ashamed" (v. 23). This suggests that the sun and the moon are among the "hosts of heaven"—heavenly rulers that parallel human kings. We tend to view the language about the sun being ashamed and the moon being confounded as a literary device, as personification, but it was probably more than that.[36]

The implication that the sun and the moon could act against God's people is also hinted at elsewhere in the Bible. The ability of the sun and the moon to harm people seems to be presupposed by Ps 121:5–6: "The sun shall not strike you by day, nor the moon by night."[37] The sun's "striking" could simply be a metaphorical reference to the effects of its scorching heat,[38] but the moon's "striking" cannot be explained so simply. An interesting case study is found in Matthew's account of the epileptic boy healed by Jesus in Matthew 17. Matthew says that the boy was "a lunatic"—*selēniadzatai*, literally "struck by the moon." The moon may have been God's creature but it was not necessarily always tame.[39]

Psalm 148:1–6

Praise Jehovah!
Praise Jehovah from the heavens;
    praise him in the heights!
Praise him, all his angels;
    praise him, all his hosts!

---

36. It is possible that the covenant that Jehovah made with the sun, moon, and stars also indicates a hint that they are more than inanimate objects. God speaks of them as covenant partners as David is his covenant partner (Jer 33:20–22).

37. Cf. Hos 5:7; Isa 49:10.

38. cf. Isa 49:10; Jas 1:11; Rev 16:8.

39. There does appear to be a tradition of a rebellion amongst the "sons of God" against God (Gen 6:1–4; Daniel 10) and of divine judgment against them (Psalm 82).

Praise him, sun and moon,
>   praise him, all you shining stars!
> Praise him, you highest heavens,
>   and you waters above the heavens!
> Let them praise the name of Jehovah!
>   For he commanded and they were created.
> And he established them forever and ever;
>   he gave a decree, and it shall not pass away.

Here we see God's heavenly choir and yet again "angels" and heavenly "host" are very closely associated with the sun, moon, and stars. It is not possible to dogmatically claim that they are identified but the association is, at very least, suggestive.

The "Host of Heaven"/"Hosts of Jehovah"

A very common epithet for God in the Hebrew Bible is "Jehovah of hosts" (*Jehovah ṣĕbāʾôt*), "God of hosts" (*ʾĕlōhê ṣĕbāʾôt*), or some other combination such as "Jehovah God of hosts" (*Jehovah ʾĕlōhîm ṣĕbāʾôt*). For instance,

> Thus says Jehovah,
> who gives the sun for light by day
>   and the fixed order of the moon and the stars for light by night,
> who stirs up the sea so that its waves roar—
>   *Jehovah of hosts* is his name . . . (Jer 31:35)

The epithet, in one version or another, appears almost 290 times in the OT. Clearly the idea was a prevalent one in ancient Israel. The "hosts" or "armies" in question are sometimes Israel,[40] but there are more than a few references to "the host/army of heaven." Sun, moon, and stars are clearly amongst the host of heaven.[41] The phrase is also used of the divine council.[42] Indeed, the link between the sun, moon, and stars and the "gods" is clear in the warnings to the Israelites not

---

40. Exod 6:26; 12:17, 41, 51; 1 Sam 17:45.
41. Gen 2:1; Deut 4:19; 17:3.
42. 1 Kgs 22:19; 2 Chr 18:18.

to worship the "host of heaven," identified as the sun, moon, and stars *conceived of as gods.*[43]

That these heavenly armies (*sĕbāʾôt*) were sometimes actively involved in warfare is suggested by the Song of Deborah in Judges 5. There we read:

> The kings came, they [i.e., the tribes of Israel] fought;
>> then fought the kings of Canaan,
> at Taanach, by the waters of Megiddo;
>> they got no spoils of silver.
> *From heaven the stars fought,*
>> from their courses they fought against Sisera. (Judg 5:19–20)

Here the stars in heaven are pictured as joining the armies of Israel in fighting against Sisera. The earthly battle had a heavenly counterpart.[44]

This idea of the stars as God's heavenly army fighting for Israel is also found in the vision in Dan 8:1–14, which depicts the empire of Alexander the Great as a goat with a horn (Alexander). The horn is broken off and is replaced by fours horns (Alexander's four generals who divided his empire after his death). The vision focuses on a "little horn" descended from one of the four horns. This is Antiochus IV, the arch opponent of Israel and Israel's God: "Out of one of [the goat's four horns] came a little horn, which grew exceedingly great toward the south, toward the east, and toward the glorious land. It grew great, even to the host of heaven. And some of the host and some of the stars it threw down to the ground and trampled on them" (Dan 8:9–10). Here Antiochus' opposition to Israel is presented as a battle against "the host/army of heaven." And he has some measure of success—some of the stars (i.e., the heavenly army) are thrown to the ground and trampled.[45] We seem to be presented with a vision that highlights the heavenly dimension of Antiochus' earthly conflict against the temple in Jerusalem. The attack on Jerusalem's temple was an assault on the very stars of heaven, on the divine council itself. Of course, this is a symbolic vision, but it is of interest because it reveals the continuing influence of the ancient association of stars and heavenly beings.

These stars/gods were made by Jehovah and so worship Jehovah. Thus Ezra prayed, "You are Jehovah, you alone. You have made heaven, the

---

43. Deut 4:19; 17:3; cf. 2 Kgs 17:16; 21:3, 5; 23:4; Jer 8:2; 19:13; Acts 7:42.

44. We may also think of the sun and the moon coming to assist the armies of Israel in battle in Joshua 10 (cf. Zech 14:5, where God's "holy ones" may well be the armies of heaven).

45. Cf. the assault on the stars in Isa 14:13.

heaven of heavens, *with all their host*, the earth and all that is on it, the seas and all that is in them; and you preserve all of them; and *the host of heaven worships you*" (Neh 9:6; cf. Ps 148:1-3).[46]

Does the Bible Strip the Sun, Moon, and Stars of Their Divinity?

It is common for Bible scholars and theologians to claim that one of the innovations of the Old Testament is that it divested astral deities of their divinity. Here, for instance, is Denis Lamoureux: "the biblical authors, through the Holy Spirit, stripped these astronomical bodies of their divine status and made them mere creations of the Hebrew God."[47]

Now there is indeed a very interesting shift in emphasis in biblical literature, when it is compared with other ancient Near Eastern literature, away from a focus on their deity of astral bodies. We shall consider that in a moment. But this shift in emphasis is not a result, I suggest, of biblical authors rejecting the idea of the sun, moon, and stars as divine. What they *unanimously* and *emphatically* rejected was any idea that humans should *serve and worship* these astral gods. I suggest that it is *this* radical and decisive move that explains the theological shift in the biblical literature. The sun, moon, and stars may be gods, but they are created by Jehovah, are under his control, are appointed by him to serve humanity (giving light and overseeing the rhythms of time), and their glory serves to point to his greater glory. These are the things that interest the writers of the texts that became Scripture. Biblical writers have no interest in identifying specific stars with specific deities (except when condemning Israelites for worshipping stars as gods). The identification of stars with gods is, in biblical religion, generic rather than specific. Perhaps the worry was that an over-interest in the stars would lead to their being worshipped. And to worship the stars, in effect, upsets the order of creation and effectively makes them idols and even demons.

---

46. The Apocalypse, in the New Testament, also seems to make links between heavenly beings and stars. At the start of the book good angels are stars: "As for the mystery of the seven stars that you saw in my right hand, and the seven golden lampstands, *the seven stars are the angels of the seven churches*, and the seven lampstands are the seven churches" (Rev 1:20). Later we see a bad angel like a fallen star: "And the fifth angel blew his trumpet, and I saw *a star fallen from heaven to earth*, and he was given the key to the shaft of the bottomless pit" (Rev 9:1). Of course, we are in the world of highly symbolic visions here, but it is parasitic upon the older association of stars and gods that we have already identified. The link was a natural one.

47. Lamoureux, *Evolutionary Creation*, 127.

So I am suggesting that the *relative* disinterest in the Hebrew Bible in the deity of astral bodies is rooted in the fact that Israel was forbidden to offer them cultic devotion and *not* in a desire to strip them of their status as gods. Even as "gods" they were a part of creation. In biblical writings the astral bodies did not lose their deity so much as have it put in its proper place—they are servant gods, not gods to be served.[48]

God and the Sun, Moon, and Stars

Given this shift away from worshipping and serving astral entities, how did the biblical writers think of the sun, moon, and stars? Ancient Hebrews seemed impressed by the vast number of the stars[49] and by their inaccessibility to humans.[50] They were considered to be beautiful[51] and awe inspiring.[52] Several theological themes seem to be prominent.

Astral Entities as Created

First and foremost, Jehovah is *never* identified with any astral entity nor with their totality. Rather, the sun, moon, and stars are entities *created by Jehovah*.[53]

> [Give thanks] to him who by understanding made the heavens,
>> for his steadfast love endures forever; . . .
> to him who made the great lights,
>> for his steadfast love endures forever;
> the sun to rule over the day,
>> for his steadfast love endures forever;
> the moon and stars to rule over the night,
>> for his steadfast love endures forever (Ps 136:5, 7–9)
>
> It is he who sits above the circle of the earth,
>> and its inhabitants are like grasshoppers;

---

48. See Philo, *Special Laws* 1.13–20 (LCL).
49. Gen 15:5; 22:17; Exod 32:13; Deut 1:10; 10:22; Neh 9:23; 1 Chr 27:23; Nah 3:16.
50. Obad 4.
51. Song 6:10.
52. Ps 8:2–4.
53. Pss 74:16–17; 104:1, 19–20; Jer 31:35.

> who stretches out the heavens like a curtain,
>> and spreads them like a tent to dwell in;
> To whom then will you compare me,
>> that I should be like him? says the Holy One.
> Lift up your eyes on high and see:
>> who created these?
> He who brings out their host by number,
>> calling them all by name,[54]
> by the greatness of his might,
>> and because he is strong in power
>> not one is missing. (Isa 40:22, 25–26)

As created beings the sun, moon, and stars are called to worship their creator: "Praise him, sun and moon / praise him, all you shining stars!" (Ps 148:3).[55] Rather then being the *objects* of worship, they *offer up* worship.

Astral Entities under the Command of Jehovah

This sovereign creator exercises absolute control over the creation, including the sun, moon, and stars:

> all the inhabitants of the earth are accounted as nothing,
>> and *he does according to his will among the host of heaven*
>> and among the inhabitants of the earth;
> and none can stay his hand
>> or say to him, "What have you done?" (Dan 4:35)

Jehovah, as creator of the sun, moon, and stars is also the one who controls them. He "brings them out by number . . . not one of them is missing." He is the one:

> who commands the sun, and it does not rise;
>> who seals up the stars;
> who alone stretched out the heavens
>> and trampled the waves of the sea;
> who made the Bear and Orion,
>> the Pleiades and the chambers of the south;

---

54. Cf. Ps 147:4.
55. Neh 9:6; Ps 69:34.

who does great things beyond searching out,
and marvelous things beyond number. (Job 9:7–10)

God's control over the astral entities is demonstrated in the story of Hezekiah's illness and the sun standing still to enable Joshua's army to keep fighting (see chapter 1).

Astral Entities as Testimony to the Fidelity of Jehovah

God set the sun, moon, and stars in the sky in their right places and appointed them to give light and heat and to regulate time; to govern the day and night.[56] This was all part of establishing the boundaries and limits of the order of creation.

The movement of the sun, moon, and stars is *predictable*, and this did not fail to make an impression on ancient Israelites. The sun rises and sets at the right time each day,[57] the moon goes through its predictable cycles such that Israel's calendar was regulated by it,[58] and the constellations move across the sky in a regular manner throughout the night and over the course of the year. All this was attributed to God's command and manifested his faithfulness to creation: God "set [the sun, moon, and stars] in place forever and ever, he gave a statute (*ḥoq*) that will never pass away" (Ps 148:6). God is even said to have made an unbreakable *covenant* (*bĕrît*) with the sun, moon, and stars to guarantee that day and night will come at their appointed times.[59] So for Jeremiah and the psalmist divine covenant and its accompanying statutes and laws regulated the behavior of celestial entities. The ever-enduring stability of the stars thus became a model for things that last in perpetuity.[60] And this is why the darkening of the sun, moon, and stars was seen as such an ominous sign of coming judgment.[61] It seemed to suggest the very unweaving of the creation order itself and indicated the cosmic dimensions of judgment.[62]

---

56. Gen 1:17–18; Pss 104:19–20; 136:7–9.
57. Ps 19:4b–6; Eccl 1:5.
58. Ps 104:19.
59. Jer 33:20–22.
60. Pss 72:5, 17; 89:36; Jer 33:20–22.
61. Isa 13:10; Ezek 32:7; Joel 2:10, 31; 3:15; Amos 5:8; 8:9; Luke 21:25; Matt 24:29.
62. Isa 34:4.

Astral Entities as Manifesting the Glory of Jehovah

As the work of God, the heavens manifest something of his divine splendor.

> The heavens declare the glory of God;
> > the skies proclaim the work of his hands.
> Day after day they pour forth speech;
> > night after night they reveal knowledge.
> They have no speech, they use no words;
> > no sound is heard from them.
> Yet their voice goes out into all the earth,
> > their words to the ends of the world. (Ps 19:1–4, NIV)

> Jehovah, our Lord,
> > how majestic is your name in all the earth!
> > You have set your glory above the heavens....
> When I look at your heavens, the work of your fingers,
> > the moon and the stars, which you have set in place,
> what is man that you are mindful of him,
> > and the son of man that you care for him? (Ps 8:1, 2–4)

Astral entities are inherently glorious creations—they are so bright, so beautiful, so elevated and inaccessible to humans, and so long-lasting. Indeed their glory is a differentiated glory. Paul puts it like this: "There is one glory of the sun, and another glory of the moon, and another glory of the stars; for star differs from star in glory" (1 Cor 15:41). But the glory of the sun, moon, and stars is *nothing* compared to the glory of Jehovah.[63] Perhaps this idea is what Job is getting at when he says, "Behold, even the moon is not bright // and the stars are not pure in his eyes" (Job 25:5). The point is that the moon *is* bright and the stars *are* pure, but to God *even these* glorious entities are as nothing. Yet their glory is a sign pointing to God's transcending glory and thus they "declare the glory of God."

Astral Entities and the Rhythms of Creation

Consider the primary creation account in the canon—Genesis 1.[64] There we read:

---

63. Isa 60:19–20.
64. It is primary canonically, not in that it was written first.

PART II—A TOUR OF THE BIBLICAL HEAVENS

> And God said, "Let there be lights in the expanse of the heavens to separate the day from the night. And let them be for signs and for seasons, and for days and years, and let them be lights in the expanse of the heavens to give light upon the earth." And it was so.
>
> And God made the two great lights—the greater light to rule the day and the lesser light to rule the night—and the stars. And God set them in the expanse of the heavens to give light on the earth, to rule over the day and over the night, and to separate the light from the darkness. And God saw that it was good. And there was evening and there was morning, the fourth day. (Gen 1:14–19)

Many have suggested that the fact that the names "sun" (*shemesh*) and moon (*yārēaḥ*) are not mentioned is because those words were also the names for ancient Near Eastern deities and the text wishes to distance itself from such ideas. Thus, they are simply described as "the greater lamp" and "the lesser lamp"; and the stars seem to be thrown in as a mere afterthought. On top of that, it is pointed out that these celestial entities are not created until the fourth day (Wednesday). Does this imply some kind of snub to those with "higher" views of astral entities?

Perhaps this is so, but I am not convinced that polemic is at the front of the author's mind. Given the structure of Genesis 1,[65] Day Four would have been the first appropriate opportunity to create the sun, moon, and stars, for they inhabit the light and dark time slots created on Day One. That they are not named but are referred to by the term "lamp"/"light" (*māʾôr*) may not be a intended as a snub—after all, biblical writers have no aversion to the words "sun" and "moon" in creation accounts elsewhere—but for a quite different reason. Many scholars have suggested that the cosmos in Genesis 1 is being portrayed as a cosmic *temple*. The use of the term *māʾôr* for sun, moon, and stars may be a deliberate allusion to the "lamps" in the tabernacle. Every other occurrence of the word *māʾôr* in the Torah refers to the lamps in Israel's tent of meeting.[66] Philo suggested that the seven-branched lampstand in the tabernacle was a symbolic representation of the seven wandering stars (the plants visible to the naked eye). So it may well be that any polemic in Genesis 1 is more of a side effect than a primary intention of the author.

The *cultic* association of the sun, moon, and stars—that they are the lamps in God's cosmic temple—brings attention to a central focus of the

---

65. Days One to Three being concerned with creating habitats and days Four to Six being concerned with filling them.

66. Exod 25:6; 27:20; 35:8, 14, 28; 39:37; Lev 24:2; Num 4:9, 16.

author: "Let them be for signs (*'otot*) and for seasons (*môʿădîm*), and for days and years." The word translated here as "seasons" (*môʿădîm*) is always used in the Torah to refer to *religious festivals*, sacred seasons, and not merely the natural seasons of the year. The sun and the moon are given important assignments vis-à-vis Israel's cultic festivals. It may be that the sun and moon are assigned roles over two kinds of time: *sacred time* (signs and festivals) and *ordinary time* (days and years).

With regard to natural time we may note that the stars were used to predict the seasons. They were also used to tell the time at night (when sun dials are not much help) and allowed an accurate prediction of when sunrise would happen. So they functioned somewhat akin to calendars and clocks.

With regard to sacred time we should note that ancient Israel used a lunar calendar and that its "appointed festivals" (*môʿădîm*) were regulated by this calendar.[67] Thus Passover, Unleavened Bread, and Tabernacles all occur on a full moon. The "new moon" (*ḥodeš*), the first day of the month, was also celebrated as a religious festival.[68] What is fascinating about the creation of the sun, moon, and stars in Genesis 1 is that part of the *reason* that God made them was to regulate the rhythms of Israel's worship—natural time and sacred time were linked.

Celestial Signs

In the ancient Near East one major belief about the sun, moon, and stars was that they provided signs and omens concerning the future. Biblical religion in ancient Israel stands out for shying away from omens and astrology. Nevertheless, significant events were often thought to be accompanied by unusual phenomena in the astral sphere.[69] The birth of Jesus the Messiah is a wonderful game-changing event foretold by the celestial realm—in Matthew by a wandering star and in Luke by the hosts of heaven[70]—but the majority of heavenly signs were signs of coming judgment. This is most obvious in prophetic and apocalyptic texts. Consider the fol-

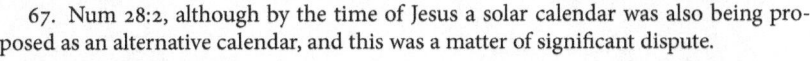

---

67. Num 28:2, although by the time of Jesus a solar calendar was also being proposed as an alternative calendar, and this was a matter of significant dispute.

68. Num 10:10; Ps 81:3[4].

69. Rev 12:1.

70. Matt 2:1–2, 9; Luke 2:8–14.

lowing signs of judgment marked by the darkening of the sun, moon, and stars:

> For the stars of the heavens and their constellations
> > will not give their light;
> the sun will be dark at its rising,
> > and the moon will not shed its light. (Isa 13:10)

> When I blot you out, I will cover the heavens
> > and make their stars dark;
> I will cover the sun with a cloud,
> > and the moon shall not give its light. (Ezek 32:7)

> The earth quakes before them;
> > the heavens tremble.
> The sun and the moon are darkened,
> > and the stars withdraw their shining . . .
> The sun shall be turned to darkness, and the moon to blood,
> > before the great and awesome day of Jehovah comes. (Joel 2:10, 31)

Indeed, the prophets can even speak of the destruction of the astral entities!

> All the host of heaven shall rot away,
> > and the skies roll up like a scroll.
> All their host shall fall,
> > as leaves fall from the vine,
> like leaves falling from the fig tree. (Isa 34:4)

One thinks also of the New Testament account of the darkness that came over the land at the time of Jesus death[71] and also Jesus' own teaching about ominous astral signs that will accompany the coming of the Son of Man.[72] Similarly, the book of Revelation speaks of signs in which "the sun became black as sackcloth, the moon became like blood" (Rev 6:12) and in which "a third of the sun was struck, and a third of the moon, and a third of the stars, so that a third of their light might be darkened, and a third of the day might be kept from shining, and likewise a third of the night" (Rev 8:12).

---

71. Luke 23:44–45.
72. Matt 24:29; Luke 21:25.

The new age, by contrast, was thought to be marked by increased light. This may be via an intensification of the light from the sun and the moon[73] or it may be because Jehovah's glory will replace the sun and the moon as the main source of light:

> The sun shall be no more
>   your light by day,
> nor for brightness shall the moon
>   give you light;
> but Jehovah will be your everlasting light,
>   and your God will be your glory.
> Your sun shall no more go down,
>   nor your moon withdraw itself;
> for Jehovah will be your everlasting light,
>   and your days of mourning shall be ended.
> (Isa 60:19–20; see Rev 21:23; 22:5 for a NT appropriation of this oracle)

It is not that the Isaianic prophet is imagining a future in which there is no sun or moon[74] but rather that the light of God's glory will be so intense and constant that they will no longer be necessary as a light source. Similar to the way in which a torch is no longer necessary if someone turns on the floodlights.

EXCURSUS: STAR SIGNS IN THE BOOK OF REVELATION

Bruce Malina and John Pilch, in their social-scientific commentary on Revelation, argue that the entire book of Revelation is an astral vision in which stars and constellations play leading roles. According to them, John is an astral prophet and most of his visions are based upon mystical interpretations of signs in the sky. His visions are, in effect, a prophetic voyage around the sky in which he is able to interpret the meaning of the stars. Given the relevance of this approach to our topic I wanted to take an example of just one of John's visions to illustrate their proposal.

Revelation 4–5 offers a vision of the throne room of heaven. John is taken by the Spirit through a door in the firmament into God's heaven (4:1). At the center of this vision is the throne of God, surrounded by twenty-four

---

73. Isa 30:26.
74. New moons, for instance, are thought to continue, Isa 66:23.

thrones of the elders (4:4). Around the throne on each side were four "living creatures" full of eyes and with wings. One was like a lion, one like an ox, one like a man, and one like an eagle (4:6–8). John then saw "the Lion of the tribe of Judah" (5:5) who "was a lamb standing as though it had been slain" (5:6).

Now the invisible events on the other side of the skydome are reflected in the stars. The vision is dominated by the throne at the center of the cosmos. The notion of a constellation associated with the cosmic throne, a throne that the other stars circled around, was ancient and widespread. The throne was jasper and carnelian, the yellowish color associated with the pole star, the *central* star proper to the divine throne.

Around the throne are the twenty-four thrones of the elders, dressed in white and wearing crowns. Pilch and Malina see these as significant astral beings known in the Hellenistic period as decans. The decans were powerful star gods who dominate every ten degrees of the circle of the zodiac. There were consequently thirty-six of them. Why does Revelation only have twenty-four? The astrological reasoning here is rather complex. Suffice it to say that, in fact, it was common to picture twenty-four decans representing the twelve hours of day and the twelve hours of night. They embrace the whole cosmos in the course of a day and a night, watching over everything.

From the throne came lightning and thunder and before the throne were seven torches of burning fire (4:5). In Greco-Roman religion lightning and thunder are associated with the stars/gods Saturn, Jupiter, and Mars, but here with the throne of the God of Israel at the center of the cosmos. The seven torches are the seven stars in the vicinity of the pole—namely, the constellation of Ursa Major.

The sea of glass like crystal before the throne is the solid sky dome we have encountered before. This suggests that the sky, as Ezekiel had also noted, was made of a crystal substance. God's throne is above it.

The living creatures are modeled on the entities from Ezekiel's vision that we encountered earlier. And here, as there, they are constellations (with the eyes representing stars). Malina and Pilch suggest that they represent the constellations that lie opposite each other along the celestial equator (a projection of the earth's equator onto the sky)—Leo (the lion), Taurus (the bull), Scorpio (who has a human face in the Babylonian tradition), and Pegasus (the constellation pictured in Babylonian astrology as a thunderbird, the flying eagle). Each of these constellations contains a royal star (linking them to the throne) and they lie at roughly 90 degrees from each other, representing the whole vault of the sky. The pole star throne lies at their center.

The Lion of Judah is announced and John turns to see a Lamb. This is the constellation Aries, which has from time immemorial been represented as a male lamb with its head turned back. Malina and Pilch think that the reverted head suggests that the neck is broken, and yet the lamb still stands. This makes it an obvious symbol for Jesus.

The point of all this is simply that the sky for John the seer was rich in Christian meaning when the Spirit could open his eyes to see it. This way of looking at stars is something Christians have long forgotten.

It is time now to go higher up, through the doors in the firmament, and into the highest heaven itself—into the presence of the God of Israel and of Jesus.

6

Brighter than a Thousand Suns

God's Heaven

Up

THERE IS A (DISPUTED) story that when Russian cosmonaut Yuri Gagarin made the first manned flight into space in 1961 he said, "I looked and looked and looked but I didn't see God." And all the sensible people laughed because only a silly person thinks that heaven is *literally* up in the sky—that if you flew in a space rocket you could reach it. Right?

Biblical authors *did* think that heaven was literally up in the sky, which is why, among other things, God "looks down" from heaven[1] and why Jacob's ladder with its ascending and descending angels stretched between earth and sky.[2] One ascends to heaven and descends from it. And this was not merely metaphorically "ascending" and "descending." When the prophet Elijah was taken from the earth chariots and horses of fire appeared and Elijah "*went up* by a whirlwind into heaven" (2 Kgs 2:11). Even more clearly, Jesus himself *literally* went up into the sky to heaven.

> And when he [Jesus] had said these things, as they [the disciples] were looking on, he was lifted up, and a cloud took him out of their sight. And while they were gazing into heaven as he went, behold, two men stood by them in white robes, and said, "Men of Galilee, why do you stand looking into heaven? This

---

1. Deut 26:15.
2. Gen 28:12–17.

Jesus, who was taken up from you into heaven, will come in the same way as you saw him go into heaven." (Acts 1:9–11)

There can be no doubt about the direction of heaven here. Now, of course, we need to appreciate that this story of the ascension is laden with symbolism. All that language about going in clouds into heaven, the presence of God, has overtones of a vision of the prophet Daniel in which "one like a son of man" comes "with the clouds of heaven" before God, "the Ancient of Days." He was given "dominion, glory, and a kingdom" (Dan 7:13–14). The story of Jesus' ascension is intended to remind the audience of Daniel's vision and to communicate that Jesus is this "one like a son of man" figure, this victorious one coming before God to reign. That is the meaning of the ascension story—Jesus is ascending into God's presence to rule as Lord. But just because the story has symbolic meanings we should not suppose that the early church saw the story as *only* symbolic and did not think that Jesus literally went up into the sky. It is not either/or; it is both/and. He did literally ascend and that literal act was deeply meaning-full.[3]

The passage from Acts 1, quoted above, also reminds us that the early church expected Jesus to *literally* descend from the sky too ("in the same way you saw him go"). This image is perhaps most overt in one of Paul's letters:

> For this we declare to you by a word from the Lord, that we who are alive, who are left until the coming of the Lord, will not precede those who have fallen asleep [i.e., died]. For the Lord himself will descend from heaven with a cry of command, with the voice of an archangel, and with the sound of the trumpet of God. And the dead in Christ will rise first. Then we who are alive, who are left, will be caught up together with them in the

---

3. As an interesting speculative aside, Tarah Van De Wiele has suggested to me that, "In ancient Near Eastern thought, an opening in the sky was largely presumed to be directly over the temple where the god resided, so in the case of Israel, above the Lord's temple, or more accurately the sky above Jerusalem. Now, I love this because it adds a cosmic layer to why Jesus did not ascend right after the fact of his resurrection in Galilee, but rather traveled to the Mount of Olives, under the sky of Jerusalem. Remember also that Stephen in Acts 7:56 sees Jesus standing before God through the opening in the sky over Jerusalem." (Email dated March 26, 2014.)

clouds to meet the Lord in the air, and so we will always be with the Lord. (1 Thess 4:15–17)

Here the picture is of a victorious king returning to his city and the joyful inhabitants rushing out to meet him so as to welcome him into the city. (It is probably not about flying off to heaven in "the rapture."[4]) But I think we have every reason to think that Paul expected Christian believers to literally rise up into the air to meet Jesus as he descended from heaven.

All of this is simply to say that biblical heaven was *up*. But there is a lot more to say about heaven other than that it was above the earth.

Heaven: God's House, God's Temple

First and foremost, heaven is the primary location of God's presence in the cosmos. This idea was hardly unique to Israel. All ancient people thought that deity inhabited the heavens. For instance, as we have already seen, the Sumerians believed that the highest heaven belonged to and was inhabited by Anu, though he shared it with other gods (e.g., 300 Igigi and Ishtar). It was here that divine assemblies of gods were convened by the king of the gods. The middle heavens, beneath Anu's heaven, belonged to Enlil and were inhabited by the Igigi gods and Marduk/Bel (god of thunderstorms). The lower heavens, visible to humans, were inhabited by astral deities—the sun, moon, and stars.

We know little about how Mesopotamians imagined the interior of the highest heaven to look. From passing comments we can discern that it was thought to be entered through gates and to have a courtyard and shrines to house important gods. In all likelihood it was understood to be a great temple complex. This would make sense because gods lived in temples. As the Lord said to Moses, "And let them [Israel] make me a sanctuary, *so that I may dwell in their midst*" (Exod 25:8). Heaven was the ultimate sanctuary; the dwelling place of divinity par excellence.

The Bible similarly presents God's heaven as a temple dwelling place. Indeed, the temple in Jerusalem in which God dwelt was understood to be a replica of the true heavenly temple. This idea is rooted in the Old Testament but comes out most clearly in the New Testament book of Hebrews. The author of the book of Hebrews contrasts the role of the high priest in the Jerusalem temple with the role of Christ in the heavenly temple. "For Christ

---

4 To the best of my knowledge there are *no* biblical texts that teach a rapture of the kind found in some sections of the contemporary church. The idea of a rapture appears to be based on a misunderstanding of texts like 1 Thessalonians 4 and Matt 24:36–44.

has entered, not into holy places made with hands, which are copies of the true things, but into heaven itself, now to appear in the presence of God on our behalf" (Heb 9:24). The high priest enters the presence of God once a year in the temple, but that important and awesome event is merely a pale reflection of what Christ did. He entered the *actual* holy of holies—the presence of God *in heaven itself*. The Jerusalem temple and the sacred objects in it are merely "copies of the heavenly things" (Heb 9:23). All of this is to underscore that first and foremost heaven is a temple, and that means that heaven is a house for deity.

What marks the biblical cosmos off from the various pagan cosmoses was that *only one* God dwells in heaven. There may be other divine beings there (the sons of God, angels, cherubim, seraphim) but they are all in a *wholly different league* from Jehovah. They are not other beings of the same kind, potential rivals.

But in the ancient world temples were not simply houses for gods—they were royal palaces from which gods ruled. The same is true for the Bible—when Jesus enters the sanctuary of heaven he comes before "the throne of grace" and sits down "at the right hand of the throne of the Majesty in heaven."[5]

The Throne Room of the Universe

"Heaven is my throne and the earth is my footstool" (Isa 66:1). When biblical writers seek to paint a picture of heaven it is always an image of a throne room. It is from heaven that God rules over the cosmos. We have already seen something of this in the chapter on stars, because the stars in some way manifest the reality of the invisible heaven beyond the sky dome. The throne of God is the central image of heaven in the numerous Jewish visions of heaven. Revelation chapter 4, discussed at the end of the last chapter, is a classic instance.

> After this I looked, and behold, a door standing open in heaven! And the first voice, which I had heard speaking to me like a trumpet, said, "Come up here, and I will show you what must take place after this." At once I was in the Spirit, and behold, a throne stood in heaven, with one seated on the throne. And he who sat there had the appearance of jasper and carnelian, and around the throne was a rainbow that had the appearance of an emerald. Around the throne were twenty-four thrones, and seated on the thrones were twenty-four elders, clothed in white

5. Heb 4:16; 8:1; 12:2.

garments, with golden crowns on their heads. From the throne came flashes of lightning, and rumblings and peals of thunder, and before the throne were burning seven torches of fire, which are the seven spirits of God, and before the throne there was as it were a sea of glass, like crystal. And around the throne, on each side of the throne, are four living creatures, full of eyes in front and behind: the first living creature like a lion, the second living creature like an ox, the third living creature with the face of a man, and the fourth living creature like an eagle in flight. And the four living creatures, each of them with six wings, are full of eyes all around and within, and day and night they never cease to say,

"Holy, holy, holy, is the Lord God Almighty,
who was and is and is to come!"

And whenever the living creatures give glory and honor and thanks to him who is seated on the throne, who lives forever and ever, the twenty-four elders fall down before him who is seated on the throne and worship him who lives forever and ever. They cast their crowns before the throne, saying,

"Worthy are you, our Lord and God,
to receive glory and honor and power,
for you created all things,
and by your will they existed and were created."

There are numerous points that could be observed here but the following will suffice. Notice first that John has to go *up* to get to heaven. No surprise there. Most importantly, observe how the entire scene is *dominated* by the divine throne. It is the first thing John observes on his arrival and everything else in the vision is orientated around that throne, either pointing to it or coming from it. The throne is the center of everything, at the very heart of the cosmos. And the rest of the book of Revelation bears this out as the future of creation unfolds in the decrees of the one who sits upon the throne. Finally, as an aside, remember the different aspects of this vision because several of them will become clearer as we proceed.

Again, the notion of heaven as a throne room is not unique to Israel. All the ancients thought that the gods ruled from the heavens. What is unique is Israel's belief that *only Jehovah* rules over the cosmos. There is *only one* throne in the biblical heaven. He may delegate tasks to the divine council or to angels but they merely act as his agents, mediating his divine rule.

Heaven Is Inhabited by Heavenly Creatures

As we have already seen in the chapter on stars, heaven in inhabited by a range of heavenly creatures.

The Divine Council

First, there is the divine council. We have already said quite a bit about the council so I will only add a little to that.

There are two or three stories in the Old Testament in which readers are given a sneak glimpse into the divine council chamber. In the first, the prophet Micaiah is brought before Ahab, king of Israel, and Jehoshaphat, the king of Judah, to speak a word from God concerning whether they should join forces and go into battle against the Syrians. All the other prophets had said that the Lord supported such a plan. Micaiah also said, "Go up and triumph; Jehovah will give [Ramoth-gilead] into the hand of the king" (1 Kgs 22:15). Ahab suspects a lie—for this prophet has a reputation for prophesying only bad news for the king—and he presses Micaiah who then switches his message and proclaims coming defeat.

Now prophets were people who had been granted access in the Spirit to the divine council and were thus authorized to speak in the name of Jehovah.[6] At this point in the story Micaiah gives what is possibly the only biblical account from a prophet of his visionary experience of standing in the divine council:[7]

> And Micaiah said, "Therefore hear the word of Jehovah: I saw Jehovah sitting on his throne, and all the host of heaven standing beside him on his right hand and on his left; and Jehovah said, 'Who will entice Ahab, that he may go up and fall at Ramoth-gilead?' And one said one thing, and another said another. Then a spirit came forward and stood before Jehovah, saying, 'I will entice him.' And Jehovah said to him, 'By what means?' And he said, 'I will go out, and will be a lying spirit in the mouth of all his prophets.' And he said, 'You are to entice him, and you shall succeed; go out and do so.' Now therefore behold, Jehovah has put a lying spirit in the mouth of all these your prophets; Jehovah has declared disaster for you." (1 Kgs 22:19–23)

---

6. Jer 23:18, 22.

7. Isaiah 6 may also be a prophetic vision of being in the divine council. While Isaiah only mentions seeing God and the seraphim, note God's words: "who will *I* send and who will go for *us*?" God is likely addressing the council.

The second story is from the prologue to the book of Job. There we have a scene set in heaven. It was a day when the sons of God came to present themselves before Jehovah. Among them was a member of the court who is called the satan (*hassātān*). "The satan" is not a name like "Bob" (or Satan) but a job title like "the builder." It means *the accuser*. The role of the accuser in the council seems to be some kind of testing role. He wanders throughout the earth and instigates trials that test the quality and truth of various people. In the prologue we see a conversation between the accuser and Jehovah about a righteous man called Job. The accuser suspects that Job's devotion to God is skin deep; anyone with such a blessed life could seem so righteous. But take away some of the benefits and his true colors would show. God grants him permission to do just this. So the accuser leaves God's presence and returns to earth where he causes a series of calamities to befall Job; yet Job does not curse God. At the next meeting of the divine council, the accuser returns to heaven and argues that stronger tests of Job's integrity are required. He is given permission to carry out these tests too.

The character of the accuser is ambiguous in the Bible. In the book of Job he is a member of God's council and seems to play a constructive, albeit unpleasant, role in God's governance of the cosmos. In the prophet Zechariah he seems to play a similar role, accusing Joshua the high priest, although there he is rebuked by the angel of Jehovah.[8]

In the book of Chronicles Satan (not *the* satan this time) opposes Israel by inciting David to number Israel, an act that brings divine judgment on the nation.[9] This seems to be in an act of opposition to God, with Satan playing the role of enemy, yet even that is not clear because the equivalent story in Samuel says that it was *God* who had incited David to number Israel and incur divine wrath![10] Chronicles may simply be presenting the accuser as an agent of God to test David. David failed.

This ambiguous role of seeming to constantly accuse and oppose God's people takes on a whole new emphasis by the time of the New Testament. There Satan is a proper name and he is the enemy of God par excellence. Yet even then God can cause Satan's work to serve his own purposes, as when Paul mentions a "messenger [lit. angel] of Satan" that was given him—we are unsure what it was—to keep him humble and so to reveal God's power in him.[11] This "angel of Satan" was, in an indirect and redirected way, an angel of God.

---

8. Zech 3:1–2.
9. 1 Chr 21:1.
10. 2 Sam 24:1.
11. 2 Cor 12:1–3.

What else can we say about this elusive divine council? A case can be made that they seem to be assigned governance by Jehovah over the seventy nations of the biblical world. Recall that there were seventy sons of El, the chief god, in the Canaanite divine council. In biblical literature, these seventy "gods" are assigned to rule the seventy nations. This we infer from the following: The table of nations in Genesis 10 lists *seventy* nations and, according to Deut 32:8, the number of nations is fixed according to the number of the "sons of God": "When the Most High gave to the nations their inheritance, when he divided mankind, he fixed the borders of the peoples *according to the number of the sons of God*." This suggestion is reinforced by Psalm 82 in which the sons of God are berated by God for not "doing justice" in the nations. Daniel 10, with its references to the heavenly rulers of Greece and Persia, may also fit with this idea. The heavenly princes of Greece and Persia in Daniel 10 may have been thought of as members of the divine council.[12]

Yet, despite all we have said, biblical authors do not devote a lot of attention to the divine council. The reason being that Jehovah is seen as omnicompetent, leaving the council a very reduced role in Scripture. God, after all, does not need anyone to advise him on the right course of action. He is wisdom itself and needs no counselors.

> Who has measured the Spirit of Jehovah,
>   or what man shows him his counsel?
> Whom did he consult,
>   and who made him understand?
> Who taught him the path of justice,
>   and taught him knowledge,
>   and showed him the way of understanding? (Isa 40:13–14)

Paul, echoing Isaiah, asks rhetorically, "Who has understood the mind of the Lord so as to instruct him?" (1 Cor 2:6) and doxologizes, "Oh, the depth of the riches and wisdom and knowledge of God! How unsearchable are his judgments and how inscrutable his ways! 'For who has known the mind of the Lord, or who has been his counselor? Or who has given a gift to him

---

12. Interestingly, Deut 32:8 and 9 are set up as a contrast: After Babel (Gen 10–11) God has given the nations to the "sons of God" to rule, *but Israel* he has kept as his own inheritance. That is why Israel is forbidden to worship the gods of the nations, for while the worship of astral gods has been allotted to the nations by Jehovah, Israel is his own possession (Deut 4:19). This handing over of the nations to rule by the sons of God may be a punitive act of God on humanity—distancing himself from the nations by working through intermediate spiritual powers. The worship of the sons of God by the nations is certainly regarded as misguided.

that he might be repaid?" (Rom 11:33–35). The divine wisdom by which God created is personified as a companion working alongside God[13] but it is clearly *God's own* wisdom that is spoken of and not a member of the divine council.

The biblical divine council does not serve to supply a lack in God but to mediate God's wise plans to the rest of creation. They are pictured as sounding boards for God, as suggesting ideas as to how God's plans may be put into practice, and as offering to execute his will in the world. In this latter capacity they may have been assigned roles overseeing different nations with the task of implementing divine justice. Furthermore, kings in the ancient world had councils, so to an ancient audience the divine council served to paint a picture of God as the King of Creation. But for the most part they are invisible, lost behind the dazzling brightness of the divine glory.

Angels and Archangels

Second, there are the messengers of God, the angels. The Greek word *angelos* (as the Hebrew *māl'ak*) means "messenger" so it is no surprise that messengers, the angels, carry messages from God to people. Such angels can sometimes initially appear indistinguishable from humans (so presumably they did not have wings!),[14] but most times they appear in heavenly glory, striking awe and fear into the hearts of those who see them! One thinks immediately of Gabriel's appearance to Mary to tell her of Jesus' coming birth, but there are many other instances. Their clothing is universally pictured as white garments, sometimes dazzlingly white like lightning.[15]

These angels are also the astral "hosts" or "armies" of God. As such they fight for God and his people. We have already seen them in this role in our tour of the stars.

---

13. E.g., Prov 8.
14. E.g., Gen 18 (cf. Heb 13:2); Josh 5:13–15.
15. Matt 28:3; Mark 16:5; Luke 24:4; John 20:12

In both of these roles angels move across the boundaries between heaven and earth, "ascending and descending" as Jacob saw in his dream.[16]

In later texts in the period before Jesus certain angels were seen to have more prominent roles and are even named. In the Bible we see the archangels Michael and Gabriel named. Michael is usually presented as some kind of warrior archangel[17] while Gabriel, who is not called an archangel in the Bible, is primarily a messenger who brings or interprets divine revelations.[18] In some texts from the Second Temple period we find more archangels named and more roles that they play. For instance, *1 Enoch*, a text written prior to the time of Jesus, names seven:

> And these are the names of the holy angels who watch.
>
> *Uriel*, one of the holy angels, who is in charge of the world and Tartarus.
>
> *Raphael*, one of the holy angels, who is in charge of the spirits of men.
>
> *Reuel*, one of the holy angels who takes vengeance on the world of the luminaries.
>
> *Michael*, one of the holy angels, who has been put in charge of the good ones of the people.
>
> *Sariel*, one of the holy angels, who is in charge of the spirits who sin against the spirit.
>
> *Gabriel*, one of the holy angels, who is in charge of paradise and the serpents and the cherubim.
>
> *Remiel*, one of the holy angels, whom God has put in charge of them that rise.
>
> *These are the names of the seven archangels.*
>
> (*1 Enoch* 20)

Other Heavenly Creatures

Third, there are a range of other heavenly beings: cherubim, seraphim, and the twenty-four elders from the book of Revelation. Little is known about these but we'll take a quick peek at Cherubim and Seraphim.

---

16. Gen 28:12. Cf. John 1:51.

17. Dan 10, Jude 9, and Rev 12.

18. Dan 8:15–27 and 9:21–27 (appearing to Daniel); Luke 1 (appearing to Zechariah and Mary).

PART II—A TOUR OF THE BIBLICAL HEAVENS

Cherubim

Cherubim are emphatically *not* cute babies with wings! They are awe-inspiring heavenly beings—winged creatures that seem to serve two purposes in the Bible. First, they serve as guards posted at important gateways, such as the entrance to the garden of Eden.[19] There they are armed with flaming swords to ensure that no humans enter, lest they access the tree of life. (As an aside, the motif of a tree between two cherubim was widespread. The drawing above is an example from an Assyrian ivory carving.)

Heavenly creatures that guard important gateways were common in the ancient Near East. Here is a picture of a lamassu, an Assyrian protective deity with the bull or lion's body, a human head, and eagle's wings. These creatures were often posted at city gates. Other similar hybrid creatures populated ancient Near Eastern cultures.

19. Gen 3:24.

Second, Cherubim serve God by holding up his heavenly throne: God "sits enthroned above the cherubim."[20] Cherubim thrones were popular in Canaan and Phoenicia in the Late Bronze and early Iron Ages. So the image of God's throne was probably akin to the picture below of the King of Megiddo on his cherubim throne. Although its prime location was in heaven, this throne was not necessarily static—in Ezekiel's visions it was more of a throne *chariot* carried by the Cherubim, first to Babylon and then to Jerusalem.[21]

Ancient images of cherubim show them with the body of a lion or panther or bull, the wings of an eagle, and the head of a human. As such they were seen as strong, fast, and intelligent. Ezekiel's vision of the living creatures in chapters 1 and 10 was an unusually detailed vision of Cherubim.[22] At first Ezekiel's gaze is captivated by the presence of these awesome winged astral creatures. So overpowered is he by this experience that he struggles to put it into words (his Hebrew is something of a mess in chapter 1). These Cherubim, these living creatures, these astral deities had a vague human appearance but with four wings, four faces (human, lion, ox, eagle), four

20. 2 Kgs 19:14-15; Isa 37:16; Pss 80:2; 99:1.
21. Ezekiel 1; 10.
22. Ezekiel 1 calls them living creatures but Ezekiel 10 consistently calls these same creatures Cherubim (see esp. 10:20).

hands, and hoofed feet. They flashed with bright fire, moving fast, and lightning burst forth from their presence. Each was located on an eye-rimmed crystal wheel that enabled them to move in any direction and their beating wings made a sound like thundering waters.

Then Ezekiel heard a voice from above the firmament over their heads and his attention was drawn up to a crystal-like throne.[23] What he sees there makes him forget the mysterious Cherubim. He sees "a likeness with a human appearance. And upwards from what had the appearance of his waist I saw as it were gleaming metal, like the appearance of fire enclosed all around. And downwards from what had the appearance of his waist I saw as it were the appearance of fire, and there was brightness around him" (Ezek 1:27). This kingly figure enthroned above the Cherubim was surrounded by the "appearance of the likeness of the glory of Jehovah" like a rainbow (Ezek 1:28).

Notice how Ezekiel struggles to describe what he sees. Everything is couched in carefully qualified terms—it had the *appearance* of this or that. Even the divine glory he saw was only "the appearance of the likeness of the glory." But it was enough to make him fall flat on his face in awe and terror.

Seraphim

Seraphim appear only once in the Bible—in Isaiah's vision of the Lord in his temple throne room. The name "seraphim" means "burning ones" but it is unclear why they bear this name. They fly above God's throne, each having six wings: two are used to fly, two are used to cover their faces (because of God's blinding glory), and two are used to cover their feet (perhaps a euphemism for genitals).[24] They call to each other, "Holy, holy, holy is Jehovah of Hosts; the whole earth is full of his glory" (Isa 6:3). One of these seraphim flew to the terrified Isaiah with a burning coal from the altar and touched it to the prophet's mouth to cleanse his unclean lips.[25]

Having seen how heaven is presented in biblical literature we can turn finally to consider some other important biblical ideas concerning it.

23. Ezek 1:26. We see God riding on a cherub in Ps 18:10 also.
24. As in Exod 4:25; Judg 3:24; Isa 7:20.
25. Isa 6:5–7. Might this be why they are "burning ones"?

Some Final Reflections on Heaven

Heaven is (Usually) Inaccessible to Terrestrial Beings

An obvious fact about heaven is that, although it is the very heart of the cosmos, terrestrial beings such as humans cannot see it (except indirectly via the stars) and certainly cannot enter it.

There are rare exceptions to this—Enoch and Elijah are taken up into heaven and some prophets and visionaries are granted temporary access in order to bear witness to what they have seen. Visionary accounts of ascents into heaven were well known around the time that the New Testament texts were written; indeed, the book of Revelation itself is one such account. Now, most of the visionary reports that we have of heaven appear to be just that—visions. However, Paul spoke of someone (most scholars think he referred to himself) who "was caught up to the third heaven—whether in the body or out of the body I do not know, God knows" (2 Cor 12:2).[26] What is interesting here is not whether Paul's experience of heaven was embodied or disembodied—and he was certainly uninterested in knowing which—but that he could *conceive* of it being embodied. It was a live option for him to imagine a *body* temporarily visiting heaven.[27] We tend not to think of heaven in such concrete ways.

However, all of the above are the very much the exceptions to the rule. The rule is that heaven is invisible and utterly inaccessible to terrestrial beings.

Heaven is Created

God *created* the heavens and the earth and at the end of this age will create a renewed heavens and a renewed earth. Both heaven and the "divine" creatures that inhabit it are *created* and are utterly dependent on God for their existence. As such, they are not divine in the same sense that the creator is divine. Their divinity, if we may call it that, is derived.

---

26. This reference to "the third heaven" is the only hint in the Bible of more than one level in God's heaven. (Unless the first heaven is the atmosphere and the second heaven is the astral plane; in which case "the third heaven" is simply what we call "heaven").

27. 2 *Enoch* 2 seems to envisage a bodily ascent to heaven and *The Ascension of Isaiah* 6:11 envisages a non-bodily ascent.

PART II—A TOUR OF THE BIBLICAL HEAVENS

Heaven Is Where God's Will Is Done

God's heaven is also presented in the Bible as the sphere of creation in which God's will is done, in contrast to the earth, where it often is not. This contrast is perhaps clearest in Matthew's Gospel, and nowhere more so than in the Lord's Prayer:

> Our Father in the heavens,
> May your name be hallowed [on earth as in the heavens]
> May your kingdom come [on earth as in the heavens]
> May your will be done on the earth as in the heavens. (Matt 6:10)

The phrase "on earth as in the heavens" qualifies all three of the requests. The assumption is that in heaven God's name *is* hallowed, God's kingly rule *is* exercised unopposed, and God's will *is* done. In this regard heaven is *unlike* the earth. However, the disciple is to pray that the earth comes to resemble heaven in this respect.

The Future of Heaven and Earth is One of Unity

For the biblical writers the creation is always dual—"heaven and earth," visible and invisible—and the existence of one side of the duality without its counterpart would be almost inconceivable. However, the vision of the future of creation found in some biblical texts seems to be one in which the duality between heaven and earth is overcome, not through the elimination of one of the pair, but by their merging.

For Matthew's Gospel the end will be when God's will is done both on earth and in heaven, when the antithesis between above and below is ended and the "kingdom of heaven" (Matthew' preferred terminology) has come to earth.

The book of Revelation contains a vision of the end in which the seer sees a *uniting* of heaven and earth.

> And I saw the holy city, new Jerusalem, coming down out of heaven from God, prepared as a bride adorned for her husband. And I heard a loud voice from the throne saying, "Behold, the dwelling place of God is with man. He will dwell with them, and they will be his people, and God himself will be with them as their God." (Rev 21:2–3)

As the vision of chapters 21 and 22 is gradually unveiled we see that this heavenly Jerusalem is the very heavenly temple dwelling place of God, the location of his throne. And yet here it is *on the earth!* If you cast your mind back to the cylinder of holiness on page 12 then we may imagine this end-time vision as one in which sheol is emptied and annihilated,[28] and the vertical gap between the top and bottom of the cylinder is collapsed—God's holiness and glory fill all things completely. This seems to represent a radical dissolving of the division of creation into heaven and earth; a whole new phase in the existence of creation—what the Bible calls "new creation."

Heaven Cannot Contain God

Heaven is not eternal in the sense that God is. It is, if you will, the dimension of creation that serves as an interface between God and the rest of creation. As such, even though biblical writers will regularly speak of God dwelling in and ruling from heaven they are also aware that God is "bigger" than heaven. In fancy language, God transcends not only the earth *but heaven itself*. As Solomon so beautifully put it in his prayer at the dedication of the spectacular temple he had built: "But will God indeed dwell on the earth [in this temple]? Behold, *heaven and the highest heaven cannot contain you*; how much less this house that I have built!" (1 Kgs 8:27).

The paradox of God's dwelling in the temple in Jerusalem captures in a scaled-down way this same tension. The Bible holds together the idea that God dwells in the Jerusalem temple with a resistance to the idea that God's presence can be contained there. God's presence is everywhere, even outside the Promised Land, even to the ends of the earth, and even in sheol![29] More than that, God's presence is in heaven, while the temple is on earth. So while God's presence *is* in the temple, it is not there in quite the same way that it is in heaven.

Some texts speak obliquely of the temple as "the place that Jehovah your God will choose *to make his name dwell*" (Deut 26:2). This way of speaking beautifully captures the balance. It speaks of God's real presence in the temple (for in ancient thinking the *name* of a person is profoundly connected to the person; it was no mere label) while at the same time pushing against a simplistic understanding of that presence. There is a subtle distance inserted between God and the temple in the very words that speak of his dwelling in it—he causes *his name* to dwell there. Israel's theologians are seeking to speak of the reality of God's presence but also of the way in which God's presence is unlike any other presence. Words fail when God is the topic under discussion.

28. Rev 20:13–14.
29. Ps 139:7–12.

PART II—A TOUR OF THE BIBLICAL HEAVENS

The paradox fundamental to biblical thinking is that God is present in the temple while transcending the temple. And the same paradox is found on the cosmic scale. God dwells in heaven, but heaven cannot contain God, for in the end heaven is an aspect of creation but God is the creator.

PART III

The House of God: Temple and Cosmos

7

God's in the House

The Temple and the Biblical Cosmos

The Bible ends with a vision of "a new heaven and a new earth."[1] However, what the prophet John actually sees in the vision is not what we might expect: not oceans and mountains, nor fields and rivers, but a city. Down from heaven descends the new Jerusalem, and its presence marks the dwelling of God with humanity[2] for this city is, in fact, a temple city. It is not merely a city that *contains* a temple (like Jerusalem), but the city itself *is* a temple.

The temple-city connection comes out in various ways, but the following will be enough to make the point: (a) the city is a vast cube, the same dimensions of the holy of holies (the innermost part of the temple);[3] (b) the city is composed of precious stones and gold, elements used in the construction of the temple and items associated with it;[4] (c) the city has no temple in it to contain God's presence, for God's glory and presence fill it as they fill the holy of holies;[5] (d) God's throne is in it and from this throne flows life-giving water, feeding the lush tree of life[6]—all these are temple images, as we shall see. The question is this—why would a vision of a temple count

---

1. Rev 21:1.
2. Rev 21:3.
3. Rev 21:16.
4. Rev 21:18–21.
5. Rev 21:11, 22–23.
6. Rev 22:1–2.

PART III—THE HOUSE OF GOD: TEMPLE AND COSMOS

as a vision of a new heaven and a new earth? Has the Bible not got its wires crossed? This part of the tour will explore that question.

The basic pattern of the tabernacle shown by God to Moses on Mount Sinai was simple enough. It was composed of three sections: (a) an outer courtyard, containing a large altar for sacrifices and a laver containing water, (b) a chamber called the holy place, containing a seven-branched lampstand, a table for bread, and an altar for burning incense, and (c) a central chamber, the holy of holies, containing the ark of the covenant.

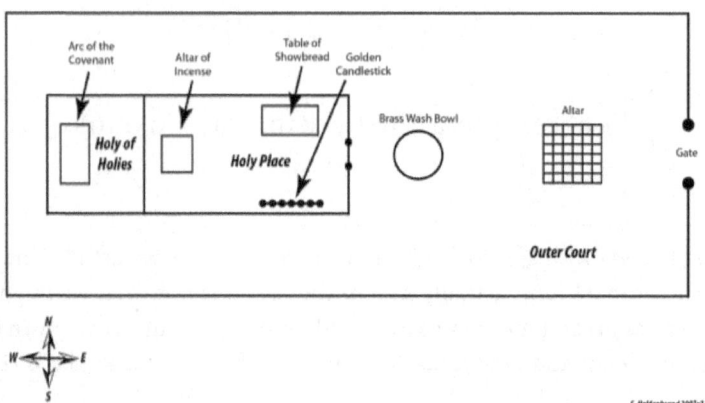

The outer court was open to all Israelites, the holy place to all priests, and the holy of holies to the high priest, though only on one day per year. This same basic pattern was retained later in the temple built in Jerusalem by Solomon.

The ancient world was awash with temples dedicated to a wide array of deities. Every ancient culture had its gods and its temples. Israel did not invent the idea of a temple; they inherited it. In fact, the temple in Jerusalem had overt non-Israelite input: it was built with imported Phoenician materials[7] and furnished by Hiram, a skilled metalworker from Tyre.[8] A quick comparison of the three-part structure of Israel's temple and of its furnishings will reveal that there were many similarities between the biblical temple and temples across the ancient Near East.

What was really distinctive about Israel's temple was that, uniquely in the ancient world, it had no statue of the deity in it, for Jehovah had

7. 1 Kgs 5:1–18.
8. 1 Kgs 7:13–45.

expressly forbidden such a thing. Nevertheless, Israel's temple did share much in common with other temples, and it is helpful to briefly note a few things about temples in the ancient Near East in our attempt to better grasp the Bible's temple.

The Meaning of Temples in the Ancient Near East

Temples and Mountains

There is a strong association between sacred hills and temples in the old world (see chapter 3). Egypt is famously flat but most of the great Egyptian temples claimed that within their courts was the primeval mound upon which the creator had made the world. The temple-mountain association is so strong that Ramesses III, addressing the god Ptah-Tatenen, can say that the temple of Medinet Habu has been built "on the mountain," even though it is located on a completely flat plain! In the equally flat world of Mesopotamia the great ziggurats functioned as symbolic mountains, staircases to heaven. If we move to locations closer to mountains we find gods such as Ba'al dwelling in a temple on Mount Zaphon and El inhabiting a temple on his own mountain. The association is fairly simple—mountains bridge the chasm between the heavens and the earth and temples symbolically serve this same function. Temples were cosmic mountains.

PART III—THE HOUSE OF GOD: TEMPLE AND COSMOS

Temples, Gardens, and Water

Temple gardens were found throughout Mesopotamia and Egypt. Trees could represent gods or a mystical and fertile life-source (like the tree of life in the Garden of Eden). Trees are also strongly associated with water in temples and are often shown as sources of water in iconography. Many temples also have other sources of water linked with them. There are ritual basins of water, sacred pools and lakes, and even springs of water. Water in this context, like the trees, was seen as a symbol of the life that gushed from the gods to sustain the world. Temples were quite literally zones of *vitality*. The flourishing of the land may depend on what went on in the temple.

This section of a wall relief from seventh-century BC Assyria shows all three aspects of temples very clearly. The temple itself is at the top of a mountain, water flows from an aqueduct around the temple grounds, and lush trees can be seen planted all about.

Temples as the House and Palace of a God

It almost goes without saying, because it is so blindingly obvious, that first and foremost a temple was the house of a god. Gods lived in temples and ruled from temples. Thus temples were always the temple of Marduk or El or Artemis or Ishtar or Ba'al or whoever.

Within a temple was found a cult statue of the deity to whom the temple was dedicated—an idol. The idol was not simplistically identified with the deity, as if the deity was the idol and nothing more, for the god or goddess was understood to reside in heaven or in the underworld or wherever. The idol was thought of as just a statue until it was ritually "activated" and, as we might say, "online." Once "activated," the spirit of the god or goddess was thought to inhabit the statue such that people could worship him or her by means of worshipping the idol. Functionally speaking, the idol *was* the god or goddess; nevertheless, the god or goddess could not be *reduced to* the statue. After all, most of these deities had numerous cult statues in various locations so the god must have been thought of as transcending any single idol.

The various biblical authors had a very low view of such idols because Jehovah, the living God, could not be represented by something so static and lifeless as a statue. A metal or stone image (ṣelem) of a god cannot see or hear or act and so cannot represent the living Jehovah.[9] The only authorized image (ṣelem) of God in Scripture is humanity; thinking, hearing, seeing, speaking, acting humanity, filled with the Spirit of God.[10] In Genesis 1, human beings are created to be the equivalent in creation of the cult statue in a temple! That is an *astonishing* claim.

Temples as Gateways to Heaven

Ancient Near Eastern temples were symbolic representations of heaven (and sometimes of the whole cosmos). The Babylonian creation myth *Enuma Elish* says of the building of Marduk's temple: "He shall make on earth the counterpart of what he brought to pass in heaven." That is to say that the temple of Marduk was intended to be an earthly model of heaven. In Egypt also temples were made "like the heavens" or "the likeness of the heavens."

As images of heaven, temples served as gateways to heaven. In Egypt when the gates of the sanctuary were opened each day the words "The gates of heaven are opened" were uttered. The person entering the sanctuary itself says: "I enter into heaven to behold [name of god]." The temple was a place where the line between heaven and earth got very blurry and fuzzy.

We see the same thing if we travel east to Mesopotamia. The picture below of the sun god is a case in point. On the left we see the Babylonian king (the middle figure) led by a priest towards a symbol of the sun god on a table in the temple. However, the sun god himself is seen as present on

---

9. Pss 115:1–8; 135:16; Isa 44:9–20; 46; Jeremiah 10.
10. Gen 1:26–28.

his throne (far right). At the bottom of the image one can see the heavenly ocean (what Genesis would call "the waters above") and Mercury, Mars, Jupiter, and Saturn. So are we in a temple on earth or are we in heaven with the sun god? Both, because the temple served as a gateway into heaven itself.

Perhaps we can imagine this as in *some* ways like a 3D video conference call. If we were able to have such a call with someone on the other side of the world there is a sense in which we are clearly in a different place from that person—we are thousands of miles apart. Yet there is another sense in which we are in the very presence of that person—we see and hear them in real time. Are we in the same place or not? No, but yes. In *virtual* reality we are. The video image of the person we speak with is not the person and yet it mediates the person's presence to us. That gives us at least some inkling as to how ancient thought that temples functioned. They were considered "thin places" in which the distance dividing heaven and earth was collapsed, allowing communion between the spheres.

The Meaning of the Temple in Ancient Israel

Temple and Mountain

The Jerusalem temple is, as we have already seen, located on Mount Zion, also referred to as "the holy mountain"[11] and "the mountain of Jehovah."[12] And although, at less than 750 meters, Zion is not a big hill—even the hills around it are higher—to the authors of the Bible it is the biggest of hills because it is the site of the temple. Clearly this height was not understood in a crudely literal way; anyone could see that Zion was smaller than the Mount of Olives or Mount Scopus. Rather, as the gateway between heaven and earth it was the mountain par excellence; the mountain that caused other mountains to look on with jealousy;[13] the mountain that in the last days would rise up above other mountains thereby manifesting its true identity.[14] As the gateway between heaven and earth, when pilgrims "ascend the hill of Jehovah"[15] they are not merely ascending a hill, they are ascending heavenwards.

Temple and Garden

Ezekiel thought that the garden paradise of Eden was located on a holy mountain.[16] This reflects the close association of temples with both mountains and gardens. Eden itself is presented in Genesis as a garden temple—a lush paradise (containing a life-giving tree) in which God dwelt and fellowshipped with human beings.

While there is no indisputable mention in the Bible of an actual garden around the temple in Jerusalem,[17] the temple is decorated with a lot of garden imagery. It is, symbolically at least, a garden paradise in which God and Israel can fellowship.

---

11. Pss 2:6; 3:4; 15:1; 43:3; 48:1; 99:9.

12. Ps 24:3.

13. Ps 68:15–16.

14. Isa 2:2; Mic 4:1.

15. Ps 24:3.

16. Ezek 28:13–16.

17. Pss 52:8 and 92:12–13 seem to imply that trees were planted around the temple complex.

PART III—THE HOUSE OF GOD: TEMPLE AND COSMOS

Temple and Water

Although the temple had sacred basins of water for use in rituals,[18] Zion had no natural water source (though there was a spring at its foot, called the Gihon). However, as a temple it was spoken of as if it did:

> There is a river whose streams make glad the city of God,
> the holy habitation of the Most High. (Ps 46:4)

And prophets could envisage a future restoration of the temple in which a miraculous life-giving stream would flow out from the temple itself into the land causing even the Dead Sea, lifeless because of all the salt in it, to burst with fish.[19] This temple river mediated the life of God from heaven via the temple to creation; it speaks of the idea of the temple as a sphere of *life*.

Temple as God's House and Palace

The Jerusalem temple was regularly referred to as a "house" (*bayit*) for Jehovah.[20] This is the ordinary word for a house—a place in which someone lived. But, of course, the resident of this house was no ordinary resident; it was the "King of Glory."[21] So the house must be understood as a royal palace (the words *bayit*, "house," and *heykal*, "temple" are both used of royal palaces). It was the earthly location of God's heavenly throne. This throne was located in the innermost sanctuary of the temple, the Holy of Holies. There lay the ark of the covenant with two vast golden cherubim looming over it. It is likely that these cherubim were thought of as supporting the divine throne. The biblical language of Jehovah sitting "enthroned above the cherubim"[22] refers to this idea. However, the throne itself, like the one who sat upon it, was not visually represented in the temple.[23] The ark of the covenant, on the other hand, was most likely understood to be Jehovah's footstool.[24] (A royal cherubic throne and footstool can be seen in the picture on p. 131.)

---

18. 1 Kgs 7:23–26, 38–39.
19. Ezek 47; Joel 3:18; Zech 14:8; Rev 22:1–2.
20. E.g., Pss 5:7; 23:6; 26:8; 27:4.
21. Ps 24:7.
22. Pss 80:2; 99:1; 1 Sam 4:4; 2 Sam 6:2.
23. Alternatively the wings of the cherubim, which touched each other, may have formed the seat.
24. Pss 132:7; 99:5; 1 Chr 28:2

Temple as the Gateway to Heaven

Just as elsewhere in the ancient world, Israel's temple was understood to be a location where the chasm between heaven and earth narrowed enabling real communion between the deity and the people. This blurring of the boundaries is such that in some biblical texts it is impossible to know for sure whether the text is referring to God in the heavenly temple or the earthly temple. Many of the references to God sitting enthroned above the cherubim, for instance, could refer to the cherubim in the Jerusalem temple or those in heaven or both. Or consider Isaiah's famous vision:

> In the year that King Uzziah died I saw the Lord sitting upon a throne, high and lifted up; and the train of his robe filled the temple. Above him stood the seraphim. Each had six wings: with two he covered his face, and with two he covered his feet, and with two he flew. And one called to another and said:
> "Holy, holy, holy is Jehovah of hosts;
> the whole earth is full of his glory!"
> And the foundations of the thresholds shook at the voice of him who called, and the house was filled with smoke. (Isa 6:1–4)

Was Isaiah caught up to the heavenly temple in a vision or was this a vision of God in the earthly temple? It is impossible to tell—the lines between the two are very blurry at times because the earthly temple functioned as a gateway to heaven.

Although the distinction between heaven and the temple was fuzzy, in Israel's sacramental worldview it was not completely erased; biblical authors *did* still make a distinction. The temple, after all, was thought of as a copy of the reality, based on the revelation of God to Moses on Sinai.[25] This distinction comes out, for instance, in Solomon's prayer at the dedication of the temple in which he voices his amazement at the gracious mystery of God's choosing to dwell in the temple—if even the actual heavens cannot contain the transcendent

---

25. Heb 9:23–24.

God, how can the little temple he has built hope to do so![26] They cannot, and yet he presences himself in both.

The Temple as Microcosm of the Cosmos

> He built his sanctuary like the high heavens,
>   like the earth, which he has founded forever. (Ps 78:69)

In this psalm God is pictured as the one who built his own house[27] (in the ANE gods were often spoken of as the founders and builders of their temples), but what is interesting is that this house is compared to creation. This is no accident but is fundamental to the symbolism of the temple, for the temple is *a model of the universe*. As Josephus said regarding the items of the tabernacle: "Every one of these objects is intended to recall and represent the nature of the universe" (*Ant.* 3:180). Different scholars have worked out the details of the comparison differently, but the proposal I find most convincing is the following: (a) the outer court corresponds to the terrestrial sphere of earth and sea, (b) the holy place represents the sky, and (c) the holy of holies stands for God's heaven itself.

The Outer Court: Land and Sea

In the courtyard of the temple we find several clues concerning its meaning:

First, there is a large bronze basin containing water, appropriately called "the sea."[28] This "sea," representing the cosmic ocean, was cylindrical, perhaps reflecting the notion of a circular sea we have found elsewhere. This sea is not the unconstrained chaos prior to the ordering activity of creation; rather, it is the *bounded* sea; it is water as a good part of creation when kept in its place.

Second, there is an altar that in the earliest versions of the temple was to be composed of earth or uncut stone.[29] This suggests some kind of earth symbolism.

Third, the rim of the large water basin was decorated with two rows of gourds,[30] perhaps suggesting the plant life found on earth. Furthermore,

---

26. 1 Kgs 8:27.
27. Pss 87:1; 147:2; Exod 15:17.
28. 1 Kgs 7:23–26, 44; 2 Chr 4:2–10.
29. Exod 20:24–25.
30. 1 Kgs 7:24.

it was standing upon twelve oxen, possibly gesturing towards the animal life on the earth and its fertility. These oxen were in groups of three, facing north, south, east, and west—the four points of the compass, the four corners of the earth.[31]

The outer court was a place that any ritually clean Israelites could go to. It was holy, but it was the least holy part of the temple. This fits with the idea that it represents the terrestrial plain.

The Holy Place: The Sky

The most obvious astral symbol in the holy place is the seven-branched lampstand. As we have seen, aside from the fixed stars, the ancients could see seven bright lights in the sky with the naked eye—the sun, the moon, Mercury, Venus, Mars, Jupiter, and Saturn. It is likely that the seven lights on the candlestick represented those astral lights.[32] As we saw in chapter 5, Genesis 1 refers to the sun and moon as "lights," using a word only ever used elsewhere of the lights in the temple. This association of the astral lights and the temple lights was no accident. We should also note that the curtain separating the holy place from the outer court was blue, purple, and scarlet and was held up by blue loops—all sky colors.[33]

However, the symbolism of the holy place is a little ambiguous, for it seems to contain not only sky symbolism but also garden symbolism. The lamp stand may be seen as a stylized tree of life, and we can find floral decorations on the curtains and on the walls and, of course, there is bread on the table, and bread is made from grain. Doesn't this mixing of symbols mess up the neat picture I am presenting? No. You will recall that temples were associated with mountains that reached up to the heavens and with a garden paradise. Remember too that Ezekiel thought of Eden's garden as located on God's mountain. So a paradisiacal tree of life in the sky is not as odd as it may seem at first blush. The garden paradise goes all the way up.

31. 1 Kgs 7:25.
32. A link explicitly made by Josephus and Philo.
33. Exod 26:36; 27:16; 36:11, 37; 38:18.

PART III—THE HOUSE OF GOD: TEMPLE AND COSMOS

The Holy of Holies: Heaven

The link between the holiest place and heaven is beyond dispute. The curtain separating the holy place from the holy of holies was decorated with cherubim, symbolic of those heavenly creatures that guard the divine throne. Its colors of blue, purple, and scarlet were those of the sky (indeed, it may have represented the sky-dome).[34] Within the chamber itself was God's cherubic throne[35] and his royal footstool, the ark of the covenant.[36] This was the dwelling place of God, the divine throne room. Appropriately, humans cannot see into this heavenly chamber and are not permitted to enter it. The one exception is the high priest one day a year, and even then only when surrounded by a thick cloud of incense, obscuring his sight.[37]

So the temple is the cosmos writ small. When the priests and the high priest move around the temple performing their sacred duties, they are symbolically moving around the biblical cosmos. This may help explain why the temple was so central to ancient Israel and why its desecration and its destruction by pagan nations were understood as such catastrophic events. The destruction of the temple—first at the hands of Babylon and later at those of Rome—was in a very real sense, the end of the world.

The final vision in the book of Revelation now makes a little more sense. Not only was the temple the biblical cosmos writ small, the biblical cosmos was the temple writ large. In other words, in the world of the Bible *the cosmos is God's house*. As Philo put it, "The whole universe must be regarded as the highest and, in truth, the holy temple of God" (*Spec.* 1.66). As such the biblical cosmos is a sacred place indeed.

---

34. Exod 26:1, 31; 36:8, 35.
35. 1 Kgs 6:23–28; 2 Sam 6:2; 2 Kgs 19:15; 1 Chr 13:6; Pss 80:1; 99:1.
36. 1 Chr 28:2; Pss 99:5; 132:7–8; Isa 66:1; Lam 2:1.
37. Leviticus 16.

8

Christ's in the House

Jesus and the Biblical Cosmos

> But grace was given to each one of us according to the measure of Christ's gift. Therefore it [Scripture] says, "When he ascended on high he led a host of captives, and he gave gifts to men" [Ps 68:18]. (In saying, "He ascended," what does it mean but that he had also descended into the lower regions of the earth? He who descended is the one who also ascended far above all the heavens, that he might fill all things.) (Eph 4:7–10)

In the text above we are presented with Jesus as one who "descended" and "ascended" *so that* he might fill all things. Jesus traverses all the regions of the biblical cosmos and fills it all. This part of the tour considers Jesus' relation to the different parts of the cosmos and to the whole of it.

The *Logos Asarkos:* From Heaven

Some of the New Testament authors spoke of Jesus' heavenly origins prior to his life on earth. The theological phrase for this is *Logos asarkos* (lit. "Word without flesh"). John's Gospel is an especially important source for such thinking, with its prologue setting forth the work of the divine Word in creation and *then* the coming of that same divine Word in human flesh.[1] This divine Word "prior to" its coming as Jesus was "with God" and "was

---

1. John 1:1–14.

God."[2] Another way of saying that is to say that the Word was "in heaven," although actively at work in the earth as "the light of humanity"[3] and working in the history of Israel. And John's Jesus does indeed speak of his own coming from heaven: "No one has ascended into heaven except he who *descended from heaven*, the Son of Man" (John 3:13). "You are from below; I am from above. You are of this world; I am not of this world" (John 8:23). John's Christ also talks of the glory that he shared with the Father before the foundation of the world.[4]

Paul too writes, albeit sparingly, of heavenly existence for the Son prior to his life on earth. The classic instance is the opening of the Christ hymn in Phil 2:5–11. Here Jesus was in the form of God but did not consider his equality with God a thing to be grasped onto but instead willingly emptied himself and was born on earth in the likeness of men, in human form. Because he willingly made himself low God highly exalted him. So again we find this descent-ascent narrative beginning and ending with the Son in heaven.

The New Testament authors are also agreed that the divine Son was the one through whom God the Father created the universe in the beginning and the one who holds the universe in being at each and every moment of its existence. Consider the following witnesses from different branches of the early Jesus community:

- *John:* "All things were made through him [the Word], and without him was not anything made that was made." (John 1:3)
- *Paul:* "For by him [the beloved Son] all things were created, in heaven and on earth, visible and invisible, whether thrones or dominions or rulers or authorities—all things were created through him and for him. And he is before all things, and in him all things hold together." (Col 1:16–17)
- *Hebrews:* "Long ago, at many times and in many ways, God spoke to our fathers by the prophets, but in these last days he has spoken to us by his Son, whom he appointed the heir of all things, *through whom also he created the world*. He is the radiance of the glory of God and the exact imprint of his nature, and *he upholds the universe by the word of his power.*" (Heb 1:1–3)

---

2. John 1:1.
3. John 1:4.
4. John 17:5.

Notice the ongoing role of Jesus in holding the universe in being—"in him all things hold together"; "he upholds the universe by the word of his power." So Jesus is related to the cosmos in the first instance as its creator and sustainer. As such he inhabited heaven with the Father.

The Logos Incarnate: To Earth

Central to Christian faith is the notion that the divine Logos became a real human being—"the Word became flesh" (John 1:14). As we have just seen, this incarnation is spoken of as a divine descent from heaven to earth.

As Jesus, the Logos interacted with the different spheres of the terrestrial realm. He was baptized in the *river* Jordan; he went into the *wilderness* to face and overcome the temptations of the devil; he went up *mountains* to deliver his divine teaching like Moses, to pray, and to be transfigured; he went into *villages and towns* to preach and heal; and he walked on the *sea* and calmed the waves, demonstrating his power over the chaotic waters. The climax of his story—his death, resurrection, and ascension—took place in and around *Jerusalem*, the holy city at the center of the biblical earth. In all this Jesus was Emmanuel, God with us here on earth.

Christ's Further Descent into the Earth: To Hades

The descent to earth was not the end of Christ's descent. When he died on the cross he "descended into hades,"[5] as the Apostles Creed puts it. Indeed, it is worth noting that historically this belief was not considered an optional extra by the church but a *non-negotiable* part of orthodox Christian faith. To deny it is, strictly speaking, heresy.

The New Testament itself contains some somewhat murky passages that became the basis for the belief in the descent of Christ into hades.

- The Christian tradition observed that Jesus compared his three days in "the heart of the earth" to Jonah's three days in the belly of the fish.[6] And, as noted in our tour of the sea, Jonah spoke of this in terms of being in sheol/hades.

---

5. The Latin of the Athanasian Creed says *descendit ad infernos*, descended into the inferno, from which the more recent notion of Christ descending into hell comes. But, strictly speaking, it is hades and not hell into which Christ descends.
6. Matt 12:40.

PART III—THE HOUSE OF GOD: TEMPLE AND COSMOS

- In Peter's sermon on the Day of Pentecost he sees a prophetic anticipation of Christ's resurrection in the words of Psalm 16. Peter says, "God raised him up, loosing the pangs of death, because it was not possible for him to be held by it. For David says concerning him, '. . . For you will not abandon my soul to hades, or let your Holy One see corruption . . .'" (Acts 2:24, 27). So for Peter, Christ went to hades but God did not permit him to remain there.

- There is mention in 1 Peter of Christ proclaiming to the spirits in prison. It appears from the context that this refers to the sinners who died during the time of Noah's flood, and Christ's proclamation to them occurred when Christ was "put to death in the flesh."[7] The location of this victorious declaration would thus be hades. Later in the same letter we read, "For this is why the gospel was preached even to those who are dead, that though judged in the flesh the way people are, they might live in the spirit the way God does" (1 Pet 4:6). This too appears to envisage Jesus proclaiming the good news to the dead in hades.

- Paul sees Christ's death as a means of defeating death and hades,[8] and the book of Revelation presents Jesus is the one who has the keys of hades and death by virtue of being the one who lives and was dead.[9] So it was Christ's presence in hades and then God's rescue of him from there that forever broke the locks on the gates of death.

While both the biblical texts and the tradition are somewhat ambiguous on the details of Christ's descent there is a clear agreement that it was a key part of his conquest of death and the breaking of its power over humanity. The famous Orthodox icon of the resurrection shows Christ standing over hades with its gates broken beneath his feet. Christ is reaching out his hands to Adam and Eve (representing humanity) and raising them from the dead.

Christ's presenting himself in hades and then breaking out was also the means by which he can be said to be Lord of *all*, the one before whom every knee shall bow, even those under the earth:[10] "For to this end Christ died and lived again, that he might be Lord both of the dead and the living" (Rom 14:9).

7. 1 Pet 3:18–21.
8. 1 Cor 15:55.
9. Rev 1:18.
10. Phil 2:10–11.

Christ's Ascension: To Heaven

Christians often speak nowadays of the death and resurrection of Jesus as if they are the heart of the narrative; the ascension is treated as a mere afterthought. However, for New Testament authors the ascension of Jesus is of *critical* importance. The ascension spoke of Jesus' completed work of atonement and his reign at God's right hand, as well as his ongoing high priestly ministry of intercession. The Jesus of the early *ekklēsia* was the risen *and ascended* Lord, ruling from heaven.

The Ascended Jesus as Lord and King

A dominant theme associated with Jesus' ascension is that he has been exalted to the throne of God in heaven and is now ruling over all things. The passage from the Old Testament that is quoted more than any other in the New Testament is Psalm 110. Verse 1 in particular had a big impact. In it David says, "Jehovah says to my Lord: 'Sit at my right hand, until I make your enemies your footstool.'" The "Lord" to whom Jehovah spoke was universally understood by the early Messiah-followers to be Jesus. As such, the ascended Jesus is often spoken of having sat down in heaven *at the right hand* of God.¹¹ Here, for instance, is part of Peter's sermon on the Day of Pentecost:

> This Jesus God raised up, and of that we all are witnesses. Being therefore *exalted at the right hand of God*, and having received from the Father the promise of the Holy Spirit, he has poured out this that you yourselves are seeing and hearing. (Acts 2:32–33)

The right hand of God was a position of power and honor and authority; a position of ruling with God over creation. Some texts speak directly of Jesus' own throne,¹² while the book of Revelation goes so far as to speak of "the throne [singular] of God and of the Lamb" (Rev 22:1). Jesus was sitting *on God's own throne!* Pressing for absolute consistency in the images is a mistake. Both pictures point to the same notion—that Jesus has been elevated as God's co-regent. Philippians 2:9–11 famously put it this way:

> Therefore, God has highly exalted him and bestowed on him the name that is above every name, so that at the name of Jesus every knee should bow, in heaven and on earth and under the earth, and every tongue confess that Jesus Christ is Lord, to the glory of God the Father.

The "name above every name" is God's own holy name—YHWH! Notice too the allusion to a prophecy in the book of Isaiah in which Jehovah says:

> Turn to me and be saved,
>   all the ends of the earth!
>   For I am God, and there is no other.
> By myself I have sworn;
>   from my mouth has gone out in righteousness
>   a word that shall not return:
> "To me every knee shall bow,
>   every tongue shall swear allegiance." (Isa 45:22–23)

In Philippians 2 Paul is saying that God's commitment to bring it about that every knee bow and every tongue swear allegiance *to him* is fulfilled *in the ascension of Jesus* to divine dominion. When creatures bow down to Jesus and confess him as Lord they are bowing down *to God* and confessing *him*. Their worship of Jesus is not in conflict with their worship of God but

---

11. Matt 26:64; Mark 14:62; 16:19; Luke 22:69; Acts 2:33; 5:31; 7:56; Rom 8:34; Eph 1:20; Col 3:1; Heb 1:3; 8:1; 10:12; 12:2; 1 Pet 3:22.

12. Matt 25:31; 19:28.

is "to the glory of God the Father," the one who exalted Jesus from death. The ascended Jesus, in other words, is ruling over creation *as God*. He is "Lord of lords" and "King of kings." And he will continue to rule until God has finally placed all his enemies under his feet—the last enemy to fall will be death itself. Then he will hand the kingdom over to the Father and God will be "all in all."[13]

The Ascended Jesus as High Priest

The book of Hebrews sees the ascension of Christ in terms of the ministry of Israel's high priest. The high priest was a mediator who would represent God before the people and the people before God. When, on the Day of Atonement, he entered into the very heart of the temple, into the holy presence of the God of Israel, he would offer the blood of the sacrifice for the purification of sins and he would intercede for the people.[14] Jesus is the great high priest who enters heaven itself (not merely a representation of it on earth) on behalf of his people.[15] He offers his own life-blood to make atonement. And because his sacrifice is so perfect it only needs to be offered once, rather than repeatedly.[16] So unlike Israel's high priest Jesus can then *sit down* in the divine presence; his work of atonement is complete.[17] Thus, for the book of Hebrews the ascension of Jesus was necessary to complete his work of atonement. (This may surprise those used to thinking of the work of atonement as completed when Jesus died.) Now that he has gone into heaven itself sin has been dealt with once and for all. Now he lives to intercede for the people of God.[18]

Jesus Location between the Ascension and Return

For New Testament authors Jesus is no longer here on earth. His location is in heaven. However, there are some important things that need to be said to qualify this sense of absence. First, Jesus said that in his absence he would send another counselor like himself to be with his disciples, the Spirit.[19]

13. 1 Cor 15:25–28.
14. Leviticus 16.
15. Heb 9:24.
16. Heb 7:27; 9:11–28.
17. Heb 8:1; 1:3; 10:11–12.
18. Heb 6:20; 7:25–28; 8:1–6.
19. John 14:16.

The divine Spirit that indwells the disciples is the Spirit of Christ, and he mediates the presence of the absent Christ to the disciples. As such he is "Christ *in you*, the hope of glory" (Col 1:27). This is why Jesus could promise his disciples just prior to leaving them that he would be with them always, even to the end of the age.[20] So Jesus is absent in so far as he is in heaven, but he is present with his people through the Spirit that lives in them.

Second, believers are united to Jesus through baptism and participating in the Lord's Supper.[21] These sacred rituals were seen by Paul as bringing about a mysterious but very *real* communion with Jesus. Indeed, so strong was the union of believers and the absent Jesus that the church is spoken of as the *body* of Christ on earth.[22] In other words, Christ is still present on earth through the Spirit-filled community of the church.

So for New Testament believers Christ is not simply absent; he is present in his absence and absent in his presence. This paradox marks a New Testament understanding of the present relation of Christ to the terrestrial realm.

Christ's Return to Earth—New Creation

The angels who were with the disciples when Jesus ascended told them, "Men of Galilee, why do you stand looking into heaven? This Jesus, who was taken up from you into heaven, *will come in the same way as you saw him go into heaven*" (Acts 1:11). In other words, he would bodily descend from the sky. He would return to rule the earth, presumably from Jerusalem (not Wales).

The return of Jesus was often spoken of as the *parousia* (literally, the presence). After the years of absence, the presence of Jesus was associated with the final judgment, with its separation of saints and sinners,[23] and with new creation.[24] New creation was the transformation of the whole created order, the unification of heaven and earth, and the final defeat of sin and death.

---

20. Matt 28:20.
21. Rom 6:3–11; 1 Cor 10:16.
22. Rom 12:4–5; 1 Cor 12.
23. For instance, see the parables in Matt 13:24–30; 25:1–46.
24. Revelation 21–22.

Christ *as* the Cosmos

God created and sustains the cosmos through his Word, and the Word-made-flesh, Jesus, inhabited and exercised dominion in each sphere of the cosmos. As such he is Lord of *all*. But there is more to say about the Christ-cosmos connection than this. There is the surprising notion that *Christ represents the whole cosmos in his human body*. In this sense Christ *is* the cosmos and its destiny is linked to his destiny.

The book of Genesis taught that humans are the pinnacle of creation and, as icons of God, rule over creation on behalf of God. The fate of creation was thereby linked to the fate of human beings. Humanity out of sync with God has creation-wide implications, and humanity liberated likewise ushers in the liberation of all creation.[25] Humans were representatives of creation. In the thought of the early Christ-followers Jesus was a Second Adam—a human as God intended humans to be.[26] And this Second Adam succeeded where the first Adam had failed. As the true human, the true Adam, Jesus represented all humanity, but *as such* he also represented the whole universe.[27] His resurrection was thus the resurrection of all humanity and of all creation. In biblical language the resurrection is "new creation." Thus when New Testament authors speak of the salvation of people and of the cosmos they think of it in terms of new creation; that is, being united with Jesus and sharing in his resurrection life.

We can also see this cosmic Jesus idea indirectly in the notion of Jesus in his own body being like the temple in Jerusalem. In John's Gospel Jesus speaks of "this temple" being torn down and raised up. His audience thought he spoke of the temple in Jerusalem but, John tells us, the temple he spoke of was his body.[28] This is no surprise to his audience because earlier in the Gospel he had spoken of how "the Word became flesh and *tabernacled* among us" (John 1:14). This is an allusion to the tabernacle in the wilderness during the days of Moses, the precursor to the temple. As God tabernacled with Israel so the Word now tabernacles with Israel in the body of Jesus. Paul sees the church, through its union with Christ, as the temple

---

25. Rom 8:19–24, read in context.

26. Rom 5:12–21; 1 Cor 15:20–23.

27. There is an affinity between this idea and the ancient Greek philosophical proposal that the human being is a microcosm of the cosmos. Some ancient Greeks from at least the fifth century BC embraced this notion, and it remained popular among Neoplatonists—pagan, Jewish, and Christian—well into the Middle Ages. One certainly finds it in some of the early church fathers.

28. John 2:18–22.

of God and as the body of Christ.[29] As we saw in the last part of the tour, the temple was a scale model of the cosmos. Put simply, *Christ as temple = Christ as cosmos*. And, through union with Christ, the church too was seen as the temple/body symbolically representing the whole cosmos.

The Christ-cosmos connection possibly also comes out when we consider Jesus as the book of Hebrews presents him—as high priest. There are some grounds for maintaining that Israel's high priest, when dressed in his holy garments, symbolically represented not only the nation of Israel but also the whole universe.[30] Certain Jews from around the time of Jesus clearly made this connection.[31] The same fabrics, metals, and precious jewels are used in the construction of both the garments and the tabernacle, and just like the tabernacle, the garments contain elements that seem to have some links to different parts of the cosmos. For instance, images of pomegranates, representing the fertile earth, were sewn into the bottom of the robe; the main robe was of a blue color, like the daytime sky; there were jewels on the ephod and the breastplate that represented the twelve tribes of Israel but also, arguably, the twelve constellations. (The link between gems and the heavens is paralleled elsewhere, as is that between the Israelites and stars.[32]) The ephod and breastplate were woven from colors that could link to the sky (blue, purple, scarlet) and the stars (gold);[33] the square breastplate on the high priests chest may be intended to pick up on the square dimensions of the holy of holies. God's presence is further suggested by the Urim and Thummin, tools used for discerning God's will, and the gold sign on the turban inscribed with the words "Holy to Jehovah." Ecclesiasticus speaks of the glory of the high priest on Yom Kippur in ways that picture him as manifesting divine glory just as creation does:

---

29. Rom 12:4–5; 1 Cor 11:29; 12.

30. The garments are described in Exod 28.

31. Wis 18:24; Josephus, *Ant.* 3.180, 183–87; Philo, *Vit. Mos.* 2.117–26, 133–35, 142–43; *Spec.* 1.95; *Fug.* 110; *Som.* 1.215.

32. Gems are associated with the crystal floor of the heaven in which stars were fixed, although a connection with *stars themselves* is not clear. The twelve sons/tribes of Israel could be linked to stars, as was the case when God promised to multiply Jacob's children as the stars of heaven (Gen 26:4; Exod 32:13; Deut 1:10; 10:22; 28:62; 1 Chr 27:23; Neh 9:23), or in Joseph's dream in which his eleven brothers were stars (Gen 37). Daniel also says that the righteous of Israel will "shine like the brightness of the sky above ... like the stars forever and ever" (Dan 12:3). So seeing the gems as representing Israel as star-like is certainly a possibility.

33. Alternatively, Josephus (*J.W.* 5.212–13) linked the colors to the four elements: blue for air, purple (made from the secretion of sea snails) for the sea, red for fire, and the white linen coat for the earth (as linen was made from a plant). The gold was not one of the four elements but the heavenly glory.

How glorious he was when he came out of the Most Holy Place! He was like the morning star shining through the clouds, like the full moon, like the sun shining on the Temple of the Most High, like the rainbow gleaming in glory against the clouds, like roses in springtime, like lilies beside a stream, like the cedars of Lebanon in summer, like burning incense, like a cup made of hammered gold and decorated with all kinds of jewels, like an olive tree loaded with fruit, like a cypress tree towering into the clouds. (Sir 50:5–10)

All this suggests that the high priest is functioning in the temple as an Adam figure—a human representing the whole creation to God and representing God to the whole creation. It further suggests that when Jesus ascended to heaven as the Son of Man, riding on the clouds of heaven, he was entering heaven as a high priest surrounded by a cloud of incense, as on the Day of Atonement. Again, for those with eyes to see, all this suggests that Jesus ascends as a high priest into heaven on behalf of the whole created order. *Creation ascends in him.*

This final part of the tour has sought to show how the story of Jesus is fundamentally interconnected with the contours of the biblical universe. His narrative is played out on all the stages of both heaven and earth. He moves between the highest heaven and the pit of sheol and back again. "He who descended is the one who also ascended far above all the heavens, that he might fill all things" (Eph 4:10). But more than that, the story of that cosmos is fundamentally interwoven with the story of Jesus—he created it and sustains it; he rules it and is present throughout it; and he is the one who bound its destiny to himself in his own body thereby enabling it to share in his own new creation resurrection life.[34] The future of the biblical cosmos is the future of Christ. Here we see "the mystery of [God's] will, according to his purpose, which he set forth in Christ as a plan for the fullness of time, to unite all things in him, things in heaven and things on earth" (Eph 1:9–10).

---

34. Rom 8:20–21.

PART IV

Can WE Inhabit the Biblical Cosmos?

9

How Can We Inhabit the Biblical Cosmos Today?

CLEARLY MODERN PEOPLE, CHRISTIANS included, can visit the biblical cosmos as tourists. We can imaginatively try to feel our way into it—temporarily suspending our modern understandings of the cosmos—in order to better understand it. And such visits are important if we are to understand Scripture in its original contexts. So far in this guide we have been tourists in the biblical world. But can we actually *inhabit* it? Can the biblical conceptions of the cosmos become our own? My answer to this question is both no and yes.

A Dead End—Fundamentalism

I suggest that it is simply not possible for a modern Christian, even a fundamentalist, to believe the cosmos to have the exact physical structure that biblical authors believed it to have. By this I mean that it is not really possible, short of severe self-delusion, to believe that the earth is flat, that the sky is a solid dome beyond the stars with waters of chaos above it, that beneath the ground is the world of the dead, that heaven is literally up, and that the stars are divine beings.

I know that many Christians claim that the Bible is scientifically accurate on all matters on which it touches and that they are prepared to reject the findings of mainstream science to hold onto a seven-day creation that took place six to ten thousand years ago, but, as we have seen, this does not go nearly far enough. If fundamentalists really were to have the courage of their convictions then we would see membership of the Flat Earth Society boosted significantly. What happens instead is that this is a bridge too far, even for hard-line fundamentalists, and biblical texts are thus reinterpreted to fit with modern cosmology. For instance, Isaiah's phrase "the circle of the earth" (Isa 40:22) is taken as proof that the Bible authors actually believed in a planetary globe—proof, we are told, of its inerrancy. However, in this tour we have seen that such interpretations are implausible.

So I really do not think we can inhabit the biblical cosmos *in the same way* that ancient Israelites or Second Temple Jews (including the authors of the New Testament) did. The world can never feel the same again after Copernicus. The cosmology of the Bible is ancient and we are not; it's as simple as that.

A Step in the Right Direction—Divine Accommodation

Most biblical scholars and theologians do recognize the gap between biblical and modern cosmologies. Many argue that God accommodated his revelation when speaking to ancient people. He adapted his communication to their understandings of the world. After all, his goal was communication, and if he had spoken to them about particle physics and the like they would not have known what was going on. Here, for instance, is Denis Lamoureux: "in order to reveal spiritual truths as effectively as possible to the ancient peoples, the Holy Spirit used their ancient phenomenological perspective of nature. That is, instead of confusing or distracting the biblical writers and their readers with modern scientific concepts, God descended to their level and employed the science-of-the-day."[1] And listen to Paul Seely:

> The divine intent of this picture [in Genesis 1] was not to communicate natural science, but to teach the fact that the God of Scripture is Creator and absolute Sovereign over the supposedly independent forces of the natural world. This is an important revelation which men still need today. Of course, the ancient science employed in giving this revelation cannot be completely harmonized with modern science . . . We need simply to see with Warfield that divine inspiration does not bestow omniscience, and hence God has sometimes allowed his inspired penmen to advert to the scientific concepts of their own day. . . . The divinely intended message of Genesis 1 does not err.[2]

---

1. Lamoureux, *Evolutionary Creation*, 110.

2. Seely, "The Firmament, Part II." Online, no page numbers. The citation is from the conclusion.

So it is being claimed that God accommodated his self-revelation to the ancient world and that Christians have had little trouble updating their theology since then. And that is fine, as far as it goes. I see no problem with appealing to divine accommodation. Indeed, I think that the instinct is fundamentally correct. However, I want to argue that more is going on here.

A Third Way: The Metaphysical and Metaphorical Truth of Myth

It seems to me that God is communicating his truth not merely *in spite of* the "wrong science" *but in and through it*. And, I suggest, God can *still* speak truth through these ancient ideas, and while they may not be scientifically true, they point to important metaphysical truths that remain as true today as they ever were.

Unlike the biblical authors and their original audiences, we cannot take some of their beliefs literally any longer. That option is not open to scientifically literate people. But "beyond the desert of criticism" there is a second naïveté in which the text can again disclose divine truth and God can speak afresh. This is not a return to a pre-scientific view of the world but is rather a *post*-critical retrieval—a willingness to let God speak anew *precisely through* the strangeness of the ancient text. We cannot simply strip away the out-of-date views and throw them away like the peel of an orange in order to get to the ripe juice of revelation contained within. I believe that God wants to speak to the modern world through the insights of ancient cosmography.

Karl Barth reminded us that the theological task is not to simply repeat what the apostles and prophets said but to say what *we* have to say in the light of what the apostles and prophets said.[3] The fact is that we know a lot of things about the earth, the sea, and the sun, moon, and stars that the biblical authors did not. Indeed, our entire cosmology has undergone some major shifts. The task of thinking biblically about the heavens and the earth is not simply exegeting biblical teachings about them (what the apostles and prophets said) but also asking what it means for *us* to affirm such things in light of what we now know. What does it mean for *us*, with all our scientific knowledge, to speak of chaos monsters, star gods, an underworld, heaven in the sky, and a living universe? Is there even a place for such talk? That is what we will explore in these final chapters.

---

3. Barth, *Church Dogmatics* I/2, 16.

10

The Cosmic Temple Today

God and the Cosmos Today: The Cosmic Temple

In the West we no longer live in a civilization with temples, so isn't all that biblical temple theology irrelevant today? Not at all. Although most of us Westerners no longer come across temples in our daily lives, the ideas embodied in ancient temples are perfectly intelligible to us. Temples were houses for gods, and we know what a house is. Indeed, they were royal palaces from which gods ruled, and we know what palaces are and what rulers are. Temples were also paradisiacal gardens, and that Edenic memory still lingers in our postmodern world. Temples were microcosms of the cosmos and we well-understand the idea of a model. Even the belief that the gap between the earthly and heavenly temples can be partly collapsed in ritual, enabling communion, is not entirely foreign to the modern age with its communication technologies.

The idea of the cosmos as a temple in no way depends on ancient cosmography in order to get a grip on the imagination. If anything, to consider creation as a beautiful palace created by God to inhabit is a profoundly inspirational way of thinking about the universe today. It adds new layers of meaning to the belief that creation is *good*. God is no deistic entity who started the universe off and then left it to its own devices—God is *here*; the cosmos exists as God's dwelling place. As such it should be treated with reverence by creatures. For this reason many contemporary Christian thinkers have welcomed the recovery of the biblical belief in the temple-cosmos. It speaks right to the heart of the meaning of creation.

THE COSMIC TEMPLE TODAY

But in what manner does God inhabit this temple? Scripture speaks of the divine presence in creation in three modes: God's particular presence, God's ubiquitous presence, and God's presence in heaven.

God's particular presence: God's appears to Moses in a burning bush and in the storm atop Mount Sinai, he is present with the Israelites in a pillar of cloud and of fire, he comes in theophanic glory at the dedication of Solomon's temple, and he is there on the Day of Pentecost in the outpoured Spirit descending to indwell the disciples. The Bible will regularly speak of divine presence in this particular mode.

Scripture also speaks of divine absence from particular places at particular times. In Ezekiel's visions the presence of God can *leave* the temple just as easily as it can inhabit the temple.[1] Likewise, many a psalmist can lament God's absence from his people and pray for God's return. However, this "absence" was not understood in a crude way. In the very next breath after lamenting divine absence, biblical writers can lament God's wrathful presence. So adversity can be imagined *both* as God being absent and as God being *all too present*, but present *as assailant* rather than as the source of blessing and protection. So divine absence was not literal absence so much as the absence of a specific mode of presence, the absence of God's presence *in blessing*.

God's ubiquitous presence: At the same time, the Bible's authors speak of God as one who hears what is said anywhere and everywhere, who can manifest himself anywhere and everywhere, and, indeed, as one who is actually at all places in all times. There is nowhere a person can go to escape the holy presence.

God's presence in heaven: Finally, God inhabits creation by being present in creation's throne room in heaven. And God's mode of inhabiting heaven is conceived of in the most intense form. There he is *continuously present in all his manifest glory*. On earth one may be oblivious to the divine presence, but in heaven such ignorance is impossible.

These modes of divine presence should be understood as modes of the presence of the divine Trinity. The Spirit is present everywhere[2] and yet manifest in special ways in specific places and times.[3] The divine Logos is ubiquitous and yet in the humanity of Christ is always in a single spatio-temporal location. And both the Spirit and the Christ are said to come down from heaven, their home. Yet talk of their com-

---

1. Ezek 8–11.
2. Ps 139:7–12.
3. Acts 2:1–5; 4:31; 8:17; 10:44–46; 19:6.

ing down should not be taken to suggest that they are no longer found there too. The Father is present in general and particular ways through the persons of the Son and the Spirit. All of which is to say that the language of divine presence has a Trinitarian grammar.

God's Presence in His Temple

God's Ubiquitous Presence

Now a contemporary Christian account of God's inhabiting creation would need to pay attention to these differing biblical modes. It seems to me that the most fruitful approach to the issue is not actually a new one but a very old one—the classical approach of Christian Platonism.

In the classical Christian tradition God is the cause of the existence of the cosmos, the source of its be-ing. Now we are very familiar with the idea of causation within the creaturely sphere—event (or person) A causes event B—but God was not thought of as a cause of the same kind as creaturely causes. God was a cause of a *fundamentally different kind* operating at a *fundamentally different level* from all other causes. You see, God was not *a* being, not even a mere supreme being; God was *Being Itself*, the overflowing Source of all creaturely being. The whole cosmos only had any existence at all, any be-ing, because God donated being to it. God caused creation to share, in a limited and finite way, in his own infinite Be-ing.

God is not only Being Itself, but Beauty Itself, Goodness Itself, and Truth Itself. Creation displays being, beauty, truth, and goodness—it has to or it is literally *nothing* at all—but all its being, beauty, truth, and goodness are *derived* from God. Creation "participates in" God in order to *be*. (The notion of "participation" is, of course, a metaphor. There is no way to speak of these surpassing truths without metaphor.) Consequently, the meaning and existence of the world are *not grounded in the world itself* but in the world's transcendent Source, God.

By way of (woefully inadequate) illustration: imagine a beautifully crafted lantern with a light in it. The patterns from the lantern are projected onto the walls round about. These patterns are not the lantern but their very existence at each and every moment depends and draws on the lantern. The patterns on the walls may look rather different from the lantern itself but they still image something of its reality. God is the lantern and the patterns are creation. Creation participates in God's being as the patterns participate in the lantern. Of course, this illustration falls down at many levels because the relation between God and creation is unique and not exactly like any inner-creational relations. Nevertheless, so long as this illustration is treated with caution it is of some help.

Let me immediately draw attention to one weakness of the lantern analogy. God is not one more object in addition to the universe, another "thing" in the inventory of reality (trees + birds + oranges + rocks + God). God is not *a* being, a thing existing in time and space. God is the Source and Ground of all that is. As Paul puts it, in God "we live and move and have our being."[4] In this God is *not* like the lantern. If you find this all a bit mind-blowing and hard to comprehend, that is as it should be. We are speaking of *God* here, not Superman.

Anyway, what this means for divine presence in creation is, first of all, that God is ubiquitous, *immanent within everything*. God is there at the deepest and most fundamental level of the reality of all things, closer to us than our own breath. Yet at the same time, the God who is immanent in all things is the *transcendent* God. God is neither part of the universe nor its totality, and the universe is not God. Every instance of creaturely be-ing, beauty, truth, and goodness are dim manifestations of the divine. As such, all reality points beyond itself to its creator.

So God is not present in a place by filling up space in that place in the same way that a plant or an animal or a mountain does. God is not present in a place as an object in addition to the created objects already there. Rather, God is present "in" the created objects themselves.

This discussion of divine presence needs putting into christological perspective, and for that we turn to John's Gospel. The early church saw the opening of John's Gospel—in which Jesus was said to be the divine Logos through whom God created all things—as a major theological key to understanding the universe.

John's words about the divine Logos would have resonated with both Greco-Roman and Jewish thought of his day. In Greek philosophy the word *logos* (meaning "reason" or "word") had been used by philosophers since Heracleitus in the sixth century BC to refer to the divine Reason, analogous to the reason in human beings, that was manifest in the order of the cosmos. Later Stoics saw the whole of reality permeated with and structured by the Logos, the soul of the universe. To the Platonists Logos was the divine mind that transcended the world, yet was immanent everywhere in the world. The Hellenistic Jew Philo of Alexandria brought this Platonic philosophy together with biblical theology. Philo's Logos was the divine Reason through which God created and ordered all things. And humans, said Philo, could

---

4. Acts 17:28. Paul is here quoting Epimenides, the Greek poet philosopher, with approval.

only know God through this same Logos.[5] The author of John's Gospel was picking up on this set of ideas and blending it with the Old Testament teachings that God created the universe through divine Word (Let there be . . .) and through divine Wisdom.[6] Creation, says John, was indeed granted being through the divine Word/Reason/Wisdom and is filled with the light of this Word/Reason/Wisdom:

> In the beginning was the Word (*Logos*), and the Word was with God, and the Word was God. He was in the beginning with God. All things were made through him, and without him was not any thing made that was made. In him was life, and the life was the light of men. (John 1:1–4)

So far any philosophically inclined Roman or any educated Jew would say "Amen." The radical claim in John's prologue is his assertion that this divine Logos "became flesh" in the person of Jesus.[7] This particular man is the key to the cosmos—the one through whom it came into being and remains in being. Jesus, the Logos, is the Reason/Word/Wisdom underlying all things and holding them in being as intelligible realities.

This insight, central to Christian Platonism, remains as relevant to Christian thought today as ever it was, and shifting conceptions in cosmology don't in any way make it outdated. In short, God is present in all things in creation *through the Logos*.[8]

God's Particular Presence

So much for ubiquity. But what of particular presence? If God is dwelling everywhere what would it mean to say that God is here (and, by implication, not there) or to pray for God's presence to come down? Here we need to think in terms of the importance not simply of divine presence but of *manifest* divine presence.

Because of the way in which all creation directly participates in God, all of creation has the potential to manifest God. In other words, all creation

---

5. Philo's Logos was also the archetypal man in the image of God, God's firstborn son, a high priest, etc. Philo's thought bears more than a few similarities with NT thinking about Jesus.

6. Creation by divine Word: Genesis 1; Ps 33:6. Creation by divine Wisdom: Prov 3:19; 8:22–31. Indeed, Word and Wisdom were linked (Wis 9:1; Sir 24:1).

7. John 1:14.

8. The ubiquity of the Spirit is especially associated with life, and we will come to it later.

has sacramental potential, the ability to mediate divine reality and to act as a sign pointing Godward. Remember the way in which the physical temple in Jerusalem was a "thin place" in which the gap between it and the heavenly temple was closed during the performance of sacred ritual (see chapter 7). The priests ministering in the temple were ministering in heaven. The Jerusalem temple thus served to mediate sacramentally invisible divine reality to ancient Israelites. In just the same way, to conceive of the *whole cosmos* as a temple is to conceive of it as a place in which the visible and "ordinary" point beyond themselves to the invisible dimensions of reality, and in which at key moments God can manifest his invisible glory *through the visible*. The ordinary is, in fact, extraordinary, charged with the grandeur of God. Thomas Traherne, a seventeenth-century poet and priest, expressed this well: "Your enjoyment of the world is never right, till every morning you awake in Heaven; see yourself in your Father's palace; and look upon the skies, the earth, and the air as celestial joys: having such a reverend esteem of all, as if you were among the angels."[9] Here is Elizabeth Barret Browning, writing in the nineteenth century:

> . . . Earth's crammed with heaven,
> And every common bush afire with God;
> But only he who sees, takes off his shoes,
> The rest sit round it and pluck blackberries.[10]

This is very important for contemporary appropriations of ancient biblical cosmology. God can open our spiritual eyes to discern his presence in some phenomenon or other, and that phenomenon is able to mediate truth and meaning as well as divine action.

The biblical God is a God who acts within this world, both what we call "the natural world" and what we call the human world of "history." It is easy for a modern reader to pick out particular passages of the Bible in which, for instance, God causes some specific weather event to occur. We then imagine that the Bible's God is an interventionist God leaving the world to run itself most of the time but stepping in periodically to manipulate things, acting in the world as one cause among others. This, of course, would raise all sorts of issues for thoughtful contemporary Christians. Is this a God of the gaps who is wheeled in to explain events that science cannot yet explain? And if science can explain an event in terms of natural causes, does that mean we no longer have grounds for thinking God was involved?

---

9. Traherne, *Centuries of Meditations*, #28.
10. Browning, *Aurora Leigh*, Book 7, Part 86, lines 61–64.

However, this biblical language of divine action is more sophisticated than we may realize. God is certainly seen to be the cause of weather, say, but not at the level of fiddling around with weather patterns from time to time. In Scripture God is understood as the cause of *all* weather, from devastating storms to refreshing rains. And not just weather but all natural events from the growth of crops to human reproduction to geological happenings to animal birth, survival, and death. And all historical events too—including the free choices of human agents. In all these happenings the Bible is content to speak simultaneously of causes that are intrinsic to creation and of God as the transcendent cause.

Take plant reproduction—is this an event with natural causes open to scientific study or does God cause it? Yes. In Gen 1:11–12 plants are commanded to be fruitful according to their kind. This clearly indicates immanent causation within the world—the kind of thing that modern science studies. Yet the Bible also speaks of God causing plants to grow.[11] According to Christian Platonism this makes perfect sense—God infuses the world with the dignity of internal powers that operate as causes within it. Yet those very internal creational causes depend upon divine grace. There is no opposition between the causes considered in physics, chemistry, or biology and divine causation, for *they operate at different levels.*

In the language of theology, God is the *primary* cause of all that is, but he works in creation through *secondary* causes. Modern science is only concerned with matters of secondary causation, and so God does not feature in scientific explanations, *nor should he.* Primary causation is the subject of metaphysics, and while, by the nature of the case, it is not subject to empirical observation, it is no less real than the secondary causation studied by the empirical sciences. Indeed, it is *more* real, because it is that which enables secondary causes to exist at all. (If this distinction between God and creation had been properly adhered to by atheists and religious believers in contemporary discussions many of the arguments about a supposed conflict between science and religion would be dissolved in a stroke.)

Let's get back to the question of God's particular presence. Take a thunderstorm passing over ancient Israel. It will have been seen as sent by God and possibly, in the right context, even as a theophany, a manifestation of God's very presence. But why would this be problematic? Sure, we moderns can give a meteorological explanation of the storm but that has no bearing on the question of divine causation or of divine self-manifestation. And why can't a storm be a very appropriate symbol to communicate truths

---

11. 1 Cor 3:7. Paul was using the plant here as a metaphor for the church, but the verse still reflects his view about plant growth.

about God—the one with awesome power beyond human control; the one who utters his thunderous battle cry on behalf of his people and who sends his lightning arrows to defeat their enemies. Israelites did not think that God *was* the cloud but that God came in and through the cloud, because creation, sharing in the divine Logos, can reveal the creator. God's presence in creation is ubiquitous but can be made *manifest* through certain parts of creation on certain occasions. (And remember too that the cloud hid him as much as it revealed him. This warns us always to put a conceptual distance between God and the natural event through which he is revealed.)

In sum, God can co-opt any natural event in the world in order to reveal himself because all creation derives its being from him and can reveal something of his glory, albeit in very different degrees. Thus all creation can mediate divine revelation. That is why the psalmists can see God's hand in everything from the shining stars to the eagle feeding her young, from the thunderstorm to the deliverance of the exodus, from the birth of a child to the growth of a tree. So God can manifest his presence in certain times and places and communicate meaning to those whose eyes he opens. In a very meaningful sense God can be said to be present in particular locations at particular times in a *special* way.

Similarly, while in a general sense any event could be said to have God as its primary cause, particular creational events can also be said to mediate *special* divine action. Some people have argued that behind the biblical stories of the plagues of Egypt and the path through the Red Sea lie historical events that can be given a scientific explanation. Let's suppose, for the sake of argument, that this is the case. Such a scientific explanation can never communicate the *meaning* of the event, merely its secondary causes. The Bible tells us the meaning—God was rescuing his people from slavery. Regularly in Scripture "normal" events in the natural world are the means by which God reveals himself and acts.

God can be present in particular human choices in a special way too. Human freedom also depends on the divine gift, so in one sense all human choices are ultimately caused by God. However, here things are somewhat more complex. We should not take this to mean that human choices have no integrity of their own, nor that God makes people do things that they do not want to do. Humans are free, in varying degrees, to do what they want to do. And the truth is that humans often exercise their freedom in ways incompatible with the truth, goodness, and beauty of God. God does not directly will these human volitions.

So human choices often fall short of God's will. Yet *even then* God can act through those unforced bad choices. Let's take an example. Joseph was sold into Egypt by his brothers; yet he was able to discern the action of God in the event: "As for you [brothers], you meant evil against me, but God meant it for good, to bring it about that many people should be kept alive, as they are today" (Gen 50:20). So the *same* event, the selling of Joseph into slavery, can be simultaneously viewed *both* as an action resulting from human choices, in this case bad choices, *and* as an act of God.[12]

But if God is the primary cause of all things, then why pick out some events and not others as instances of special divine action? Isn't a cow breaking wind as much a "divine action" as the plagues of Egypt? Here we might, if we dare, use an analogy from our own actions. In performing a specific act, I may perform all sorts of other acts that are not my intended goal but are simply acts that must occur for me to perform the act I intend to perform, or side effects of it. For instance, I wish to move a piece in a chess game in order to make the winning move. That act requires all sorts of other things to happen in my brain and in the muscles of my body, especially my arm and fingers. These events in my body set off a whole network of small but significant changes in the environment around me. I was a cause for all of these events, but they were not all the goal of the action. Some were simply a means to an end, and others were not even that. Most of us think that it makes sense to describe moving the chess piece as a special effect, even though in one sense it was only one of countless effects I just caused. But it is not like the others. Singling it out from the rest is essential to understand the *meaning* of what I just did. Why can we not think of divine action in a similar way?

A brief word on miracles is necessary. We tend to think of miracles as events that "violate the laws of nature" and consequently have no scientific explanation. The Bible does not frame things in those terms. Miracles are (a) astonishing acts of God that (b) serve to bring about some of God's kingdom purposes in creation and (c) act as signs pointing to important divine truths. As astonishing acts they are very much out of the ordinary and wonderful but not necessarily scientifically inexplicable. If there were scientific explanations for them, it would not affect their status as miracles one jot; they would not cease to be wondrous truth-disclosing acts of God. I

---

12. Isa 10:15–19 provides another good example.

am not suggesting that all miracles can be explained by science; my point is simply that it would not matter if they were.

These issues are exceptionally complex, and I am painfully aware that I have not dealt with the objections to this account. However, now is not the time to lose ourselves down the rabbit hole. I am interested only in making a few initial explorations into the manner in which we can think of God inhabiting his temple cosmos.

Humanity and Particular Presence

Space prohibits a long discussion of this critical topic. Suffice it to say that, as mentioned in chapter 7, human beings in Genesis 1 are created as the image or icon of God (or perhaps, if the overtones are not too shocking, the idol of God) in the cosmic temple. Temples contain images of deities and the cosmic temple is no exception. Humans are to be filled with the divine glory and to mediate the rule of God on earth. This is a *breathtaking* vision of humanity and one that suffuses the biblical metanarrative. Spirit-filled humanity is a very distinctive mode of God's particular presence in creation and is very much tied up with the notion of creation as a temple.

Sin corrupts this human icon of God, making humanity a broken vessel. The story of redemption is, in one important sense, simply the story of the restoration of the divine image in humanity, enabling us to function as bearers of divine glory. Our eschatological destiny is thus, in the language of classical Christian theology, deification (*theōsis*). This is not about us "becoming God" (which is an incoherent notion, if taken in a strictly literal sense) but it is about a union with God of such intimacy and profundity as to enable us to function as the divine image we were made to be.

Christ, Church, and the Cosmic Temple

In some patristic thinking, the archetype "image of God" is the divine Logos itself, the second person of the Holy Trinity. So we could say that humanity is created in the image of the image-of-God. To illustrate this idea, think of the Logos as a hand and humanity as a rubber glove that has been modeled on that template. So Adam is only "image of God" in a derived and secondary sense, albeit in a real and significant sense. This is why humanity is a fitting receptacle for the Spirit. Being filled with the fullness of God is our raison d'être.

The incarnation of the Logos as Jesus of Nazareth is like the hand putting on the glove.[13] Jesus is thus the perfect image of the invisible God *both* as the divine Logos *and* as the perfect human being. As such Jesus is Emmanuel, God with us, the unsurpassable manifestation of particular divine presence in the temple of the cosmos.

More than this, as we saw earlier, Christ's human body represents the temple itself and thus the whole universe. His body is, in other words, a symbol of the universe. So the future of the cosmos is written in the risen body of Jesus. To "see" his resurrection body is to glimpse the destiny of the world. All things were made by him and *for* him and will find their destiny in union with him. The good news is that the perfection of the material world in Jesus' resurrection body will be the future of the whole created order as it is liberated from its slavery to decay. As the glory of God tabernacles in the body of Jesus so it will tabernacle in the "body" of the renewed creation, and the glory of the Lord will cover the earth as the waters cover the sea.

In the New Testament, the notion of Christ's body as the temple is also closely linked with the idea of the community of Christ, his body on earth, as a temple for the Spirit of God. The church as such, though its union with Christ, is another special instance of particular divine presence in the earth. It is a new humanity imaging God as it is gradually conformed by the Spirit to the image of Jesus, the Second Adam. It is the body of Christ, and thus the temple of God, and, as such, it too represents the cosmos in the process of transformation. The final liberation of the community of God, for which we wait in groaning and anticipation, will usher in the liberation of the whole creation that we discussed above. Why? Because when the human icon of God that represents the whole cosmos is rescued and completed, then that which it represents can itself be redeemed and reach its fulfillment.

Here we are standing at the top of a mountain with unexpected and mind-expanding views on the land round about us. Nothing can look the same again. There is *so much* that needs to be said here, but having sown the seed I must leave that to your own explorations.

God's Heavenly Presence

And what of heavenly presence? This can be thought of as the ubiquitous manifest presence of God in the invisible realm of creation. Of course, this presence does not directly impact humans, as we are not in heaven, but that does not mean that the heavenly presence of God is not fundamental to

---

13. This analogy, as all analogies, is weak at several points and so should be treated with care.

Christian theology. To understand this we need to say a little more about the continuing relevance of biblical teaching about heaven. That is the focus of our next chapter.

11

The Biblical Heavens Today

Heaven above the Sky Today

Can We Believe in a Heaven "Up There"?

CHRISTIANS HAVE A LONG tradition of making the adjustment and translation from biblical to contemporary cosmologies, often without realizing it. In the history of Christianity, ancient Israelite cosmologies soon gave way to Ptolemaic cosmologies, which dominated Christian thought for many hundreds of years.[1] Most Christians did not even notice that a shift had occurred. And once Copernican cosmology finally supplanted the Ptolemaic, Christians had little trouble adapting to that either.

As cosmological beliefs shifted, talk of the sun "rising" and "setting" was easily retained as a metaphor, as was biblical language about a three-decker universe, heaven being "up," and the earth having four corners. And while no one thought any longer that heaven was *literally* "up" above the sky, speaking and acting *as if* it was up continues to dominate Christian engagement with heaven. We, unlike our biblical ancestors, understand such talk *only* metaphorically or metaphysically, but that move away from literal interpretation was surprisingly easy for Christians to make.

Remember, in the biblical texts the *symbolic meaning* of all that talk of heaven being "above" had always been the most important thing about such language. Height and depth vocabulary often spoke of relative importance and rank, and biblical authors had no trouble speaking of certain people and places being "raised up" or "brought low," without feeling the need to

---

1. Ptolemaic cosmology was still earth-centric but recast the earth as a globe.

understand such language in a simplistic literal way. We too commonly use height talk non-literally: "she *went up* in the public's opinion," "he has been *elevated* to a senior lectureship," "she is *high up* in the company," "he *raised* the stakes." For Bible authors, the idea of heaven being "above" the rest of creation meant that heaven was the most important dimension of the created world because it was from heaven that God ruled over all things. Picturing heaven as "up" serves *exactly the same purpose today*.

Interpreting language of the high heaven non-geographically does not threaten the heart of the biblical teaching at all—the truth Scripture pointed to was always that heaven is invisible and inaccessible to humans and yet is at the heart of creation because divine life and rule flow from it. Whether heaven is also literally above the sky (as biblical writers thought) or not (as we think) is incidental to the truth Scripture gestures towards.

So can we still believe that heaven is "up there"? In every way that matters we most certainly can.

The model of the tabernacle as a mini-cosmos also suggests a different way of imagining heaven in relation to earth. In the tabernacle one does not go *up* to God's presence but *in*. The holy of holies is the innermost heart of the temple. In the same way, perhaps we might speak of heaven as the invisible depths of creation containing the divine presence at the center of things. Both of these sets of language—above and within—are helpful in communicating something of the mystery of heaven. Neither of them should be taken as descriptions of the *physical* location of heaven. Heaven has no *physical* location.

So what of the biblical images of heaven as a throne room filled with creatures located in different places around it? Is there an actual chair positioned above the sky? Is heaven, in other words, a sky palace with spatial dimensions that could be measured? Christians have always resisted such an idea. While heaven may be symbolically represented in such ways, Christian theology has strongly rejected the notion that God has an actual body that can sit in an actual chair, because if he did he would be limited and thus not infinite. As such he would not be God but a mere god. There is no question that the Bible does sometimes picture God as having a giant body (with arms, hands, feet, a face, and so on) and as sitting on a royal throne, but such language has rightly been understood in the tradition as metaphor and symbol.

The book of Exodus helpfully alerts us to the care needed interpreting language about God. Chapter 33 tells us that "Jehovah used to speak with Moses face to face, as a man speaks to his friend" (Exod 33:11), but in the conversation between the Lord and Moses that immediately follows this comment, God says, "You cannot see my face, for man shall not see me and live" (Exod 33:20). This was no careless oversight on the part of the book's final editor. Rather, the text is flagging up that language about *God* should not be read in a naïve way. Scripture can talk about God *as if* he has a body but it does not follow that such talk can be taken at face value (please excuse yet another terrible pun). Thus, in the tradition, both heaven and its inhabitants fill up no space at all.[2]

An analogy that may take us some, though not all, of the way in thinking about this issue is that of the relation of mind and body. We are material beings but we are also minded, conscious beings. This area is a philosophical quagmire, but while a precise philosophy of mind is ever elusive, a solid case can be made that there are several dead ends to avoid. The current fashion of trying to reduce the mind to matter is one of those dead ends—a road to nowhere. To take one version of such an approach, mind-brain identity theory, it is clear that the qualitative difference between electro-chemical events in my brain and my conscious experiences of hearing a musical chord, of seeing yellow, of following a logical train of thought, and so on, is about as obvious as anything possibly can be. My point is simply this: we are beings that have a dual nature—body and soul, if you like.[3] The body is visible and tangible—it can be measured by scientific instruments and the like. The consciousness is not material and is directly accessible to no one but the subject him- or herself. And yet, we know as clearly as we know anything that our consciousness is a reality. To doubt it is literally incoherent. We also know that body and mind are fundamentally intertwined. We know that material, visible bodily events impact conscious experience; in particular, we know that brain events are inextricably connected with mental events. We also know that mental events, such as making decisions, have bodily manifestation.

Now imagine that some alien scientist wanted to study and explain the behavior of human beings. It could study all the physical, chemical, and biological events and all the behavior of the human "bio-machines" and explain things quite neatly without reference at all to consciousness. Such explanations are fine as far as they go, and yet we know that they *cannot* be complete, they cannot say everything that needs saying, because we know at a primal level that without reference to consciousness one will not have fully understood human behavior. Yet, oddly, unless the alien scientist already

---

2. Although heaven has no space, we may still be able to speak meaningfully of the "space" of heaven if we use such language in a metaphorical way. Indeed, such talk may be essential.

3. I ought to say that the rejection of materialism need not mean that one is forced to embrace substance dualism of a Cartesian kind. The problem may need radically reframing. For starters, we may need to reconsider what we mean by matter.

knew about consciousness (which, of course, it would, being conscious itself), it would not obviously have any grounds from its empirical observations for postulating consciousness to explain anything.

We might think of the relation between heaven and earth as *in some ways* like the relation of body and soul. Creation, like a human being, is a dual reality with visible and invisible aspects. These cannot be reduced to each other without remainder, but neither can they be separated as self-contained realities that can operate independently of each other. Heaven and earth, like soul and body, are fundamentally intertwined. Furthermore, we might study the physics, chemistry, and biology of the world and think that there is nothing left to say, and yet, in biblical thinking, this would be an error akin to that of the alien scientist's ignoring of consciousness.

We can develop the analogy further.

- *Where*, we might ask, is the mind? Is it inside your head? No. It is nowhere, and yet it is as real as real can be and is fully embodied in a particular space and time—so too with heaven.

- More than that, we tend to think of there being a certain priority of mind in the mind-body relation, even if the body makes an essential contribution to mind, just as Scripture sees a certain kind of priority of heaven in the heaven-earth relation. Heaven is creation in its openness to the transcendent God, just as the soul is the dimension or aspect of a human person that is open to that which is beyond the material, even in its material manifestations.

- Just as the mind-body relation is deeply confounding, so too the heaven-earth relation is riddled with mystery. This should not surprise us, nor should it cause us to reject the reality of heaven, any more than it would cause us to reject the reality of consciousness.

As helpful as this heaven/mind analogy may be, I do not think that we can press it too far, and I offer it as nothing more than a way of starting to get some vague initial grasp of the dual nature of creation.[4]

Heaven speaks of the as-yet-unrealized possibilities of creation in its transparent openness to divine glory. It is right now what all creation will be in the fullness of time, filled with the glory of the Lord. The future of all creation thus unfolds from above, drawing that which is below towards the fullness of its possibilities.

---

4. The idea of heaven as the soul of creation has some similarities to Plato's proposal in the *Timaeus* of a "world soul" that infuses the "body" of the cosmos.

PART IV—CAN WE INHABIT THE BIBLICAL COSMOS?

The Ascension of Jesus

There are some aspects of modern cosmology that require us to rethink the biblical narrative of Jesus' movements around the cosmos. The ascension and return of Jesus in particular require some reflection. These two beliefs were closely linked with the notion of heaven literally in the sky. The loss of that notion does raise questions about how we are to think of these fundamental Christian teachings today.

We often struggle to make sense of the image of Jesus literally rising into the sky. In our minds there is no heaven in the sky for him to reach. He would simply keep on going up, up, up, past the moon, onto Mars, then outwards beyond the solar system. As with the Voyager satellite, one might ask questions about how far he has got now. Has he reached the next nearest star to our sun? And all that would just be silly and very trivial. It would utterly miss the point of the ascension. As Calvin remarked, "What? Do we place Christ midway among the spheres? Or do we build a cottage for him among the planets? Heaven we regard as the magnificent palace of God, far outstripping all this world's fabric."[5]

So belief in a literal ascension to heaven, a belief that helped ancient Christians to understand the meaning of the Jesus story, can be unhelpful to modern ones. Indeed, it can end up losing its meaning.

The problem here is not simply solved by making heaven a non-physical place. This is because in Christian thought Jesus has not stopped being human and, as such, has not stopped being embodied. For Christian theology matter matters and bodies are important. Bodies are not just like cars that our souls drive about in, but are basic to our full humanity. That is why orthodox Christianity has always envisaged eternal life as the resurrection of the body rather than some kind of disembodied existence. So it matters that Jesus is *still* an embodied human. Here, for instance, is Tertullian (d. 225 AD), "Jesus is still sitting there at the right hand of the Father, man, yet God . . . *flesh and blood*, yet purer than ours."[6] Similarly Irenaeus speaks of "the ascension into heaven *in the flesh*."[7]

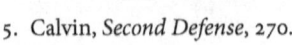

---

5. Calvin, *Second Defense*, 270.
6. Tertullian, *On the Resurrection of the Flesh*, ANF, vol. 3, 51.
7. Irenaues, *Against Heresies* 1.10.1.

But bodies occupy space, so *where* is Jesus' body now? This question was not such a problem for the old biblical cosmology. The body went up, through the windows of the sky dome, into heaven—a "space" above the sky. If one asked where Jesus' body was one could point upwards.[8] That option is no longer open. Jesus' body is not "up there." Indeed, it is not any-where in the modern cosmos. So what can modern Christians say about this?

One suggestion has been to abandon the belief that Jesus is still embodied in a particular body.[9] That, however, is an exceptionally high price to pay, and it has negative knock-on repercussions for the whole of Christian theology. So the task for theology is to show how one can still embrace the bodily existence of Jesus in heaven alongside modern understandings of the cosmos. I do not intend to solve that problem here, but I will say a few words that point us in the right direction.

One factor that needs to be born in mind is that Jesus was resurrected, not reanimated. That is to say, his body was not simply brought back to life; it was *radically transformed*, "flesh and blood, *yet purer than ours*" as Tertullian put it. The biblical authors stress both the continuity and the discontinuity between the pre-resurrection and the post-resurrection body of Jesus. That it was the *same* body was testified to by the fact that the tomb was empty and that the risen Jesus bore the scars from his crucifixion. That it was a transformed body was indicated by certain unusual properties— it was not always immediately recognized by those who knew him,[10] and while it was no ghost and could be touched and eat food, it could appear out of nowhere, even entering locked rooms, and vanish into thin air.

St. Paul tries to capture this notion of transformation in resurrection:

> But someone will ask, "How are the dead raised? With what kind of body do they come?" You foolish person! What you sow does not come to life unless it dies. And what you sow is not the body that is to be, but a bare kernel, perhaps of wheat or of some other grain.

---

8. As noted in chapter 6, St. Paul could contemplate the possibility of his being bodily present in heaven.

9. Various different theologians proposed different versions of this. Most influentially Luther argued that Jesus' body shared in the properties of his divine nature and so was omnipresent. For Luther, Jesus' body was literally everywhere in the cosmos.

10. According to Mark's Gospel, Jesus was not recognized by the two on the road to Emmaus because he appeared to them in *"another form"* (Mark 16:12)! Wow. (Even if the scholarly consensus that Mark 16:9–20 is not part of the original Gospel of Mark is correct—and I am convinced that it is not—these verses still testify to an early Christian view on the matter.)

> But God gives it a body as he has chosen, and to each kind of seed its own body. For not all flesh is the same, but there is one kind for humans, another for animals, another for birds, and another for fish. There are heavenly bodies and earthly bodies, but the glory of the heavenly is of one kind, and the glory of the earthly is of another. There is one glory of the sun, and another glory of the moon, and another glory of the stars; for star differs from star in glory. So is it with the resurrection of the dead. What is sown is perishable; what is raised is imperishable. It is sown in dishonor; it is raised in glory. It is sown in weakness; it is raised in power. It is sown a natural body; it is raised a spiritual body. If there is a natural body, there is also a spiritual body. (1 Cor 15:35–44)

The apostle's agricultural analogy is that of a seed sown (the body that dies) and the wheat that grows from it (the resurrection body). There is a clear connection between the seed and the wheat—the wheat grows from the seed—but there is also an obvious and radical *difference*. Paul contrasts the perishable, dishonored, weak, and natural body (the seed) with the imperishable, glorious, empowered, spiritual (or Spirit-animated) body of the resurrected person (the wheat). Jesus' resurrection body is not a seed but a full-grown plant, not a natural body but an eschatological body, a "new creation," the bodily mode of the end-time uniting of heaven and earth.

The fact of the matter is that the early Christ-believers thought that Jesus' resurrection body was currently the *only* such body in the whole creation. Until the general resurrection of the dead at the Last Day, there are no other instances of resurrection bodies for us to study. Immediately we see that we need to be very careful in assuming that we know the properties of such a transformed body, of what is and is not possible for it. We simply know *next to nothing* about the matter (again, excuse the pun). At very least this should warn us against dogmatism in declaring that Jesus' body could not inhabit heaven now that heaven is no longer thought of a spatial location in the cosmos.[11] Indeed, arguably Christians have every reason to think that Jesus' resurrection body can indeed exist in a heavenly mode—because Scripture declares that it does. A certain level of pious agnosticism is not inappropriate. Here is Augustine:

---

11. It has not actually been thought of as a literal "space" for almost the entirety of Christian history. While it was upwards, once one passed beyond the outer spheres one entered a "space" that was conceptual rather than physical. So the issue of the ascension of Jesus' flesh has been something Christians have insisted on against the mainstream from almost the start. To educated Greeks the notion was insane, yet for the church it was non-negotiable.

> [T]he question as to where and in what manner the Lord's body is in heaven, is one which it would be over-curious and superfluous to prosecute. Only that we must believe that it is in heaven. For it pertains not to our frailty to investigate the secret things of heaven, but it does pertain to our faith to hold elevated and honorable sentiments on the subject of the dignity of the Lord's body.[12]

But there is possibly another way of thinking about the issue. Here I am completely speculating, but allow me to throw some ideas around. Jesus has an eschatological body, an end-time transformed body. It is a body that belongs in the future age, not in this age. Perhaps we can think of Jesus "ascending" *into the future*, the new age. We could still speak of this in terms of ascending into heaven, in that the new age is one in which heaven and earth are unified, and that environment is precisely the one that Jesus' resurrection body is "fitted for." His new body is a uniting-of-heaven-and-earth-body that finds its natural habitat neither in the present earth nor in the present heaven. In this speculation the body of Jesus is not located anywhere in the cosmos *now* because it exists in the future.

This suggestion, if it has any plausibility, would require some important qualifications:

- First, God has poured out the "Spirit of Christ" into believers and the Spirit mediates the presence of Jesus into the current this-age reality of the church. So Jesus remains accessible here for us now and always, even to the end of the age.
- Second, the eschatological body of Christ is mediated by the Spirit into the present through the eucharistic elements—the bread and wine. So his body is here sacramentally.
- Third, believers are baptized in the Spirit into Christ's body, the church. It too is the body of Jesus in the here and now. But all of these realities are only realities because the ascended, embodied Lord is enthroned at God's right hand in the coming new creation.[13] Thanks to the gift of the Spirit, our fellowship with the risen Lord is very much a present fellowship. We encounter the risen Lord right *here* and right *now*. So perhaps it makes sense that the Bible's authors would picture the

---

12. Augustine, *Treatise on Faith and the Creed*, 6.

13. Neither church nor Eucharist are a *substitute* for Christ's body in heaven as if Christ is *only* embodied in the church and its eucharistic rites. So we cannot avoid the issue of how we think of an embodied Jesus in a non-physical heaven by appealing to Christ's body being found *here*, in the church.

absent-present Jesus as existing in an inaccessible part of the cosmos right now in a timeline that runs parallel to our own. That is, after all, the manner in which his people *experience* him.

- Fourth, there is no reason to suppose that the Spirit could not mediate the body of Christ into the "now" of heaven in an analogous way to the manner in which he mediates it into the now of earth (see above). So one could legitimately speak of Christ reigning in heaven now, even if his body is not present there in the same manner in which it is present in the new creation.

- Finally, the divine Logos who is incarnate as Jesus did not cease to be the eternal Word in whom and through whom all things consist. As such he entered space and time without ceasing to be eternal and without leaving the throne of God (language of his "descent" to earth in incarnation is not to be interpreted in a crassly literal way). Consequently the timeless Word is still experienced in every part of the cosmos, heaven included, at every time. While this last observation is not an argument for the presence of the embodied Logos in the current age, it is an argument for the presence of the Logos who is embodied.

Is this proposal right? I have absolutely no idea, so I throw it out simply in case it has potential. If it doesn't, then I can live with that. What I do know is this: the claim that Jesus has ascended to the right hand of the Father as Lord of all is true. Understanding that claim remains an ongoing task.[14]

Star Deities Today

Stars are not what they used to be. It is simply not a live option for us to believe in a solid dome above a flat earth above which God lives. We cannot believe that a literal ocean lies beyond the sun, moon, and stars. Nor can we believe that stars are literally gods. How are Christians to deal with this? Is biblical teaching on them still relevant today? Or does our scientific worldview require us to view it with mere curiosity and then move on?

Neil Gaimon, in his novel *Stardust*, imagines the village of Wall, standing "on a high jut of granite amidst a small forest woodland . . . Immediately

---

14. One final parting word on this issue: does it matter whether the historical Jesus literally went up into the sky? Not really. It does matter that he ascended *from here*. It matters that the ascension was *an event in the life of Jesus*. The story of going into the sky tells us the truth about what the ascension *means* and so the church believes it. Whether the historical event happened in precisely that way is not important. Did he go upwards? Maybe. Maybe not. If he did, then it was simply as a way of communicating to his disciples what was happening.

to the east of Wall is a high grey rock wall, from which the town takes its name.... There is only one break in the wall.... Through the gap in the wall can be seen a large green meadow, a stream; and beyond the stream there are trees."[15] The world beyond the wall is the magical world of Faerie. The story follows young Tristran Thorn as he transgresses the boundary keeping the two worlds apart in search of a fallen star. This star, when he finds it, turns out to be a woman—"Her hair was so fair it was almost white, her dress was of blue silk which shimmered in the candlelight."[16] But the star can only exist as a person when on the magical side of the wall. Later, after a brief trip back into Wall, Tristran heads back through the gap into Faerie:

> She was still sitting there when Tristran came back through the gap in the wall, several hours later....
> "I'm sorry," said Tristran, "I suppose I should have taken you with me into the village."
> "No," said that star, "You shouldn't have. I live as long as I am in Faerie. Were I to travel to your world, I would be nothing but a cold iron stone fallen from the heavens, pitted and pocked."[17]

In this story, the cosmos on our side of the wall is not enchanted—magic is for other worlds. Is it that the stars can be gods in the "fantasy world" of biblical literature, while for those of us who must live in the real world on our side of the "wall" we must make do with the stars as mundane material objects? Or might the divine stars of the ancient world beyond the Copernican wall offer insights into stars in our own world?

In C. S. Lewis' novel *The Voyage of the Dawn Treader*, the travelers encounter an old man with long silver hair and a long silver beard. He said,

> "I am Ramandu. But I see that you stare at one another and have not heard this name. And no wonder, for the days when I was a star had ceased long before any of you knew this world, and all the constellations have changed."
> "Golly," said Edmund under his breath. "He's a *retired* star."
> "Aren't you a star any longer?" asked Lucy.
> "I am a star at rest, my daughter," answered Ramandu....
> "In our world," said Eustace, " a star is a huge ball of flaming gas."

---

15. Gaimon, *Stardust*, 1–2.
16. Ibid., 81.
17. Ibid., 182.

"Even in your world, my son, that is not what a star is but only what it is made of."[18]

Here Lewis is hinting that there is more to stars, *even in our world*, than the sciences can tell us. Michael Ward, in his books *Planet Narnia* and *The Narnia Code*, has argued persuasively that Lewis' long-term fascination with Ptolemaic cosmology underlies all seven of the books in the Narniad. Lewis was well aware that the cosmology he felt so drawn to was, if believed literally, false. But while not factually true (in the way in which people used to think it was), it was deeply beautiful and, at an aesthetic level, was truthful. Lewis wrote, "the characters of the planets, as conceived by medieval astrology, seem to me to have a permanent value as spiritual symbols."[19] Might it be that in this capacity the divine stars of the Bible retain a permanent value and even warn us against the kind of scientific reductionism that seeks to disenchant the cosmos?

The Heavens Declare the Glory of God

Let's start with something easy. The heavens still declare the glory of God. In fact, in the cosmos of modern physics, one arguably sees even more divine glory manifest than in older cosmologies.

> The spacious firmament on high,
> With all the blue ethereal sky,
> And spangled heavens, a shining frame
> Their great Original proclaim.
> Th'unwearied sun, from day to day,
> Does his Creator's powers display,
> And publishes to every land
> The work of an Almighty Hand.
>
> Soon as the evening shades prevail
> The moon takes up the wondrous tale,
> And nightly to the listening earth
> Repeats the story of her birth;
> While all the stars that round her burn
> And all the planets in their turn,

---

18. Lewis, *The Voyage of the Dawn Treader*, 158–59.
19. Lewis, "The Alliterative Metre," 23.

Confirm the tidings as they roll,
And spread the truth from pole to pole.

What though in solemn silence all
Move round the dark terrestrial ball?
What though no real voice nor sound
Amid the radiant orbs be found?
In reason's ear they all rejoice,
And utter forth a glorious voice,
Forever singing as they shine,
"The hand that made us is divine."
—*Joseph Addison (1712)*

It is more than the regular movements of the sun, moon, and stars that points Godward, though those things do indicate God's faithfulness, it is the very light with which they shine. God is Light,[20] and the light we see in creation is a pale participation in his luminous Being. As such light itself has the potential to direct the mind towards its ultimate divine source.

> When we employ physical metaphors to describe or allude to a spiritual reality—and light is one of the most popular metaphors the world over—we tend to think of the physical referent as the most real of the two. In reality, the spiritual is higher in the scale of reality, and physical light is nothing but a shadow of God's intelligible self-communication. The true light, the light of heaven, is the archetype of which the light of the stars, and the light of torches and candles, the light that we can measure and manipulate, is a participating symbol.[21]

So the glory of the stars is not an arbitrary symbol for God's glory but one grounded in the very nature of created being. There really is an analogy between the light of stars and the divine Light. For those with the eyes to

---

20. 1 John 1:5.
21. Caldecott, *The Radiance of Being*, 24.

see, the glory of the stars remains a beautiful sign of the fullness of the glory of God.

The starlight also appropriately symbolizes the glory of the heavenly creatures that Scripture speaks of. Beings in God's heaven participate in the glorious divine Light in a fuller and higher way than do stars or lights on earth. As such they radiate heavenly light in ways purer than the light of stars.

The stars of heaven signify their divine Source both directly and indirectly: the former, because they participate directly in the divine Light; the latter, because they participate in that Light to a lesser degree than heavenly intelligences. As such they point towards God *by way of* those higher lights—the hosts of heaven. In this way stars appropriately symbolize both God's glory and the glory of angelic creatures.[22] This is metaphysics, and shifting scientific understandings of the physical organization of the cosmos don't touch it.

Stars and the Indivisibility of the Visible and Invisible Dimensions of Creation

Here is something important to notice about the stars in the biblical texts that we have been considering. The stars, closely linked with the divine council and with angels, were very clearly located in the sky but not in God's heaven (they were *this* side of the sky-dome). Yet the divine council and

---

22. Interpreting biblical images of angels in subtle and sophisticated ways is not some new invention but is deeply embedded in Christian tradition. Take Pseudo-Dionysius' book *The Celestial Hierarchies*. Dionysius is writing about the different levels of angelic beings of which Scripture speaks. These heavenly creatures were presented in numerous material forms in the Bible—men in shining outfits or creatures with animal heads and wings. These forms are not to be taken literally, says Dionysius, or we would end up with a silly view of them: "We cannot, as mad people do, profanely visualize these heavenly and godlike intelligences as actually having numerous feet and faces. . . . One would likely then image that the heavens beyond really are filled with bands of lions and horses, that the divine praises are, in effect, great moos . . ." (*CH* 2.137A, 137D).

The Bible, he says, speaks of these immaterial celestial beings in forms that we can get some grasp of as a way to help us to understand their glory. They do not actually *look* like anything, for they have no material bodies and occupy no space. Humans, however, are finite and feeble creatures, and we must approach the knowledge of these entities *indirectly*, via contemplation of the biblical symbols, symbols that simultaneously conceal the heavenly beings from the gaze of the ignorant and reveal them to the wise.

Dionysius proceeds to set forth a philosophical theology of angels that tries to "decode" the presentations of them in Scripture as images designed to explain the *meaning* of these hierarchies.

the angels inhabited God's throne room in *God's* heaven (the *other side* of the sky-dome). So the stars functioned as a link—a visible manifestation of invisible powers; a pointer beyond themselves to the transcendent power structures of the created order.

The linking function of stars meant that a complete disjunction of heaven and earth was impossible because the stars, existing in different modes on both sides of the firmament, blurred the dividing line. The stars reminded people of the *duality* of heaven and earth—that there is more to creation than can be seen with the eye—but countered any tendency towards *dualism*: the thought that God's heaven is some self-contained world disconnected from the visible creation. The "space" and "light" of heaven are connected to the space and light of the visible cosmos, and the light of the sun, moon, and stars represent that connection. There seems to me to be no reason why they cannot continue to symbolize that perennial truth, even though we now better understand their physical constitution.

Stars as Gods: The Spiritual Dimension of the Material World

The biblical writers saw a very close connection between events in heaven and events on earth. Political catastrophe, for instance, would be understood as having not simply an earthly dimension, but a heavenly one too. This link between the heavenly and earthly realm is seen in the association of astral events and events on earth; the former can announce the latter. The symbolic connection between stars and the divine council, the heavenly governors of the nations, allowed one to speak of the cosmic significance of events on earth in terms of events in the stars.

This significance to astral events could be the case even when there were no literal events in the stars to link the story to. An example: the author of Dan 8:1-14 did not imagine literal stars falling and being trampled by a goat! Rather, the vision symbolically highlights the invisible dimension of earthly political events. A critic who counted the stars in the sky before and after the events in question and said, "Ah ha! You are mistaken! There are as many stars in the sky now as there were before!" would simply have missed the point. The point is simply that mundane events are *not* mundane; that heavenly happenings lie behind/beneath/above (take your pick) earthly events. As stars appropriately symbolize those heavenly events, one can explain the cosmic significance of some major political happening by speaking of it in terms of a major astral event, even if no literal astral events of the kind are occurring. In other words, stars can function as metaphors to remind us that there are spiritual aspects to things going on in the earthly realm.

Now contemporary theology could also see creation rooted and grounded in the invisible heavenly dimensions of reality. Metaphysically speaking, earth depends on heaven. I see no reason why stars cannot still serve as signs pointing us beyond them to invisible heavenly realities, even though we no longer see stars as the actual astral bodies of gods nor believe that the future can be told from observing their movements.[23]

Stars and Time

It used to be said that ancient Israel operated with a linear view of time, shaped by its understanding of salvation history, while its pagan neighbors operated with a cyclical view of time grounded in the natural rhythms of the world. In fact, this disjunction is far too strong. Israel did come to embrace a salvation-historical linear perspective on time, but this did not entail their dropping the insights on temporality that come from the cyclical rhythms of nature. Indeed, the very cultic festivals that came to be linked to key incidents in salvation history—such as Passover, Tabernacles, and even the weekly Sabbath—were governed by cyclical, natural time. In fact, they were governed by the movements of the sun, moon, and stars. In this way Israel linked natural time and sacred time, linear time and cyclical time.

So what was the role of the astral entities in this view of time and what is the theological implication of that?

There are two important and closely connected contributions that natural time (as governed by the sun and moon) brings to sacred time: remembrance and participation.[24] The linking of annual harvest festivals to key events in salvation history meant that Israel could not forget the community-forming events of its own history. Year after year they would remember them, ensuring that the past was not lost but its significance appropriated afresh. And this remembrance was not simply a recollection of days gone by—it was *a participatory remembrance*. Each generation was

---

23. Biblical religion was very wary about astrology anyway.

24. Natural time, untamed by salvation-historical time, would cycle around but would not go anywhere new, while salvation-historical time, untamed by natural time, would fall prey to amnesia.

to recollect the exodus events as if they were the generation experiencing them. In the act of participating in the remembrance, the celebrants identify themselves with Moses' audience and submit themselves again to Jehovah, their redeemer God. In Deuteronomy Moses speaks to the generation about to enter the Promised Land (which was not the generation that left Egypt):

> And when Jehovah your God brings you into the land that he swore to your fathers . . . . When your son asks you in time to come, "What is the meaning of the testimonies and the statutes and the rules that Jehovah our God has commanded you?" then you shall say to your son, "*We* were Pharaoh's slaves in Egypt. And Jehovah brought *us* out of Egypt with a mighty hand. And Jehovah showed signs and wonders, great and grievous, against Egypt and against Pharaoh and all his household, before *our* eyes. And he brought *us* out from there, that he might bring *us* in and give *us* the land that he swore to give to our fathers. And Jehovah commanded *us* to do all these statutes, to fear Jehovah our God, for our good always, that he might preserve us alive, as we are this day. (Deut 6:10, 20–24)

Remembrance is not a simple repetition but a revisiting the past in the present with an eye to the future. It is this participatory remembrance that the natural time governed by sun and moon brings to salvation-historical linear time. In this way, Israel's time combines linear direction and repetition and cartwheels into the future.

The Christian church has, on the whole, maintained this link between sacred and natural time in the rhythms of the Christian Year. However, there is a pressure in the modern world to "liberate" humans from the constraints of the natural rhythms of time by means of technology, whether by omnipresent artificial lighting, having all fruits in season all year round, or using artificial snow domes to ski in summer or tanning booths to tan in winter.

The growth of the urban population is, in part, a factor in the partial disconnection modern people feel from natural rhythms. Harvest festivals, for instance, feel to many city people to be quaint and irrelevant to the patterns of their own lives. The rhythms of most people's work lives are not linked to seasons to anything like the degree that they were in the past. Working in a bank or supermarket or car factory or insurance company is much the same throughout the year. Modern time tends towards homogeneity, just "one damn thing after another."

There is a need to recover a deeper connection with and sensitivity to the changing seasons, marked as they are by the movements of the sun and moon. The Christian Year provides one way in which the church can continue to do that, and the fact that it is less in tune with modern life is not a reason for abandoning it but, quite the contrary, a reason to hold to it even tighter. This is the Christian Year practiced as a counter-cultural resistance to the modern blandification of time.

The celestial entities have led us from heaven to the annual cycles of the earth, so now seems to be an appropriate point to end our musings by reflecting more carefully on the challenges of inhabiting the biblical earth today. This will be the topic of the final chapter.

12

The Biblical Earth Today

Geocentric Cosmology Today

THE BIBLICAL EARTH IS the static center of the cosmos around which sun, moon, and stars move. This remained the case in the Ptolemaic cosmos inhabited by Christians for many centuries. The science of Copernicus, Galileo, and others set the earth moving and placed the sun at the center of a solar system, and later science had pushed the earth to the periphery of a *vast* universe.

No modern Christian can say with any intellectual integrity that the biblical view is literally correct. It is not. But does that mean that we simply cast it aside as a disposable husk? No. I propose that this biblical view was not merely a phenomenological perspective on how things appear from our location on the surface of the earth; it was also a means of divine communication. The notion that the earth matters to God is an important part of Christian theology. Ancient cosmology understood that centrality in a physical sense, but geocentrism can still metaphorically point to the importance of earth in God's purposes.

It is often claimed by modern people that the physical size and location of the earth in relation to the vast cosmos is proof that the earth is of next to no cosmic significance. According to the argument, we used to think that the earth was at the center of everything, but now we know that we have even less importance than a grain of sand in a desert.

The "small earth = insignificant earth" argument is weak. The cosmic significance of something cannot be determined from its size. Indeed, there are important indications in modern cosmology that the vast size of the cosmos is linked to the existence of life on earth. For intelligent life to evolve at all requires a wide range of complex and highly sensitive conditions to be met. Even slight alterations in these conditions would mean that intelligent life could never appear in the universe. The literature here is vast, and interested readers can easily follow up on the details, so I will pick out a single such condition for intelligent life—it needs a stable body, which requires an element, such as carbon, that can be stable over long periods of time. Carbon-based life is the only kind of biological life we know, and it may even be the only kind of biological life possible (alternatives to carbon, such as silicon, do not seen to be stable enough). Carbon is formed in the heart of stars. So in order for life to evolve in a universe that is even remotely like the one we live in you need time to form stars and then to form carbon. The carbon then needs dispersing when stars explode. All of this takes vast amounts of time—billions of years—and all that time the universe is expanding at a literally astronomical rate. In other words, contemporary science suggests that a universe of vast size and age may be necessary in order for intelligent life to evolve *anywhere* in it.

I am not interested in arguments for God's existence here; my point is more modest. Our vast universe could just as easily be taken to indicate the way that God chose to create intelligent biological life. If anything, this *enhances* the importance of earth.

I am not suggesting that God's cosmic purposes are all about earth—I do not believe that this is the case—but I am suggesting that modern science says nothing to demote earth's importance to God. And it is that importance that the geocentric cosmos of the ancients spoke of.

It is also worth reminding ourselves that neither biblical nor Ptolemaic cosmologies understood the earth to be the most important part of the cosmos—the heavens took that role. (In fact, contrary to the modern myth, in the Ptolemaic cosmology that dominated the Christian Middle Ages, the earth was the *least* significant part of the cosmos, being located at the center, furthest from God's heaven.)

Biblical authors were also well aware of just how astonishing it was, in light of the awesome heavens, that God should see such importance in life on earth. The psalmist stands in amazement: "when I consider your heavens, the work of your fingers, what is man that you are mindful of him, the son of man that you care for him?"[1] Why should the God of the stars care for such apparently insignificant creatures? Yet, the psalmist affirms, God *does* care. If anything, modern cosmology does not smash that hope but *amplifies*

---

1. Ps 8:3–4.

it enormously! To pray Psalm 8 now is to consider the heavens even more mind-boggling than the psalmist could have ever imagined.

The Pillars of the Earth Today: Turtles All the Way Down?

R. A. Wilson relates the following story:

> William James, father of American psychology, tells of meeting an old lady who told him Earth rested on the back of a huge turtle. "But, my dear lady," Professor James asked, as politely as possible, "what holds up the turtle?" "Ah," she said, "that's easy. He is standing on the back of another turtle." "Oh, I see," said Professor James, still being polite. "But would you be so good as to tell me what holds up the second turtle?" "It's no use, Professor," said the old lady, realizing he was trying to lead her into a logical trap. "It's turtles-turtles-turtles, all the way down."[2]

We have seen that in biblical cosmology the earth is flat, and while it is not held up on the back of a turtle it is held in place by pillars. We might well ask, "But what are the pillars standing on?" And the Bible authors never even try to answer that question. Had they done so, they would certainly not have appealed to a regress of pillars on pillars on pillars, on an on *ad infinitum*. That explains nada.

Here we may recall that obscure comment from the book of Job: "He [God] stretches out the north over the void and *hangs the earth on nothing*" (Job 26:5–7). The pillars, we might say, are suspended over nothing! So why don't they drop? Because, says Job, God has suspended them there.

When the rubber hits the road, for Bible authors the pillars simply speak of the stability of the earth: "He has set the earth on its foundation so that it should never be moved" (Ps 104:5). But the earth is utterly dependent on God, not just for its beginning but at each and every moment of its existence; it does not ground itself; it does not explain its own be-ing; and it is

---

2. Wilson, *Prometheus Rising*. The turtles story actually goes further back than William James.

not turtles all the way down. This is not a physical claim but a *metaphysical* one.

Scientific explanations by their very nature do not regress infinitely but stop at the most basic laws of nature, for those laws are that in terms of which science seeks to explain the behavior of the universe. However, there can be no *scientific* explanation as to why the laws of nature are as they are. This claim is not simply a statement about our current ignorance, as if future science will explain these most basic laws; it is a philosophical claim about what will always be the case simply by virtue of what science is and how it works. (This should not worry us, because there is no requirement built into the world that science is of no value unless it can explain absolutely everything. Such a science-explains-everything notion is not a scien*tific* one but a scien*tistic* one, and it is not only silly but *necessarily false*.)

All chains of explanation have to stop somewhere. This is widely appreciated by believers and atheists alike. For atheists these laws, the modern equivalent of the pillars of the earth, are simply brute facts. They are the way they are and there is no reason for it. End of story. The biblical worldview suggests that there *is* an explanation for the pillars of the earth but that it is of a fundamentally different kind; it is not a physical explanation, another pillar, which would only lead to an infinite regress, but a *metaphysical* one. The pillars of creation are the way they are *because God makes them the way they are*; he suspends them over nothing. And this metaphysical truth is as intelligible and important today as it ever was.[3]

The Underworld Today: Christ's Descent to Hades

There is no physical location beneath the earth in which the dead reside, so we cannot imagine Jesus *literally* going down to it. In many ways this is simply the reverse of the heaven-above-the-sky question discussed earlier. We understand perfectly well the metaphorical associations of language of "descent" and should not feel that such language loses its grip on reality if

---

3. Here we could get into long debates about who made God. But such a question, often deployed by atheists in a poor attempt to show that God is just as arbitrary a stopping place for explanation as the laws of nature, simply reflects a failure to understand what Christian theologians have classically meant by God. When the notion of God is adequately fleshed out, its superiority as a stopping point for chains of explanation is, to my mind, clear. Of course, one could choose to reject such an explanation and opt for an *ultimately* inexplicable and meaningless universe, but the price for doing so is *far* higher than most atheists have appreciated. Alas, this topic is much too large to get into here, but readers may wish to check out David Bentley Hart's fabulous book *The Experience of God*.

we do not think of sheol actually beneath the earth. What is at the heart of this talk is that Jesus was *really* dead and stood in solidarity with humanity, even in this most mysterious and dis-integrating "end."

However, we need to appreciate that this topic does not raise quite the same issues that the ascension does, because ancient Christians never imagined that Jesus' *body* literally went down into hades. His body was not thought to leave the tomb prior to the resurrection. What went to hades was some non-physical aspect of Jesus—his soul, for want of a better word. Immediately we are in the philosophically befuddling world of the philosophy of mind. It is enough to observe that the discussion does not hinge on shifts from ancient to modern cosmology. In other words, a hades that is not a place beneath the ground poses no additional problems for belief in Christ's descent to the realm of the dead.

When it comes to death there is no way to speak of its meaning that does not appeal to metaphor and myth. A simple scientific description of death is fine as far as it goes but it hardly even starts to fathom the depths of meaning and mystery. Death is something that is very difficult to get our minds around, and so we can picture it as a place, as a person, as a power, as a condition of being (or non-being), and so on. In all these ways we are fumbling around to speak of death, because speak of it we must, and in all these ways we glimpse aspects of truth, but no more.

Jesus did literally die and Jesus did really (albeit metaphorically) "descend" into death. Human experience shows us that there is no coming back from death, so picturing Jesus as descending into a dark and lifeless prison from which none escape makes a lot of sense; it speaks a lot of truth. However, Jesus was raised from the dead, so thinking of him as pioneering a prison breakout again communicates something importantly true concerning the resurrection. The loss of a literal underground zone for the dead is no threat to biblical theology. The metaphysics of Scripture can survive very happily indeed without it.

The Waters of Chaos Today

Obviously we cannot believe in physical waters above the sky or a literal creation out of water, nor can we believe in literal chaos dragons (although many biblical authors too were well aware that they were using the dragon myth in non-literal ways). It goes without saying that water itself is not at all disordered or chaotic, nor is it evil. Quite the contrary! God created the sea and God created the dragons. More than that, God is master of the sea and its monsters. He compels them to do his bidding, and they both obey him and praise him. The waters are a good part of creation when they are constrained and controlled. They are both bursting with life and necessary for life. But water and sea beasts do function as very evocative *symbols* of overwhelming and powerful chaos-inducing forces. They remind us that God's creation is good but not tame. It contains forces that are beyond human control, forces that should be treated with due respect, forces that when they exceed their bounds are destructive.

At a *metaphorical* level, dragons and wild oceans remain helpful symbols of the chaos that can invade communal and individual human worlds, threatening the order and even the possibility of life itself. The Bible uses the motif to address situations of political oppression and also what we may think of as the collapse of order and intelligible meaning in the lives of individuals. God as the warrior who fights off such monsters and pushes the water back remains one helpful image for conceiving of such situations.

At a *metaphysical* level, the dragon motif also speaks truth. The biblical models of creation picture it as something that left to itself would collapse back into chaos. The world does not sustain itself or order itself. It is *God* who "in the beginning" ordered reality according to his Logos, thereby creating cosmos, and it is God who holds the chaos at bay from moment to moment by that same Logos. But the tendency towards dis-order is inherent in the world.

We might possibly wish to raise the discussion a notch and transpose this image into the philosophical categories of being.[4] In that mode the sea represents non-being, *literally* no-thing. Read this way, the world in itself tends towards non-being, but God, through his Logos, is investing it with the powers of existence. God's ongoing ordering of the sea then speaks of the world's moment-by-moment dependence on God.[5]

Taking this approach further still we might perhaps consider evil, when portrayed in terms of watery chaos or sea beasts, as a tendency in creation to move away from being and form towards nothingness. Here I am

---

4. I am well aware that the biblical authors were not themselves thinking in such categories, but the meanings of texts go beyond the intentions of their original authors.

5. Mathematician, physicist, and philosopher Wolfgang Smith sees the insights of modern quantum physics as revealing a level of reality akin to the mythic chaos waters in Genesis 1. See Smith, *The Quantum Enigma*.

picking up on Augustine's teaching that evil is not a thing, a substance, but a *lack* in a thing, a privation. Evil is when good things fall away from their nature. On this approach, the primal sea and the out-of-control dragons can be read as symbols of meaninglessness and of the fall away from being, from what created things are intended to be. Evil so conceived has no justification or higher purpose—it has literally no meaning or sense at all. That is what is so terrible about it. Eric Perl explains the thinking here: "To explain evil, to attribute a cause to it, would necessarily be to explain it away, to deny that evil is genuinely evil at all. For to explain something is to show how it is in some way good . . . Only by *not* explaining evil, by insisting rather on its radical causelessness, its unintelligibility, can we take evil seriously as evil. This is why most 'theodicies' fail precisely insofar as they succeed."[6]

God, however, can defeat such chaos and tame the sea and its dragons. In so doing he even incorporates evil within his providential purposes and works good from it. This, of course, is to play with the biblical images in ways that go beyond anything conceived of by Scripture's authors, but such playful appropriations can still be of some value.

Sacred Geography Today

Can we still imagine that some specific places are holy places? Given God's ubiquitous presence and the sacramental power of creation to manifest God we see that he is free to manifest his reality *anywhere*. In that sense no place is more sacred than another. Nevertheless, the notion of holy places remains perfectly intelligible and relevant. First, we should note that while God is free to manifest himself anywhere, certain locations and types of location have symbolic associations that make them "fitting" as sites of revelation. Mountains, for instance, reaching towards the heavens as they do, naturally suggest to human minds the idea of drawing nearer to God. Of course, one is not physically any closer to God on the top of the mountain than at the bottom! Any idiot knows that! But the symbolism of "the mountain top" makes such locations suggestive and *potentially* holy places.

The second thing to say is that in Scripture *divine choice* is fundamental as to which sites become holy sites. The classic example is Zion—God *chose* Zion as the place where he would cause his name to dwell. He chose it to be the place where he would manifest his presence. He could have picked another mountain, but he didn't. Does this make Zion more special? Well, not in and of itself. It is no more inherently special than any other place. However, it is special in that it is the locus for important divine self-revelations.

---

6. Perl, *Theophany*, 63.

Third, certain key locations of divine appearing are swept up into the ongoing narrative of God's relationship with his people. They mark important parts of that identity-forming story and thereby become places of enduring significance, often with the continuing potential to be places of further divine self-disclose.

So the notion of holy places is not superstition but a simple acknowledgement of the above considerations. It does not amount to a denial that God can meet people anywhere. Of course he can! The God of the Bible was never contained in Zion but met people all over the place.

The notion of theologically meaningful space can also disclose metaphorical and metaphysical truth. Recall the manner in which God, in the story of the exodus, moves Israel out of slavery in Egypt, through the chaos boundary of the Sea, on through the dangerous liminal zone of the desert, towards the place of "rest." There is a venerable Christian tradition of allegorical biblical interpretation that seeks to penetrate beneath the surface level of the texts in order to discern their spiritual meaning. Now sometimes this method lacks methodological controls and flies off into cloud cuckoo land. However, it contains an important insight, and stories like the exodus show how it can work well. The exodus narrative does indeed contain subterranean meaning, and it is precisely this that enables the story to speak beyond its particularity to audiences that its authors never even dreamed of. The richness of biblical truth draws on precisely such a fullness of meaning that exceeds any and every particular reading of the text.

At the same time, the importance of holy space is never simply about general, universal truth hidden beneath the specific narrative features. It is just as much about the importance of particularity. God met *this* person in *this* place on *this* occasion. God rescues *these* people and brought them to *this* land. God is always encountered in the particular, and holy space is a way of holding on to that particularity and of refusing to let it dissolve into the abstract.

The Living Cosmos Today

We will end the book as we began, by reflecting on the life of the created order. We have seen that the biblical cosmos seems to be spoken of as if it were animate—as if rocks and mountains and seas and stars were living creatures. I want to suggest that this emphasis can serve as a helpful corrective to our tendency to view the world as a lifeless machine. I wish to briefly flag up some contemporary proposals in the area of the nature of reality (ontology) and of knowledge (epistemology) that resonate with this biblical emphasis.

Ontology: The Ubiquity of Life

Ontology is the study of the nature of reality at its most fundamental levels. One of the many dangers of modern approaches to ontology is that life is in danger of being banished from the cosmos. This is because the world tends to be understood as a self-contained machine, and life is seen as a mere epiphenomenon of the interaction of mechanical parts.

German philosopher Friedrich Schelling (1775–1805) thought that if one removed the notion of life from matter at its most basic level, then it could not be reintroduced again later. Ancient philosophy had recognized the vital dimensions of matter, but the new mechanistic philosophy saw matter as lifeless. "Since men agreed that, in the beginning, matter was dead, it was decided that death was the principle governing all things, and that life was a derivative phenomenon . . . [T]here now remained only the final and grandest task, namely, to bring nature, already dead in its innermost parts, back to life again, mechanistically."[7]

Schelling reacted against the mechanistic philosophy with its inclination to reduce biology to chemistry to physics to mathematics. Welcoming the insights of the new sciences, he nevertheless sought to place life at the center of his cosmology. He came to see matter not as lifeless stuff but as a very basic form of life with an inherent drive towards greater complexity and reaching its telos in spirit.

In a similar way Stratford Caldecott has recently explored the idea that life is a universal that all particular things "participate in" to varying degrees. This is born of the Christian Platonic vision of the cosmos. God is the Living God; he is Life Itself. Creation participates in this divine Life just as it participates in Being, Beauty, Truth, and Goodness. So in some *analogical* sense all things, even rocks, have some sharing in life, albeit it at a very far remove from the divine Source. As such life is not something alien to matter but is there from the bottom up.

This is not to say that different kinds of things are alive in the same manner. Human life differs from that of a horse, which differs from that of a rose, which differs from that of an amoeba, and so on. The "life" of a rock is that much more basic again! "C. S. Lewis, who knew and loved the medieval conception of the cosmos, described it as 'tingling with anthropomorphic life, dancing, a ceremonial, a festival not a machine.' The steps of the dance are learned from the Trinity and performed by angels."[8]

---

7. Schelling, *Bruno*, 209–10.
8. Caldecott, *Radiance of Being*, 76.

We need to be careful here. It is important to retain the distinctions between simple bodies (like rocks or water), plants, animals, and humans. It is also important to acknowledge the big gap between simple bodies, on the one hand, and entities that have a nature that can sustain itself as a system, temporarily bucking the rise of entropy (plants, animals, humans), on the other. Nevertheless, one may see what we commonly call "life" as a higher-level intensification of something that we find in much more primitive form even in "inanimate" matter.

Drawing on the work of Christopher Alexander, Caldecott sees a sliding scale of "aliveness" in which parts are linked together as mutually supporting wholes with organizing centers. Alexander identifies fifteen structural features that correlate with degrees of life, allowing him to view biological life as one example, albeit the paradigmatic one, of a universal tendency of nature.

> A stone, in other words, possesses a kind of interior life of low degree, which is related to the fact that God creates it from within, not without. It has a nature, on which God bestows existence: it receives the power of self-gift in the measure of its own essence. It plays a part in the whole, and it may be fashioned into a statue or building whose form is given it by another. Its degree of aliveness increases depending on the ways in which it receives or gives itself. A beautiful, harmonious pattern contains more self-gift than an ugly or broken one. An animal contains more kenosis than a stone, or even a statue. Thus life, for Alexander, is the radiance of being.[9]

This may perhaps be stretching the notion of life too far for comfort. Even if that is so, it is not at all crazy to suppose that inanimate things can in some ways anticipate important features that belong properly living things. As such, metaphors that speak of inanimate things as if they were living do open up genuine insights into the truth about them. Thinking of the world as fundamentally alive rather than as fundamentally dead may be just the kind of kick in the backside that the Bible can give us in the modern age.

Epistemology: Interpersonal Knowing of the Cosmos

Epistemology is the branch of philosophy concerned with knowledge, dealing with questions such as, what does it mean to say that we know something? and, how can we come to know things? Since the seventeenth century these

---

9. Ibid.

questions have been at the heart of modern philosophy. Philosopher Esther Meek argues that modern epistemology, which tends to reduce knowledge to a mere knowledge-of-information, is riddled with problems and can actually be *detrimental* to the human task of coming to know reality. This not something of mere academic relevance but impacts every sphere of human life—science, the arts, engineering, parenting, politics, economics, friendship, and so on.

Meek invites us to think of the activity of knowing, whether we are talking about physics or parenting, as akin the relational activity of loving a person.[10] In this picture knowing is the relationship between knower and known.

Meek speaks of the importance of love in truly knowing the other. Love is what motivates a knowing venture, and what guides its open and hospitable engagement with "the real." Reality woos us with a sense of wonder, and we respond with our attention. So begins a relational journey of knowledge.

The goal of knowledge is not mastery over the known or the desire to eliminate mystery but the communion or friendship of knower and known. A knowing venture requires the knower to pledge herself or himself in a committed way to that-which-is-not-yet-known. As such, it is a risk predicated on trust in the love-responsive generosity of reality. We pledge to welcome and create space for the not-yet-known and to trust ourselves to the relationship.

Meek writes, "good knowing practice involves relating to what we want to know the way we relate to another person. . . . We respect what we want to know, treating it as having worth and being worth knowing, as other than ourselves"[11] We invite the real, the yet-to-be-known, to unfold itself and we empathetically indwell that which we desire to know. We are rewarded with moments of revelation and insight, which in turn invite further communion.

Collecting information *is* a part of knowing, but it has to be situated within this wider context of love if it is not to be distorted and distorting. Knowledge is not merely informational but transformational, for knower and known. It is akin to a dance in its graceful, respectful, and engaged back-and-forth between the one who knows and that which is to be known.

Meek sees her loving-to-know approach to epistemology as grounded in the theological insight that the Triune God is essentially relational. You cannot get to a more prime level of being behind the inner-trinitarian

---

10. See Meek, *Loving to Know*; Meek, *Little Manual for Knowing*.
11. Meek, *Little Manual*, 32, 41.

relations, so relationality turns out to be at the very bedrock of being. God's creation dimly reflects that Trinitarian dynamic and can only be known appropriately when known lovingly.

It seems to me that this general approach, which I cannot hope to do justice to here, resonates deeply with Scripture's engagement with inanimate parts of the cosmos *as if* they were animate. Meek is very explicit that to know the natural world we must engage it with a loving respect akin to that due to persons. That comports well with the Bible and not so well with the epistemologies of modernity.

Living Stone

By way of final illustration let me tell you about a couple of trips to Worcester Cathedral. In 2013, Hannah, my eldest daughter, and I met with the master stonemason to talk with him about his work. He had spent thirty years working stones, and he had a real sense for the "soul" of stones. He gets them and understands their properties and their beauty. By the look and feel and sound of stones (when struck with a chisel) he can get a sense of how to work with them (and how not to). But every stone is different, and when he works with them he is tentative at first, allowing the stone to disclose something of itself as he works on it. In response to the stone's individual quirks he modifies his approach. His engagement with the stones was respectful, appreciating their spirituality and seeking to draw on it, bring it out in the work, all to the glory of God.

Not long after that, I was sitting in the Advent service in our beautiful cathedral, looking around at the candle-lit walls and reflecting on the words of the stonemason. It occurred to me that the craftsmanship of the cathedral's architects and stonemasons actually brings out something of the God-directed orientation of stones, and of the rest of creation.

All things come from God, depend on God for their being at each and every moment, and exist for God. As such, even humble stones participate in God and only make sense as what they are when seen in relation to God. But stones do not wear their God-orientated meaning on their sleeves (unless, Moses might add, inscribed by the hand of the Lord). Yet, looking around the cathedral I saw stones that led the eyes heavenward towards the invisible God; stones that were not simply co-opted to some extrinsic and alien purpose but that were fulfilling their goal or *telos* in pointing Godward; stones that cried out in silent praise to their beautiful creator. As such this human work of the stonemasons serves to point us towards the meaning not only of these stones but of all stones.

Modern Books Quoted or Referenced

Augustine. *A Treatise on Faith and the Creed*. Nicene and Post-Nicene Fathers: First Series, Vol. 3. Edited by Philip Schaff. 2nd ed. Reprint. Peabody, MA: Hendrickson, 1996.

Barth, Karl. *Church Dogmatics*, Vol. I. Part 2: *The Doctrine of the Word of God*. Translated by G. T. Thompson and H. Knight. Edited by G. W. Bromiley and T. F. Torrance. Edinburgh: T. & T. Clark, 1956.

Browning, Elizabeth Browning. *Aurora Leigh*. Oxford World Classics. Oxford: Oxford University Press, 2008.

Caldecott, Stratford. *The Radiance of Being: Dimensions of Cosmic Christianity*. Tacoma, WA: Angelico, 2013.

Calvin, John. *Second Defense of the Pious and Orthodox Faith concerning the Sacraments*. In *Selected Works of John Calvin, Vol. 2*, edited by Henry Beveridge and John Bonnet, translated by Henry Beverage. Albany, OR: Books for the Ages, 1998.

Gaimon, Neil. *Stardust*. London: Hodder, 1999.

Hart, David Bentley. *The Experience of God: Being, Consciousness, Bliss*. New Haven: Yale University Press, 2013.

Lamoureux, Denis O. *Evolutionary Creation: A Christian Approach to Evolution*. Eugene, OR: Wipf & Stock, 2008.

Lewis, C. S. "The Alliterative Metre." In *Selected Literary Essays*, edited by Walter Hooper, 15–26. Cambridge: Cambridge University Press, 1980.

———. *The Voyage of the Dawn Treader*. 1952. Reprint. London: Collins, 1995.

Malina Bruce J., and John J. Pilch. *Social-Science Commentary on the Book of Revelation*. Minneapolis: Fortress, 2000.

Meek, Esther. *A Little Manual for Knowing*. Eugene, OR: Cascade, 2014.

———. *Loving to Know: Covenant Epistemology*. Eugene, OR: Cascade, 2011.

Perl, Eric D. *Theophany: The Neoplatonic Philosophy of Dionysius the Areopagite*. SUNY Series in Ancient Greek Philosophy. New York: SUNY Press, 2007.

Pilch. John J. "The Call of Ezekiel (Ezek. 1–3): An Altered State of Consciousness (ASC) Experience." In *Flights of the Soul: Visions, Heavenly Journeys, and Peak Experiences in the Biblical World*, 30–47. Grand Rapids: Eerdmans, 2011.

Schelling, Friedrich Wilhelm Joseph von. *Bruno, or On the Natural and the Divine Principle of Things*. Translated by Michael Vater. SUNY Series in Hegelian Studies. Albany, NY: SUNY Press, 1984.

Seely, Paul H. "The Firmament and the Waters Above. Part II: The Meaning of 'The Water above the Firmament' in Gen 1:6–8." *Westminster Theological Journal* 54.1 (1992) 31–46.

Smith, Wolfgang. *The Quantum Enigma: Finding the Hidden Key*. 3rd ed. San Rafael, CA: Angelico, 2005.
Traherne, Thomas. *Centuries of Meditations*. Edited by Bertram Dobell. London: published by the editor, 1908.
Ward, Michael. *The Narnia Code: C. S. Lewis and the Secret of the Seven Heavens*. Milton Keynes, UK: Paternoster, 2010.
———. *Planet Narnia: The Seven Heavens in the Imagination of C. S. Lewis*. Oxford: Oxford University Press, 2008.
Wilson, R. A. *Prometheus Rising*. Phoenix, AZ: New Falcon, 1983.

Further Reading

What follows is simply a short selection of books that you may find helpful if you wish to look into aspects of biblical cosmography in some more depth.

Ancient Cosmography: General

Godawa, Bryan. "Mesopotamian Cosmic Geography in the Bible." The BioLogos Foundation. Online: http://biologos.org/uploads/projects/godawa_scholarly_paper_2.pdf.
Horrowitz, Wayne. *Mesopotamian Cosmic Geography*. 2nd ed. Mesopotamian Civilizations 8. Winona Lake, IN: Eisenbrauns, 2011.
Keel, Othmar. *The Symbolism of the Biblical World: Ancient Near Eastern Iconography in the Book of Psalms*. Translated by Timothy J. Hallett. Winona Lake, IN: Eisenbrauns, 1997.
Pennington, Jonathan T., and Sean M. McDonough, eds. *Cosmology and New Testament Theology*. Library of New Testament Studies 335. London: T. & T. Clark, 2008.
Seely, Paul H. "The Firmament and the Waters Above. Part I: The Meaning of *raqia'* in Gen 1:6–8." *Westminster Theological Journal* 53 (1991) 227–40.
———. "The Firmament and the Waters Above. Part II: The Meaning of 'The Water above the Firmament' in Gen 1:6–8." *Westminster Theological Journal* 54 (1992) 31–46.
———. "The Geographical Meaning of 'Earth' and 'Seas' in Genesis 1:10." *Westminster Theological Journal* 59 (1997) 231–55.
Smith, Mark S. *The Origins of Biblical Monotheism: Israel's Polytheistic Background and the Ugaritic Texts*. New York: Oxford University Press, 2003.
Stadelman, Luis J. *The Hebrew Conception of the World: A Philological and Literary Study*. Analecta Biblica 39. Rome: Biblical Institute Press, 1970.
Walton, John. *Ancient Near Eastern Thought and the Old Testament: Introducing the Conceptual World of the Hebrew Bible*. Grand Rapids: Baker Academic, 2006.

MODERN BOOKS QUOTED OR REFERENCED

Creation

Batto, Bernard F. *Slaying the Dragon: Mythmaking in the Biblical Tradition.* Louisville: Westminster John Knox, 1992.
Clifford, Richard J. *Creation Accounts in the Ancient Near East and in the Bible.* Catholic Biblical Quarterly Monograph Series 26. Washington, DC: Catholic Biblical Association, 1994.
Levenson, Jon D. *Creation and the Presence of Evil: The Jewish Drama of Divine Omnipotence.* San Francisco: Harper & Row, 1988.
Simkins, Ronald A. *Creator & Creation: Nature in the Worldview of Ancient Israel.* Peabody, MA: Hendrickson, 1994.
Smith, Mark S. *The Priestly Vision of Genesis 1.* Minneapolis: Fortress, 2010.
Walton, John. *The Lost World of Genesis 1: Ancient Cosmology and the Origins Debate.* Downers Grove, IL: InterVarsity, 2009.
Wenham, Gordon J. *Genesis 1–15.* Word Biblical Commentary 1. Dallas: Word, 1987.

Sea

Angel, Andrew. *Playing with Dragons: Living with Suffering and God.* Eugene, OR: Cascade Books, 2014.
Day, John. *God's Conflict with the Dragon and the Sea: Echoes of a Canaanite Myth in the Old Testament.* University of Cambridge Oriental Publications 35. Cambridge: Cambridge University Press, 1985.
Kloos, Carola. *Yhwh's Combat with the Sea: A Canaanite Tradition in the Religion of Ancient Israel.* Leiden: Brill, 1986.
Parris, David P. *Reading the Bible with Giants: How 2000 Years of Biblical Interpretation Can Shed New Light on Old Texts.* 2nd ed. Eugene, OR: Cascade, 2014. (On Jonah's fish.)

Land

Clifford, Richard J. *The Cosmic Mountain in Canaan and the Old Testament.* 1972. Reprinted, Eugene, OR: Wipf and Stock, 2010.
Hanson, K. C. "Transformed on the Mountain: Ritual Transformation and the Gospel of Matthew." *Semeia* 67 (1994[95]) 147–70.
Havrelock, Rachel. "The Two Maps of Israel's Land." *Journal of Biblical Literature* 126 (2007) 649–67.
Wazana, Nili. *All the Boundaries of the Land: The Promised Land in Biblical Thought in Light of the Ancient Near East.* Translated by Liat Qeren. Winona Lake, IN: Eisenbrauns, 2013.

Sheol

Alfeyev, Hilarion. *Christ the Conqueror of Hell: The Descent into Hades from an Orthodox Perspective.* Crestwood, NY: St. Vladimir's Seminary Press, 2009.

Johnson, Philip. *Shades of Sheol: Death and Afterlife in the Old Testament*. Leicester, UK: Apollos, 2002.
Laufer, Catherine Ella. *Hell's Destruction: An Exploration of Christ's Descent to the Dead*. Farnham, UK: Ashgate, 2013.
Papaioannou, Kim. *The Geography of Hell in the Teaching of Jesus: Gehenna, Hades, the Abyss, the Outer Darkness Where There Is Weeping and Gnashing of Teeth*. Eugene, OR: Pickwick, 2013.
Smith, Janet. *Dust or Dew: Immortality in the Ancient Near East and in Psalm 49*. Eugene, OR: Pickwick, 2011.
Tromp, Nicholas J. *Primitive Conceptions of Death and the Underworld in the Old Testament*. Biblica et Orientalia 21. Rome: Pontifical Biblical Institute Press, 1969.

Weather

Niehaus, Jeffrey J. *God at Sinai: Covenant and Theophany in the Bible and Ancient Near East*. Grand Rapids: Zondervan, 1995.
Wiggins, Steve A. *Weathering the Psalms: A Meteorotheological Survey*. Eugene, OR: Cascade, 2014.

Stars

Cooley, Jeffrey L. *Poetic Astronomy in the Ancient Near East: The Reflexes of Celestial Science in Ancient Mesopotamian, Ugaritic, and Israelite Narrative*. History, Archaeology, and Culture of the Levant 5. Winona Lake, IN: Eisenbrauns, 2013.
Heiser, Michael S. "The Divine Council in Late Canonical and Non-Canonical Second Temple Jewish Literature." PhD diss., University of Wisconsin–Madison, 2004. Available to buy on the author's website.
Rochberg, Francesca. "'The Stars Their Likeness': Perspectives on the Relation between Celestial Bodies and Gods in Ancient Mesopotamia." In *What Is a God? Anthropomorphic and Non-Anthropomorphic Aspects of Deity in Ancient Mesopotamia*, edited by Barbara Nevling Porter, 41–91. Winona Lake, IN: Eisenbrauns, 2009.

Heaven

Gooder, Paula. *Heaven*. London: SPCK, 2011.
Pennington, Jonathan T. *Heaven and Earth in the Gospel of Matthew*. Reprint. Grand Rapids: Baker Academic, 2009.
Rowland, Christopher. *The Open Heaven: A Study of Apocalyptic in Judaism and Early Christianity*. 1982. Reprinted, Eugene, OR: Wipf & Stock, 2002.

Ascension

Dawson, Gerrit Scott. *Jesus Ascended: The Meaning of Christ's Continuing Incarnation.* Phillipsburg, NJ: Presbyterian & Reformed, 2004.

Farrow, Douglas. *Ascension and Ecclesia: On the Significance of the Doctrine of the Ascension for Ecclesiology and Christian Cosmology.* Grand Rapids: Eerdmans, 1999.

Torrance, Thomas F. *Atonement: The Person and Work of Christ.* Edited by Robert T. Walker. Milton Keynes, UK: Paternoster, 2009.

Temple

Beale, G. K. *The Temple and the Church's Mission: A Biblical Theology of the Dwelling Place of God.* New Studies in Biblical Theology. Leicester, UK: Apollos, 2004.

George, Andrew. *House Most High: The Temples of Ancient Mesopotamia.* Winona Lake, IN: Eisenbrauns, 1993.

Hurowitz, Victor. *I Have Built You an Exalted House: Temple Building in the Bible in the Light of Mesopotamian and North-West Semitic Writings.* JSOT Supplements 115. Sheffield, UK: Sheffield Academic, 1992.

Keel, Othmar. *The Symbolism of the Biblical World: Ancient Near Eastern Iconography in the Book of Psalms.* Translated by Timothy J. Hallett. Winona Lake, IN: Eisenbrauns, 1997.

Levenson, Jon D. "The Temple in the World." *Journal of Religion* 64 (1984) 275–98.

Holiness and Geography

Jenson, Philip P. *Graded Holiness: A Key to the Priestly Conception of the World.* JSOT Supplements 106. Sheffield: Sheffield Academic, 1992.

Christian Platonism

Boersma, Hans. *Heavenly Participation: The Weaving of a Sacramental Tapestry.* Grand Rapids: Eerdmans, 2011.

Caldecott, Stratford. *The Radiance of Being: Dimensions of Cosmic Christianity.* Tacoma, WA: Angelico, 2013.

Hart, David Bentley. *The Experience of God: Being, Consciousness, Bliss.* New Haven: Yale University Press, 2013.

Tyson, Paul. *Returning to Reality: Christian Platonism for Our Times.* Kalos 2. Eugene, OR: Cascade Books, 2014.

Scripture Index

OLD TESTAMENT

Genesis

1	1, 20, 32, 36, 37, 38, 45–46, 47, 93–94, 114–15
1:1–2	20, 26
1:2	29, 36, 39
1:3–5	29
1:6–8	29, 94
1:7	30
1:8	10
1:9–13	29
1:11–12	174
1:14–19	114
1:16	96
1:17–18	112
1:17	11, 94
1:20–23	45–46
1:20	11
1:21	37
1:26–28	143, 177
1:26	11
1:28	11
2:1	107
2:5–6	62
2:8	65
2:20	11
3:24	130
6:1–4	58, 106
6:7	11
7:3	11
7:11	38, 62, 95
7:19–20	38
7:23	11
8:1–2	39
8:2	10, 62, 95
9:11–12	39
12:7	63
13:14–17	63
15:5	110
15:7	63
15:18–21	63
15:18	66
17:8	63
18	128
21:14–20	59
22	50
22:17	110
24:7	63
26:4	160
28:4	63
28:10–22	50
28:12–17	120, 129
28:17	95
35:12	63
37	160
37:35	83
42:48	83
48:4	63
49:25	61, 62
50:20	176

Exodus

3–4	52
3:1	53
4:25	132
4:27	53
6:26	107
9:18–34	93
10:14–20	52
12:17	107
12:41	107
12:51	107
14–15	39–40
14	63
14:21	47
15:11	101
15:17	148
16	59
17:1–7	59
18:5	53
18:16	101
19:1—Num 10:13	52
19:2	53
20:4	31
20:11	47
20:18	52
20:24–25	148
23:31	66
24:9–11	53
24:13	53
25:8	122
25:9	52
25:6	114
25:40	52
26:1	150
26:30	52
26:31	150
26:36	149
27:8	52
27:16	149
27:20	114
28	160
32:13	110, 160
33:11	181
33:20	181–82
35:8	114
35:14	114
35:28	114
36:8	150
36:11	149
36:35	150
36:37	149
38:18	149
39:37	114

Leviticus

16	150, 157
16:7–10	57–58
18:26–28	3
19:31	79
20:6	79
20:22	3

Numbers

4:9	114
4:16	114
8:4	52
10:10	115
13:23	64
16:23–34	78–79
28:2	115
34:1–12	65

Deuteronomy

1:7	66
1:10	110, 160
4:11	53
4:19	99, 107, 108, 127
5:4–5	53
6:10	195
6:20–24	195
8:7–9	64
10:17	101
10:22	110, 160
11:9	64
11:11–15	64
11:24	66
12	50
16:6	50
16:15	50
17:2–6	99
17:3	107, 108
18:9–14	79
26:2	135

SCRIPTURE INDEX

26:15	11, 64, 120
27:4–13	51
28:62	160
32:8–9	127
32:8	127
32:22	78
32:39	85
32:43	105
33:2	53
33:13–16	10, 62

Joshua

1:2	66
1:4	66
3	63
5:13–15	128
10	108
10:11	10, 24
10:12–14	24–25

Judges

5:5	53
5:19–20	108

1 Samuel

2:6	85
2:8	18, 22
2:10	10
4:4	146
17:45	107
23:14	59
28:11–15	79–80
28:13	101

2 Samuel

5:20	62
6:2	146, 150
22:6	87
22:16	18, 22
24:1	126

1 Kings

2:6	83
2:9	83
3:2–3	50
3:4–15	50
5:1	66
5:1–18	140
6:23–28	150
7:13–45	140
7:23–26	146, 148
7:24	148
7:25	149
7:38–39	146
7:44	146, 148
8:27	11, 135, 148
8:30	11
8:39	11
10:13–14	18
13:32–33	50
14:23	50
17:1–6	59
18:20–45	51
18:39	101
18:45	38
19	53
22:15–23	125
22:19	107

2 Kings

2:11	120
14:4	50
16:4	50
17:9	50
17:16	108
19:14–15	131, 150
20:8–11	23–24
21:3	50, 108
21:5	108
23:4	108
23:5	98

1 Chronicles

13:6	150
14:1	28
16:29–30	21
16:30	18
16:32	47
21:1	126
27:23	110, 160
28:2	146, 150

SCRIPTURE INDEX

2 Chronicles

2:3–4	28
3:1	54
4:2–10	148
18:18	107
30:27	11

Nehemiah

9:6	47, 108–9, 111
9:23	110, 160

Job

1	126
1:6	103
2:1	103
3:13–19	83
4:8	103
5:1	102
7:12	32
9:6	18
9:7–10	111–12
9:8	21, 44
9:9	95
9:13	33
10:21	80
11:8	78
12:7–9	46
15:15	103
16:22	81
17:16	78
22:11	62
22:14	20
24:19	83
25:5	113
26:5–7	20–21, 199
26:5	80, 83
26:7	20, 21
26:10	19
26:11–12	32–33, 43
28:1–11	72–73
28:12–19	73
28:24	18
30:3	59
30:8	59
31:26–28	99
37:3	18
37:7–8	102
38:4–7	103
38:4–6	21
38:4	18, 22
38:8–11	32
38:13	19
38:16	26
38:26	56
38:29	10
38:31	95
41	41
41:1–2	36
41:3–5	36
41:8	36
41:18–21	36
41:31–32	36

Psalms

1:4	93
2	54, 68
2:4	10
2:6	145
3:4	145
5:7	146
6:6	80
8	100
8:2–4	110, 113
8:8	10
9:17	83
11:4	10
11:6	93
14	83
15:1	145
16	154
16:10–11	84
16:10	80
18:5	87
18:9	93
18:10–16	33
18:10–11	93, 132
18:12–13	93
18:13	93
18:14	92
18:15	43
18:42	93
19:1–4	2, 4, 113
19:4–6	23, 112

SCRIPTURE INDEX

19:6	10, 94	76	54
23:6	146	77:16	40, 47
24:1–2	30	77:17–18	92, 93
24:3	145	78:23	95
24:7	146	78:26	92
26:8	146	78:47–48	93
26:14	81	78:48	92
27:4	146	78:69	148
29:1	101	79:2	10
29:3	30	80:1	150
29:10	30	80:2	131, 146
30:3	80, 83	81:3	115
31:17	83	82	101, 102, 106, 127
33:6	101	82:1	101
33:7	31	82:6	102
35:5	93	83:13	93
38:2	92	83:15	92, 93
40:2	78, 83	86:8	101
43:3	145	86:13	78, 80, 83
46	54	87:1	148
46:4	146	87:4	41
48	54	88:2–6	81
48:1–3	48, 54	88:3	83
48:7	93	88:5	80
49:7–14	84	88:6	80, 83
49:14	83	88:10–12	80
49:15	80, 84	88:10	83
50:1	22	88:12	80
50:3	92	88:17	62
55:8	92, 145	89:6–7	93, 102, 105
58:9	92	89:9–10	32
65:5	18	89:9	32
65:9–10	93	89:12	3
65:12	55	89:36	112
68:4	93	89:37	93, 102, 105
68:8	53	89:48	83
68:9	93	92:12–13	145
68:15–16	145	93:1	18, 21
68:18	52	94:17	81
69:34	3, 111	95:3	101
71:20	78, 83	95:5	47
72:5	112	96:4	101
72:17	112	96:10	18, 21
74	37	96:11	47
74:12	68	96:12	3
74:12–15	34–35, 40–41	97:2	93
74:16–17	110	98:7	47
75:3	18, 22	98:8	55, 63

Psalms (continued)

99:1	131, 146, 150
99:5	146, 150
99:9	145
103:16	93
104:1–3	30, 110
104:2	21
104:3	93
104:4	92
104:5	18, 22, 199
104:7	43, 93
104:13	93
104:19–20	110, 112
104:25–27	37, 41
104:25	46
104:430	92
105:32–33	92, 93
106:6–9	32, 43
106:9	40, 46
107:25	92
107:29–30	43, 92
107:33–37	60
110:1	155–56
114:3	40, 47
114:4	55–56
114:5	40, 47
115:1–8	143
115:16	11
115:17	81
132:7	146
132:7–8	150
135:5	101
135:7	38
135:16	143
136:2	101
136:3	31
136:5	110, 112
136:6	31
136:7–9	110, 112
139:7–12	135, 169
139:8	10, 78, 80
141:7	83, 87
144:6	92
146:6	47
147:2	148
147:4	111
147:8	10, 38, 93
148:1–6	106–7
148:1–5	101, 109
148:2–10	3–4
148:3	111
148:4	2, 10, 30, 47
148:6	112
148:7	46, 47
148:8	92
148:9	56

Proverbs

3:19–20	62
5:5	83
7:27	83
8	128
8:24–28	47
8:27–29	31
8:27–28	19
8:29	32
9:18	78, 83
15:11	80
16:15	38
21:6	83
25:14	38
27:20	87

Ecclesiastes

1:5	22, 95, 112
9:5–6	81
9:10	83
11:3	38

Song of Songs

6:10	110

Isaiah

2:2	145
2:2–4	54–55
5:6	38
5:14	83, 87
6	125
6:1–4	147
6:3	132
6:5–7	132
7:11	78

7:20	132	45:22–23	156
8:9	79	46	143
10:15–19	176	47:13	99
11:12	18	49:10	106
13:10	112, 116	50:2	32, 33, 43
14	83	51:3	65
14:9–15	82–83	51:9–10	40, 41
14:9	83, 87	55:10–11	10
14:10	81	58:11	65
14:11	78	60:19–20	113, 117
14:12–15	104	66:1	123, 150
14:13	108	66:23	117
14:15	78		
14:16–20	83		

Jeremiah

19	41	3:16	65
21:1	56	5:22	31
22:18	20	7:31	50
23	28	8:1–2	98–99, 108
24:21–23	105–6	10	143
26:19	85	10:12–13	30
27	37	10:12	21
27:1	35	16:9	18
28:15	83, 87	19:13	108
28:18	83, 87	23:3	65
29:1–8	54	23:18	125
30:7	40	23:22	125
30:26	117	27:3	28
31:1–6	54	31:12	65
33:20–22	55	31:35	107, 110
34:4	112, 116	33:20–22	106, 112
34:9–15	56–57	47:4	28
37:16	131	51:15	21
38:10	81, 83	51:42	39
38:18	80, 87		

Lamentations

40:3–4	60	2:1	150
40:13–14	127	3:6	80
40:21–22	19–20, 110–11	3:66	11
40:22	21		

Ezekiel

40:25–26	111	1	131–32
41:4	44	1:4–28a	102–3
41:9	18	1:22	94
41:17–20	60–61	1:26	132
43:10–11	44	1:28	132
44:9–20	143	5:5	68
44:24	21		
45:8	38		
45:12	21		
45:18	18, 101		

Ezekiel (continued)

6:3–4	56
7:3	18
8–11	169
8:16	99
10	131
26	28
26:9	39
28:13–16	51, 145
29	28
29:3–5	40
32	83
32:7	112, 116
32:17–32	83
32:21	81
32:23	78
36:11	65
36:35	65
37:1–14	85
38:10–12	68
47	62, 146
47:1–12	55

Hosea

5:7	106
6:1–6	85
10:8	56
13:14	87

Joel

2:3	65
2:10	112, 116
2:31	112, 116
3:15	112
3:18	146
4:18	55

Amos

1:9–10	28
5:8	46, 95, 112
5:25–27	98
5:26	95
8:9	112
9:2	78, 80
9:6	46

Obadiah

4	110

Daniel

4:10–11	18
4:11	18
4:35	111
7:1–8	45
7:13–14	121
7:13	45
7:18	45
8:1–14	108, 193
8:15–27	129
9:21–27	129
10	106, 127, 129
12:2	85
12:3	160

Jonah

1–2	41–42
1:17	46
2:3	42
2:5	80
2:6	42, 78, 81
2:10	46

Micah

4:1–4	54
4:1	145
6:1	56
6:2	56

Nahum

1:4	32, 33, 43, 63
3:16	110

Habakkuk

2:5	87
3:8–10	47
3:8	63

Zephaniah

1:5	99

Haggai

2:17	93

Zechariah

3:1–2	126
6:5	10
10:1	38
10:8	65
12:1	18, 21, 22
14:5	108
14:8	55, 146
14:15	102

APOCRYPHA

Wisdom of Solomon

9:1	172
18:24	160

Sirach

22:11	80
24:1	172
43:24–25	27
50:5–10	160–61

NEW TESTAMENT

Matthew

2:1–2	115
2:9	115
4:1	58
4:8	19
5–7	51
6:10	134
11:20–24	83
12:39–40	42
12:40	153
12:42	18
13:24–30	158
14:23–34	43
14:23	51
14:25–26	44
14:28–29	44
15:29–31	51
17:20	56
19:28	156
24:29	23, 112, 116
24:36–44	122
25:1–46	158
25:31	156
26:64	156
28:3	128
28:16	52
28:20	158

Mark

1:13	58
4:36–41	43
6:47–53	43–44
14:62	156
16:5	128
16:9–20	185
16:12	185
16:19	156

Luke

1	129
2:8–14	115
6:48	62
8:29	56
10:12–15	83
11:24–26	58–59
16:22–26	85–86
21:25	112, 116
22:69	156
23:30	56
23:44–45	116
24:4	128

John

1:1–14	151–53, 171–72
1:14	159
1:51	129

John (continued)

2:18–22	159
3:13	152
4:10	62
4:13–14	62
6:16–21	43
6:19	44
7:38–39	62
7:38	62
8:23	152
14:16	157
17:5	152
20:12	128

Acts

1:9–11	120–22, 158
2:1–5	169
2:24	154
2:27	154
2:32–33	156
4:31	169
5:31	156
7:36	156
7:42	108
7:56	121
8:17	169
10:44–46	169
13:47	18
17:28	171
19:6	169
27	28

Romans

5:12–21	159
5:14	87
5:17	87
5:21	87
6:3–11	158
6:9	87
8:19–24	159
8:19–22	3
8:20–21	161
8:34	156
11:33–35	127–28
12:4–5	158, 160
14:9	154

1 Corinthians

2:6	127
3:7	174
10:16	158
11:29	160
12	158, 160
15:20–23	159
15:26	87
15:25–28	157
15:35–44	185–86
15:41	113
15:54–56	87
15:55	154

2 Corinthians

11:25–26	28
12:1–3	126
12:2	133

Ephesians

1:9–10	161
1:20	156
4:7–10	151
4:10	161

Philippians

2:5–11	152
2:9–11	156
2:10–11	154
2:10	86

Colossians

1:16–17	152
1:27	158
3:1	156

1 Thessalonians

4:15–17	121–22

Hebrews

1:1–3	152, 156, 157
4:16	123
6:20	157
7:25–28	157

7:27	157
8:1–6	157
8:1	123, 156, 157
9:11–28	157
9:23–24	123, 147, 157
10:11–12	157
10:12	156
12:2	123, 156
13:2	128

James
1:11	106

1 Peter
3:18–21	154
3:22	156
4:6	154

2 Peter
1:18	52

1 John
1:5	191

Jude
9	129

Revelation
1:7	17, 19
1:18	154
1:20	109
4–5	117–19
4	123–24
5:13	86
6:12	116
7:1	18
8:12	116
9:1	109
12	59, 129
12:1	115
13	45
16:8	106
17:3	58
20:13–14	86, 135
21–22	134–35, 158
21	139–40
21:1	45
21:2–3	134
21:23	117
22:1–2	146, 156
22:5	117

www.ingramcontent.com/pod-product-compliance
Lightning Source LLC
Chambersburg PA
CBHW020408230426
43664CB00009B/1226